The Global Rise of Asian Transformation

The Global Rise of Asian Transformation

Trends and Developments in Economic Growth Dynamics

Edited by

Pongsak Hoontrakul, Christopher Balding, and Reena Marwah

First published in 2014 by
PALGRAVE MACMILLAN®
in the United States—a division of St. Martin's Press LLC,
175 Fifth Avenue, New York, NY 10010.

Where this book is distributed in the UK, Europe and the rest of the world,
this is by Palgrave Macmillan, a division of Macmillan Publishers Limited,
registered in England, company number 785998, of Houndmills,
Basingstoke, Hampshire RG21 6XS.

Palgrave Macmillan is the global academic imprint of the above companies
and has companies and representatives throughout the world.

Palgrave® and Macmillan® are registered trademarks in the United States,
the United Kingdom, Europe and other countries.

ISBN: 978–1–137–41235–5

Library of Congress Cataloging-in-Publication Data

   The global rise of Asian transformation : trends and developments
in economic growth dynamics / edited by Pongsak Hoontrakul,
Christopher Balding, and Reena Marwah.
      pages cm
   Includes bibliographical references and index.
   ISBN 978–1–137–41235–5 (hardcover : alk. paper)
   1. Economic development—Asia. 2. Technological innovations—
Economic aspects—Asia. 3. Asia—Economic conditions—21st century.
I. Pongsak Hoontrakul, editor. II. Balding, Christopher, editor.
III. Marwah, Reena, 1960– editor. IV. Pongsak Hoontrakul. Asia's
transformation for an Asian century.

HC412.G566 2014
338.95—dc23   2014026405

A catalogue record of the book is available from the British Library.

Design by Newgen Knowledge Works (P) Ltd., Chennai, India.

First edition: December 2014

10 9 8 7 6 5 4 3 2 1

To my beloved wife Toon and my sons Bank, Billet, Boom, and Birdie, and to all those who strive to improve Thailand's education system

Contents

Figures and Tables

Figures

Tables

Foreword

Over the two decades I have known Pongsak Hoontrakul, from his enrolment in the doctorate program until his retirement from Sasin Graduate School of Business Administration of Chulalongkorn University as a senior research fellow, I have been intrigued by his achievements as an individual, a businessman, a thinker, and an incisive analyst.

I remember giving him a surprised look when he told me of his decision to take a year or two off to write a book. Certainly, writing a book is always a great aspiration. And he obviously was deeply inspired!

The name of the book is surely inspiring too!

"The Global Rise of Asian Transformation: Trends and Developments in Economic Growth Dynamics."

For a while now, Asia has been under close scrutiny with regard to its future role in world economics. Is Asia really to be the center of economic growth? Is it rising and on the path to an Asian century? Will Asia make it or break it?

In this book, the author has wisely pointed out the essential paradigm shifts for Asian advantages, in particular, in geopolitics, economic power, and cyber space. I agree that with the rise of China and India and the strength of ASEAN, it is imperative that Asia commands much greater attention from the world. I found the developmental changes in the US-China relationship spelled out in this book very appealing. Through demographic change, Asia, in this century, not only portrays a large middle-class population, but it also comes with ample ability to spend, resulting in a substantial demand push from within. The author has also demonstrated how the cyber space is the new frontier benefiting the new large and young Asian population. In addition, higher education and the extended learning opportunity empower the productive generation. The window of opportunity appears to be wide open for Asia!

Nevertheless, this is still a dream in a world of complexity and dynamicity! The dream to make this century the Asian century is subject to many key issues or game changers. The book identifies political changes, energy revolution, shifts in reliance on domestic consumption versus exporting, urbanization, and infrastructure buildup as well as the ability of Asians to escape the middle income trap. All these are presented not by sector but knitted in an inducing and incisive way.

This book offers a realistic glimpse of the future of Asia in the twenty-first century.

Read it and build your dream about Asia too!

Suchada Kiranandana
Professor Emeritus and past president of Chulalongkorn University
Chairperson, Chulalongkorn University Council
Bangkok, 2014

Preface

Asia as a continent has never been conquered. There is no single Asian identity in terms of values, culture, religion, language, or most importantly, politics. After World War II, decolonization, democratization and globalization of free trade and capital have unevenly impacted countries in Asia. Industrialization and urbanization have progressed rapidly with Japan leading the pack. South Korea, Taiwan, China and some Southeast Asian countries are catching up at different speeds and with varying degrees of success. Yet the overall trend is clear. While the West has stumbled to recover from the global financial crisis of 2008, across the oceans, an Asian Century is dawning.

Also clear is that Asian countries must adapt to new realities. As the old Japanese formula of growth by exporting to the West is now being challenged, they must find new engines for growth from expanding intra-regional trade and investment, building infrastructure, and connecting people. And they must do so in a more complicated political and social environment. As countries become more prosperous, governments are facing new pressures from expanding middle classes that are making their demands felt through social media and mobile communications. Internationally, economic power is shifting from the West to the East and a new geopolitics is forming around relations between the US and China.

While this book is not aimed at providing exact forecasts, we try to identify the growth drivers and game changers that will determine how this new Asian-centered global regime will evolve. We try to analyze the factors that will create economic and political successes in some countries and those that will create failures in others.

Our extensive research has identified five megatrends that pose challenges for Asia in the decades ahead: 1) life after "quantitative easing" (QE); 2) new technologies; 3) individual empowerment and growing demands, 4) Asia's internationalization; and 5) changing demographic patterns. Additionally, we identified five game changers that can make or break the promises of the Asian Century: 1) rising pressures on ruling systems; 2) the shale gas revolution; 3) the transformation of global trade and financial flows; 4) infrastructure connectivity; and 5) human capital and "the middle-income trap." These forces will affect the fortunes of each nation differently depending on its particular domestic political and economic context.

By integrating discussion of these political, economic, and technological forces and showing their real-life workings through case studies, we hope to present a unique experience to readers, particularly the region's middle-level managers and MBA students who seek careers in Asia.

Acknowledgments

For their support over the years and during the writing of this book, I am grateful to Prof. Khunying Suchada Kiranandana, chairperson of Chulalongkorn University Council, Thailand; Prof. Denzo Horvath, dean of Schulich School of Business, York University, Canada; and Prof. Peter J. Ryan, who helped edit chapter 3. For their valuable sharing of experience, I am additionally grateful to H.E. U Htay Aung, Union Minister of Hotels and Tourism, Myanmar; H.E. Tharman Shanmugaratnam, Deputy Prime Minister and Minister of Finance, Singapore; Dr. Piyasvasti Amranand, former Minister of Energy, Thailand; Dr. Olarn Chaipravat, former Deputy Prime Minister, Thailand; M.R. Pridiyathorn Devakula, former Deputy Prime Minister and former Minister of Finance, Thailand; Mr. Kittiratt Na Ranong, former Deputy Prime Minister and former Minister of Finance, Thailand; and Dr. Julapa Jagtiani, the Federal Reserve Bank of Philadelphia. I thank Palgrave Macmillan, New York, for their superb editorial guidance of this book from beginning to end, especially Ms. Casie Vogel and Mr. Bradley Showalter.

We also are grateful to the following people for helping with the research and writing.

Prof. Klaus Schwab, Founder and Executive Chairman of World Economic Forum, Switzerland
Mr. Thierry Geiger, World Economic Forum, Switzerland
Prof. Rich E. Kihlstrom, The Wharton School, University of Pennsylvania
Prof. Michael Useem, The Wharton School, University of Pennsylvania
Prof. Deborah Lucas, MIT Sloan School of Management
Prof. Ravi Jagannathan, Kellogg School of Management, Northwestern University
Prof. Mohanbir Sawhney, Kellogg School of Management, Northwestern University
Prof. Assaf Razin, Department of Economic, Cornell University
Prof. Siqing Pen, Guanghua School of Management, Peking University
Dr. Lian Ping, Chief Economist, Bank of Communication

Prof. Toemsakdi Krishnamra, Director of Sasin of Chulalongkorn University

Prof. Suthi Ekahitanonda, Associate Director of Sasin of Chulalongkorn University

Dr. Virach Aphimeteetamrong, Chairman of Intouch Holdings Pcl

Mr. Thapana Sirivadhanabhakdi, CEO of Thai Beverage Pcl

Mr. Tevin Vongvanich, CEO of PTTEP Pcl

Dr. Pailin Chuchottaworn, CEO of PTT Group

Mr. K.K. Modi, Chairman of KK Modi Group

Mr. Peter J. Eng, particularly for his support in copyediting drafts of many chapters

Ms. Monsawart Vichityuthasart for her support in processing book production

Ms. Sucharat Sathaporn-anon, and

Mr. Chatchawan Siranyathawat, Vimanmak Noi Co. Ltd.

Contributors

Shigeyuki Abe is a professor of economics at Doshisha University, Japan. He is a chief editor of *Asian Economic Journal* and a senior research fellow at Asia Pacific Institute of Research. His current research focuses on trade, foreign direct investment, and economic integration in Asia. Books he has coedited include *East Asian Economies and New Regionalism*. He received his PhD from the University of Hawaii at Manoa.

Htay Aung has been Minister of Hotels and Tourism, Myanmar, since 2012. He has more than 23 years of experience in the tourism industry. He has an MA in tourism administration from George Washington University, United States.

Christopher Balding is an associate professor of business and economics at the HSBC Business School of Peking University Graduate School. He is the author of *Sovereign Wealth Funds: The New Intersection of Money and Power*. His research on international trade and finance has appeared in leading international journals. Prior to entering academia, he worked for a private equity firm.

Jonathan A. Batten is a professor of finance at Monash University, Australia. He has participated in technical assistance projects funded by the Asian Development Bank and the World Bank and was a visiting research fellow at the Bank for International Settlements. He is the editor of *Emerging Markets Review*, and an editor of several other business and financial journals.

Ye Bin is a postdoctoral researcher in Graduate school at Shenzhen, Tsinghua University, China. He received his PhD at the Harbin Institute of Technology, China. His research field covers environmental economics and environmental management, carbon pricing, and carbon cost management. He was one of the founders of Shenzhen Carbon Trading market.

Nonarit Bisonyabut is a research fellow at the Thailand Development Research Institute. He previously served on a Thai Senate subcommittee on monetary and financial Institutions. His work ranges across a variety of topics in econometrics, macroeconomics, and development economics. He holds a PhD from the University of Wisconsin at Madison.

David Garcia is an MBA student at Peking University HSBC Business School and the chairman of Intrepid Sourcing and Services. He is currently working on supply line innovation and liability transmission between producers and suppliers. He has written on a range of topics, including green technology innovation and shadow banking in China.

Pongsak Hoontrakul is a member of the International Advisory Council of the Schulich School of Business, York University, Canada, and a member of the International Advisory Board of the International Association of Deposit Insurance, Switzerland. He is a nonexecutive director of UOL Group Ltd., Singapore. Until May 1, 2013, he published numerous papers as a senior research fellow at the Sasin of Chulalongkorn University, Thailand. Hoontrakul received a doctoral degree in finance from JDBA program in Thammasat University, Thailand.

Reena Marwah is an associate professor at Jesus and Mary College, Delhi University, India. She also has given numerous lectures in India, China, and Thailand on Indian economic development, governance, and globalization. She is the author, coauthor, or coeditor of five books, including *Contemporary India: Economy, Society and Polity*, *Economic and Environmental Sustainability of the Asian Region*, and *Emerging China: Prospects for Partnership in Asia*. Her PhD is in international business.

Chanathip Pharino is an assistant professor of environmental engineering at Chulalongkorn University, Thailand. Her research focuses on environmental systems management, low carbon energy policy, and greenhouse gas management. She is the author of *Sustainable Water Quality Management Policy: The Role of Trading: The U.S. Experience*. She holds a PhD in environmental engineering from the Massachusetts Institute of Technology.

Nat Pinnoi is the Southeast Asia Regional Manager with AF-Mercados Energy Markets International S.A. Prior to joining AF-Mercados, he spent 12 years with the World Bank in both Thailand and Washington, DC Offices managing global portfolio of clean energy investment projects. He holds a PhD in economics from Texas A&M University.

Nisanart Thadabusapa is a corporate credit analyst at Siam Commercial Bank PCL and a financial consultant for several Thai startup companies. She is a former consultant at PricewaterhouseCoopers. She has an MBA from the Sasin of Chulalongkorn University.

1

Asia's Transformation for an Asian Century: Choices and Challenges

Pongsak Hoontrakul

Introduction

A decade into the twenty-first century, Asia sees a promising future. Asian countries are catching up with the West by transforming primarily agrarian societies to industrial powerhouses. Manufacturing is driving innovation, productivity growth, and higher standards of living for hundreds of millions across Asia. In the colonial past, the Asian production and supply chains served Western consumers. But the world is evolving, and an era centered in and shaped by Asia—an Asian Century—finally may be dawning.

This chapter establishes the overall context of Asia's transformation and previews the detailed chapters and case studies to come. It discusses the historical, economic, and social context in which Asia—especially China, India, and the Association of Southeast Asian Nations (ASEAN)—has been rising while the West has been declining. We highlight the moves by these countries to extend their influence, including China's steps to internationalize its currency, and ASEAN's economic integration and free-trade pacts with global partners. We lay out the megatrends that are challenging the region: (1) life after the end of "quantitative easing" (QE); (2) the impact of new technologies; (3) individual empowerment and growing demands; (4) Asia extending from regional to international; and (5) changes in demographic patterns. These megatrends will bolster the region's world standing if governments and businesses handle them adeptly. In addition, we look at game changers that could either boost or retard productivity in the years ahead: (1) rising pressures on ruling systems; (2) the energy landscape reshaped by the shale gas revolution; (3) the transformation of global trade and financial flows; (4) infrastructure connectivity; and (5) talent, human capital, and "the middle-income trap."

What strategies should governments formulate to steer this mix of dynamic and complex forces on the right path? What strategies should businesses formulate to profit from it?

The Rise and Decline of the West

As late as the mid-1800s, Asia accounted for more than 60 percent of global gross domestic product (GDP) according to Maddison (1995). It had the largest population and land mass among the continents and rich natural resources. But the Industrial Revolution armed the West with advanced technology and military might that it used to colonize the rest of the world during the Age of Imperialism of the late nineteenth to midtwentieth centuries. Wars and coerced treaties converted Asia into a raw materials and production base for Western consumers.

The West went on to ride a roller coaster of economic and political fortunes and fates. The Great Depression (1929–1940) was followed by World War II (WWII; 1939–1945), and then the Cold War between the United States and the Soviet bloc (1945–1991). On December 25, 1991, the Soviet Union collapsed. The United States became the sole superpower.

For the next 20 years, the United States stood unchallenged. Then on September 11, 2001, Islamic militants toppled the World Trade Center, the great edifices of American capitalism. And 2008, when capital markets truly collapsed, brought the Great Recession to the United States and its allies in Europe.

Today, in the rest of the world, the United States sees continuing violence in Syria and Afghanistan, Iran's nuclear threat, and military conflict and social turmoil in the Middle East and in Africa. And among its old allies in Europe: debt crises and recessions that threaten to spread globally. Further complicating Europe's difficulties was Russia's annexation of Crimea in March 2014, triggering economic sanctions from the European Union (EU) and the United States Europe will be preoccupied with its own affairs for a long time. Meanwhile, a revolutionary shift in world economic power from the United States and Europe to Asia is emerging.

So the United States has returned to Asia, a region of relative political stability and economic prosperity. Only days after winning a second term in November 2012, President Barack Obama chose Asia for his first foreign trip, to signify the new US strategic focus—the "pivot to Asia," in which Washington is increasing ties with the region in recognition of its increased global political and economic clout.

The Rise of Asia

After WWII, "the Japanese miracle" (1955–1990) placed Asia back on the world business map. Japan's export-led model was followed by many Asian countries including South Korea, Taiwan, and ASEAN's Tigers—Singapore, Malaysia, Indonesia, and Thailand. As developed countries faced both high public debt and unsustainable fiscal deficits in the post-Great Recession, Asian economies remained relatively healthy. Of the world's total of about $11 trillion in dollar-denominated foreign exchange reserves in 2013, more than 60 percent was held by Asian countries (see Figure 1.1).

However, there may be problems on the horizon. The central banks of the United States, the EU, and Japan have used unconventional monetary measures—near-zero interest rates and QE (essentially, printing new money)—to stimulate their economies after the 2008 economic crisis. This injected an estimated $4 trillion into the global financial system, according to the International Monetary Fund (IMF).[1] The capital inflow has caused widespread surges in asset prices and appreciation of the currencies of nearly all the current account surplus countries in Asia. The groundwork has been laid for future economic crises in the region. The situation was so acute that in November 2012, even the IMF, which has long opposed capital controls, endorsed its use by the Philippines at its own discretion. In February 2014, the new head of the US Federal Reserve, Janet Yellen, continued her predecessor's reduction of "QE". When the Fed first hinted at the reductions, in May 2013, currency and stock markets in developing Asian countries including India and Indonesia plunged. How can Asia adjust to life after QE?

The Rise of China

China is using its huge reserves to build up its military might overseas, and gradually internationalizing its renminbi (RMB) currency to build up economic influence.

China has long been preoccupied with domestic security and strategic interests over buffer regions. With industrialization, the income gap between China's cities and the countryside has widened, stoking resentment. And China wants to maintain control over Manchuria, Inner Mongolia, Xingjian, and Tibet, to insulate itself from any attacks from the north (Russia) and from the west (India).

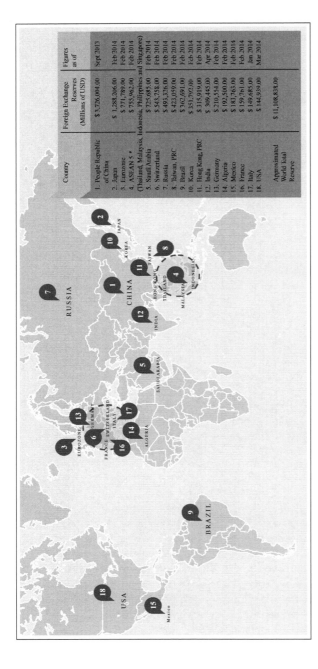

Country	Foreign Exchange Reserves (Millions of USD)	Figures as of
1. People's Republic of China	$ 3,726,000.00	Sept 2013
2. Japan	$ 1,288,206.00	Feb 2014
3. Eurozone	$ 771,789.00	Feb 2014
4. ASEAN 5 * (Thailand, Malaysia, Indonesia, Philippines and Singapore)	$ 755,962.00	Feb 2014
5. Saudi Arabia	$ 725,685.00	Feb 2014
6. Switzerland	$ 543,758.00	Feb 2014
7. Russia	$ 493,326.00	Feb 2014
8. Taiwan, PRC	$ 423,059.00	Feb 2014
9. Brazil	$ 362,691.00	Feb 2014
10. Korea	$ 351,792.00	Feb 2014
11. Hong Kong, PRC	$ 315,919.00	Feb 2014
12. India	$ 309,445.00	Apr 2014
13. Germany	$ 210,554.00	Feb 2014
14. Algeria	$ 192,500.00	Feb 2014
15. Mexico	$ 183,763.00	Feb 2014
16. France	$ 159,761.00	Feb 2014
17. Italy	$ 149,685.00	Jan 2014
18. USA	$ 144,939.00	Mar 2014
Approximated World Total Reserve	$ 11,108,838.00	

Figure 1.1 List of States by Foreign-Exchange Reserves

Notes: 1. *Thailand = $168.1bn, Singapore = $274.0bn, Malaysia = $130.6bn, Indonesia = $102.7 and Phillippines = $80.54bn.

2. Total Reserve of Greater PRC China = $ 4,632,453.00.

3. Total Reserve of the World = Over $ 11 Trillion.

(as of April 30, 2014).

Source: The list is based on IMF (International Monetary Fund) data—when available; otherwise—US Central Intelligence Agency data are indicated. For consistency; forward currency swap contracts are not included in this list until they mature, figures that include them may be higher or lower than those listed here. IMF or other outstanding loans are not shown here, and if accounted for many nations would list lower. Copyright © 2014, Pongksak Hoontrakul.

However, as China has reengaged in international trade and made itself a world factory over the last two decades, it has had to depend on the sea lanes to export its products and to import essential raw materials. China's greatest strategic fear is that the lanes in the South China Sea will be blockaded by the US Navy's 7th Fleet.

It remains to be seen how President Xi Jinping and his colleagues elected at the 18th National Congress of the Communist Party in November 2012 will respond to the US's Asia pivot. In his inauguration speech on March 18, 2013, Xi suggested that unlike the American Dream, which focuses on the wants of individuals, the China Dream focused on the well-off society.[2] On November 15, 2013, the Third Plenum of the Chinese Communist Party's Central Committee revealed a reform package including deregulation, fiscal and tax reform, easing of the one-child policy, rural development, anticorruption campaigns, and social safety nets. This package, with 60 major initiatives across almost all areas, constituted the most comprehensive and ambitious reform in the history of the People's Republic of China.

At the same time, China is jostling with the United States for the upper hand in forming new multination free-trade pacts. Beijing has been promoting the Regional Comprehensive Economic Partnership (RCEP) while Washington has been promoting the Trans-Pacific Partnership (TPP). The RCEP was developed by ASEAN and six major trading partners: China, Japan, South Korea, India, Australia, and New Zealand. Beijing's primary aim in pursuing the RCEP is a higher volume of trade and direct investment. The RCEP proposal was endorsed by the ASEAN summit in Phnom Penh in November 2012. The TPP sets higher standards for economic agreements, especially in the areas of intellectual property, labor, state-owned enterprises, and environmental issues. Singapore, Chile, New Zealand, and Brunei signed on to the TPP long before Obama was first elected. Australia, Peru, Vietnam, Malaysia, Mexico, and Canada later entered the negotiations.

China has stepped up efforts to court the ASEAN members, long-standing allies of the United States. Because of the US government shutdown, Obama cancelled plans to attend two summits in Asia in October 2013, which raised concerns about the US commitment to the Asia pivot. That same month, Chinese Premier Li Keqiang attended the China–ASEAN summit, then addressed the Thai parliament (the first foreign dignitary to do so) and the Indonesian parliament. He next visited Vietnam, China's old rival, to strengthen ties. Obama did make his Asia trip in April 2014, and signed a ten-year military agreement with the Philippines but made no progress on securing the TPP agreement.[3]

China and India

India is a center of global business and high-tech outsourcing while China exports cheap factory goods to every corner of the globe. The speed at which both countries catch up with the advanced economies will depend on how they embrace new technology given their institutional constraints.

Demographic patterns are diverging in the two countries. On average, the ratio of youth or working-age people to the total population in India will increase, whereas in China it will decrease by 2030.[4] This is due mainly to China's one-child policy introduced in 1978. These aging trends will affect both labor supply and demand. China may suffer a 130-million decline in the manual workforce by 2020.[5] Its manufacturing sector will be no longer be able to use young migrant labor without creating inflation. In other words, this will mark the end of low- to medium-value-added industrialization in China. China already is relocating some of its plants to younger neighboring countries like India and some ASEAN nations like Vietnam, Cambodia, and Indonesia.

More significantly, China's export-led model is no longer as appealing as its markets in the West are trying to revive growth. China has to shift to a more domestic-driven economy, like India's.

China and India have taken different paths to political and economic progress. India's federal republic parliamentary system is rooted in its colonial legacy and its mix of ethnic, linguistic, and religious communities. For more than 2,000 years, China's strong, centralized executive has strived for a unified nation and economic growth at the expense of civil liberty. But in both system, income disparities among the people are growing, partly because India's administration is ineffective and China's elite tends to concentrate wealth. More balanced development in the two countries will enhance world peace and economic prosperity.

The hardest question is how the two giants can cooperate peacefully. How should China invest in India? Are mergers and acquisitions one possible type of partnership? How should the United States and ASEAN constructively engage in these processes?

The Rise of ASEAN

The ten members of ASEAN collectively comprise 600 million people, or 8.8 percent of the world's population. In 2010, ASEAN's combined nominal GDP exceeded $2 trillion, making it the eighth largest economy globally.[6] Still, ASEAN seems to be running along two different tracks—one for the higher-income ASEAN 5 and another for the ASEAN-BCLMV. (ASEAN 5 comprises Indonesia, Malaysia, Philippines, Thailand, and Singapore. ASEAN-BCLMV comprises Brunei, Cambodia, Laos, Myanmar, and Vietnam. Brunei is included in this group despite its higher per capita income because while it has rich oil resources, little else of its economy is developed.)

ASEAN was formed in 1968 out of the collective security concerns of the Cold War. The first real economic integration among its members was the agreement on the ASEAN Free Trade Area, effective in 2010. The preferential tariff scheme promotes the free trade of goods and supports local manufacturing within ASEAN.

The next step is to create the ASEAN Economic Community (AEC) by 2015. The AEC deepens regional integration by allowing further free flows of services, investment, and skilled labor. Its main objectives are to promote a single market and production base; a highly competitive economic region; equitable economic development; and full integration into the global economy.

Like China, ASEAN members have had to rebalance their economies after the Great Recession weakened the West's demand for imports. ASEAN is jumpstarting local consumption and investment and implementing massive infrastructure projects (such as highways, high-speed trains, and gas pipelines) that connect ASEAN members and pool their resources. ASEAN wants a wider Asian economic integration that includes China, India, Japan, South Korea, Australia, and New Zealand.

ASEAN integration has significantly benefitted from Myanmar's democratic reforms and opening up to the world since 2011. Myanmar has lessened its dependence on China and increased commercial and other ties with other neighbors, especially India, Thailand, and the other members of ASEAN. In May 2012, Indian Prime Minister Manmohan Singh visited Myanmar. In November of 2012, Obama became the first US president to visit Myanmar after a trip to Thailand in which he had a private audience with King Bhumibol Adulyadej, the world's longest-reigning monarch. ASEAN leaders approved Myanmar to chair the regional bloc in 2014. Everyone is trying to ensure a peaceful transition in Myanmar. And everyone is jockeying for a piece of the cake there.

After going through the Asian financial crisis in 1997–1998 and the Great Recession of 2008 and the ensuing European crises, ASEAN appears ready to join almost any economic agreement that is on the table. Should ASEAN proceed on simultaneous multiple tracks with different partners? Should ASEAN focus more on Myanmar and other things closer to home? Will ASEAN split into two tracks—ASEAN 5 and ASEAN-BCLMV?

In order to compete regionally, ASEAN enterprises need a critical size and an ability to tap vital resources, especially human capital and talents after the formation of the AEC in 2015. And non-ASEAN businesses are looking for ways to make a fast footprint in the fast-growing area. Mergers and acquisitions (M&A) is one way. As a matter of fact, during 2010–2012 there were more M&A deals among or involving Asian companies than in other world regions. Most Asian conglomerates are either family-owned or state-owned, so M&A in the region can be quite challenging. The acquisition of Fraser & Neave Ltd (F&N) of Singapore toward the end of 2012 by Thai billionaire Charoen Sirivadhanabhakdi involved counter bids from two other Asian conglomerates. (See ThaiBev and F&N Acquisition case study.) With the Asian banking system full of liquidity and the region's corporate sector very fragmented, the M&A prospects for the future look quite good in the region.

As they pursue deals and expansion, Asia's businesses should anticipate more political tensions among Asian states in the years ahead. For instance, in the last quarter of 2012, a wave of anti-Japan demonstrations across China over a territorial dispute involving a few East China Sea islands resulted in a 40 percent fall in sales of Japanese vehicles in China.[7]

Five Megatrends That Will Reshape Asia (Summarized in Table 1.1)

Life After QE

The era of ample liquidity and ultralow interest rates is gradually ending. All developing countries in Asia, especially capital inflow-dependent countries with high inflation, have been pressured by the reversal of global liquidity.

But not all countries and sectors will be affected in the same way, and some may actually benefit.[8] Stock markets in North Asia will fare better than those in South and Southeast Asia. North Asian countries like South Korea and Taiwan will enjoy increased demand for their exports as the United States and Europe recover. But South and Southeast Asian countries like India and Indonesia will face higher rates for borrowing. Property prices will drop as the cost of funding rises. Potential losers include capital-intensive industries like utilities, telecommunications, and transportation; potential beneficiaries include banks, insurers, automakers, and exporters.[9]

An overview of current accounts, fiscal and debt positions, bond yields, and foreign exchange positions in the developing Asian countries was

Table 1.1   Selected mega trends 2030: Overview for Asia-in-transformation

Life after QE	The ending of "quantitative easing" by Western central banks will have pronounced financial impacts across Asia. These impacts will vary depending on each country's economic status and structure. The critical issue is how to henceforth finance growth. One possible solution: channeling funds from capital-surplus Asian countries like China to capital-deficit ASEAN members and India.
The impact of new technologies	New technologies such as cheap smartphones and social media are changing social paradigms— and Asians are the world's leading users. These technologies will accelerate economic productivity and growth and improve the quality of life of many millions, especially in the rural areas of India, ASEAN and China.
Individual empowerment and growing demands	Asians are being empowered by more widespread education and use of new communications technology. One result: Asia's growing middle classes are demanding a greater role in decision making, and more accountability from all groups, especially businesses and governments.
Asia extending from regional to international	The ASEAN Economic Community starting in 2015 is the world's newest economic bloc. Its members must adjust to new regional arrangements for free trade, services, investment, and labor, and deal as a bloc with its neighbors, particularly China and India, and the rest of the world. Many companies are anticipating this new environment with cross-border mergers and acquisitions.
Changes in demographic patterns	More than half of the world's population lives in Asia. But many Asian countries are graying— not only Japan but also developing China and Thailand. Other countries like India, Indonesia, and Vietnam will enjoy young and productive populations over the next two decades. The economic and business implications of this trend include labor supply and growth sectors catering to the elderly such as health care and drugs.

Source: Pongsak Hoontrakul, April 30, 2014.
Copyright © 2014, Pongsak Hoontrakul.

examined recently. In the medium to longer term, their currencies will depreciate because of increasing differences between local interest rates and US rates.[10] Interest rates for long-term maturity are expected to rise with a steepening yield curve.[11] This will have long-lasting impacts on infrastructure project finance, capital market development, financial crisis management, and fiscal policy. These issues will be discussed in chapter 3.

The Impact of New Technologies

Whereas the industries of the last two centuries were built on fossil fuels, the new economy firms of the twenty-first century are built on data.

This brings higher productivity. On the demand side, the "digitalization of consumption"—consumer spending on information technology (IT) goods and services—will create a virtuous cycle from increasing mobile devices penetration to higher self-creating content traffic, from expanding telecommunications networks investment to more online social interaction, from ever-enhancing digital services to further capital expenditure in software, hardware, and peopleware.[12] Growth prospects are encouraging in Asia with the rising penetration of online mobile technology and broadband usage in the region. Significant capital expenditure on the new digital business model of SMAC—social media, mobile, analytics, and cloud computing—is needed to boost growth in the new economy.[13] Needed on the supply side are high-wage jobs in content creation and software applications.

Globally, the fastest growth in social network use is in Asia. As of January 2014, China had the largest number of active social media users in the world—more than 600 million, which was more than twice the numbers in the United States.[14] This is even though the Chinese government has banned Facebook in favor of a strictly monitored local version. Indonesia, the Philippines, and Thailand were among the top seven users of Facebook globally in 2013. Across Asia, Facebook added roughly ten million users a month during the first half of 2013. In March, Indonesia had about 50 million active Facebook users, or about 20 percent of its total population. That made it no. 2 in the world after the United States.

India was projected to quickly take over the no. 2 spot; with Facebook penetration at only 5 percent of the total population of more than 1.2 billion, India has much room to grow.[15] And it has a strong local alternative to Facebook; WorldFloat.com, invented by Pushkar Mahatta, was signing up three million users a month as of May 2013. More than 80 percent of its members are from small cities and towns; they use the site to do everything that Facebook offers and more, including playing games and watching movies.[16]

The Internet-enabled mobile device or smartphone is probably the world's biggest innovation today.[17] This is particularly true for developing Asian countries (such as Cambodia, Myanmar, Vietnam, and India) where the fixed-line infrastructure is limited. Easy online access on portable devices is revolutionizing the way people conduct business. Mobile payment systems will benefit all developing countries, where mobile phone penetration outstrips the availability of banking and other financial services. Mobile connections are transforming the lives of Asia's billion-plus rural people, particularly in India, Indonesia, and China.

The social media and mobile communication revolution in Asia will bring many commercial and political challenges and many opportunities. What are the economics of wireless data? How is social media, a disruptive force, changing everyday life? What are the benefits of SMAC? What are the implications of virtual connectivity for educational systems and for human capital development? Chapters 2 and 5 discuss these questions.

Individual Empowerment and Growing Demands

Asia's rising middle classes are being empowered by greater education and wealth as well as their widespread use of the new technologies. They are making more demands of all groups, especially business and government.

Asia is now the primary driver of retail sales growth in the world.[18] Leading the pack by far is China. By conservative estimate, the number of Chinese households with incomes over $15,000 per year will rise from 11 percent of total households in 2011 to more than 40 percent in 2016. By then, China will surpass the United States as the top retail consumer in the world. With another billion-plus population, India also is attracting more interest, especially after the country in 2011 permitted overseas companies to own up to 51 percent of multi-brand retailers. Southeast Asia is also appealing to foreign retailers as those countries deepen economic integration under the AEC.

Asia's food market, worth an estimated $4.2 trillion in 2012, is the biggest in the globe, for example.[19] With higher incomes, Asians are now favoring more resource-intensive protein foods. More changes in consumer preferences are expected as these countries become richer. It is critical for companies to determine the best business opportunities in this area in terms of future growth potential. For example, retail trade is being reshaped as traditional mom-and-pop stores give way to more modern stores.[20] This shift will be discussed in chapter 7.

A common trigger of political turmoil in Asia (and globally) is the failure of government to meet the increased expectations of the middle class.[21] With more education, people demand more than just basic security; they want more choices and opportunities. They are using social media and mobile communications to connect and collectively pressure for a larger slice of the political pie. They are the ones who pay the most taxes, so they have the most interest in making government clean and accountable. In 2013, it was middle-class members who led demands for land reform in China and mass street demonstrations against a political amnesty bill in Thailand and against the controversial results of a general election in Cambodia. "The Thai Great Mass Uprising and Digital Spark" case study in the next chapter will highlight this issue.

How should companies and investors profit from this vast pool of new emerging consumers? How will a new middle-class activism buoyed by the use of social media shape Asia's political economy? These issues will be discussed in chapters 2, 5, and 7.

Asia Extending from Regional to International

While it is clear that Asian economies will become increasingly inter-locked, some countries will fare better than others from the process. Trade frictions may result. Regionalization's winners will push for more open-ing up; its losers will erect trade barriers to protect domestic industries.

The AEC starting in 2015 will be the world's newest economic bloc. One of its main aims is to unify ASEAN as a single competitive pro-duction base that will reach out to the world with magnified bargain-ing power. Many companies are preparing for this new environment by engaging in cross-border M&A. This will diversify risk, create economies of scale and of scope, allow access to new technologies, and capture new markets.

As businesses venture abroad, they face the new challenges of the deepening, integrated global supply chain. "Efficiency" has become the mantra of modern business. But the natural calamities that hit industrial areas of Japan and Thailand in 2011 upended global supply chains and taught us that efficiency can come with some risks. We now know that too much efficiency sacrifices reliability and safety. In both Japan and Thailand, core parts production was concentrated in one area and fac-tories did not store sufficient surplus parts to use in case of disruptions. The result was that the natural disasters severely impacted manufactur-ing and supplies not only in the directly hit areas but also in non-hit areas of Japan and Thailand—and worldwide.

Asian regionalization will deepen "vertical specialization" in pro-duction—the process from start to end, from design to manufacture to assembly.[22] The more interconnected the supply chain, the greater the exposure to foreign shocks or natural calamities. And perhaps due to cli-mate change, extreme weather events and natural disasters are becoming more frequent than ever.

What are the lessons to be learned from the Japanese earthquake and the Thai floods? What new kinds of contingency plans are required to prevent supply chain disruption for high-tech products?

Then there are the geopolitical aspects of Asian countries becoming more involved in the region. Bolstered by its economic dominance, China has begun to assert its influence and claims in both East and Southeast Asia.

What is the outlook for regionalization in Asia? How can India strategically counter China's influence in the region? How will Japan keep its leading regional role?

These questions will be addressed in chapter 2 (on political issues), chapter 3 (on QE and Japan), chapter 4 (on Asia's regionalization and internationalization), chapter 7 (on ASEAN), and chapter 9 (on the supply chain).

Changes in Demographic Patterns

Changes in working-age populations are closely associated with real GDP growth.[23] On average, Asia is graying and its labor pool is contracting. Demographic trends in both East Asia and Southeast Asia will significantly diverge over the next decade.[24] In Japan, almost half the population will reach 60 years of age or above during this decade. Other high-income countries like South Korea, Taiwan, and Singapore also are aging quickly; their median age is projected to exceed 40 years by 2020.[25] Even in China, the ratio of youth to the total population is decreasing. In ASEAN, labor force trends in the next decade are favorable for Indonesia, Philippines, and Malaysia but unfavorable for Thailand

Countries with young populations like India and Indonesia will enjoy "demographic dividends" such as increased productivity and savings and the ability to attract foreign investment. Mass consumption of food and drinks, education, communication, transportation, and leisure is thriving. For low-income nations like India, for example, future high demand growths are in two wheelers, mobile smart device, and cereals consumption . For medium- to high-income nations like China and Korea, for another instance, future demand growths for education, health care, and tourism remain robust. There is a growing appetite for accumulating assets including housing and savings products like mutual funds and insurance all over Asia.

Countries with aging populations like China, South Korea, and Japan will suffer labor scarcity and shrinking growth and savings pools, both on the individual and on the corporate level. Rising expenditures for healthcare and drugs provide both challenges for society and opportunities for businesses.

Demographic issues will be addressed in chapters 6 and 7.

Five Game Changers That Will Make or Break Asia
(Summarized in Table 1.2)

We can identify five game changers that, depending on how they are handled, can influence whether these megatrends result in prosperity or setbacks.

Rising Pressures on Ruling Systems

Many Asian countries like China, Singapore, and Japan (up to the last decade) have long been ruled by a single dominant party. But as people

Table 1.2   Game changers for Asia-in-transformation

Rising pressures on ruling systems	Empowered by new wealth and new technologies, Asian citizens will exert more pressure than ever on established elites and political systems. Elections do matter, but institutions matter more.
The energy landscape reshaped by the shale gas revolution	By 2020, the United States will reap great benefits from the shale gas revolution and its revitalized industrial sector. Energy independence and exports will redefine America's international trade and foreign policies. The ripple effects on Asia will be huge.
The transformation of global trade and financial flows	As the West struggles to recover, Asia is becoming the new center of global economic dynamism. China is rebalancing its economy from export dependence to domestic consumption. India is liberalizing its market. ASEAN is forming an economic community. When Asia's huge trade surplus with the West disappears, the region will no longer be able to rely on its current account surplus as a buffer against financial instability risk. The region must anticipate fast changes in the banking, finance, and capital market landscape.
Regional connectivity	A core economic growth engine for the AEC will be the major new connections from land bridges to power grids, from highways to "open skies" policies among its members and between the AEC and China and India. These linkages will change the way Asians do business and create new opportunities in industrial bases, trade, services, and property development.
Talent, human capital, and "the middle-income trap"	In order to boost productivity, Asian countries must give top priority to upgrading workforce skills. Labor costs in China and ASEAN are no longer as cheap, and countries may need to relocate production to low-cost regions like India and less-developed ASEAN countries. But the eventual goal should be to move to higher-value-added, knowledge-intensive production like in Japan and South Korea.

Source: Pongsak Hoontrakul, April 30, 2014.

become more educated and wealthier, they are increasingly challenging the establishment. Society's ideologies are becoming more diverse; political oppositions are getting stronger.

Despite its surface political stability, China faced on average about 500 protests, riots, and mass demonstrations per day in 2010.[26] In Malaysia in 2013, the opposition fiercely challenged election results that returned to power Prime Minister Najib Razak, the head of the United Malays National Organization (UMNO). After failing to win over ethnic Chinese and other minorities in the Muslim-dominant country, UMNO—the longest continuing ruling party in the world—lost the popular vote but managed to stay in power by capturing a majority in the parliament.

It appears that low-income countries with many poor, uneducated people need a strong government of one or few rulers who can effectively deliver the basic security, food, and prosperity that people want. In rich countries like Singapore, Japan, and South Korea, people want more freedom of expression or a break from the established political and business regimes. And what of middle-income ASEAN members like Thailand and Malaysia? Thailand's rural poor want a strong executive that can quickly alleviate poverty through populist programs. Its urban elite and middle class want a check-and-balance system that will not waste their tax money on corruption and state subsidies.

The key question is how Asian countries can peacefully transform their political systems as their economic systems advance and create new wealth and new demands. This will be examined in the next chapter.

The Energy Landscape Reshaped by the Shale Gas Revolution

A shale gas revolution has emerged from the technological breakthroughs of hydraulic fracturing and horizontal drilling. The United States is now on track to not only become energy independent but also surpass Saudi Arabia as the world's top net energy exporter by the end of this decade.[27] Shale assets are abundant worldwide, but the United States has the strongest prospect to produce shale gas competitively, followed by its close allies Australia and Canada. As these countries start to liquefy their gas and transport it across the Pacific, the United States will have more geopolitical leverage over China and the rest of Asia. US strategic interests in the Pacific sea-lanes will be magnified. This development will occur alongside the long-time territorial disputes in the South China Sea between China and four members of ASEAN (Vietnam, the Philippines, Malaysia, and Brunei), and in the East China Sea Islands between China and Japan. These disputes will not go away any time soon because the disputed areas may hold large energy reserves in addition to being part of a vital sea-lane.

Abundant gas will not only mean lower gas prices but also put pressure on global crude oil prices. It will rejuvenate manufacturing, particularly in petrochemical-related industries. It has already created more than a million new high-wage jobs.[28] The gas revolution will bring broad-scale macroeconomic benefits.[29] On the supply side, coal prices will be under pressure. The United States and other shale-exploiting countries will invest trillions of dollars in shale infrastructure and capital spending, creating a virtuous structural growth cycle. On the demand side, lower carbon emissions may be possible. Abundant, inexpensive, and clean gas energy will encourage people to switch to hybrid or gas engine cars. US industrial sectors including energy-intensive manufacturing will be revitalized.

Not all countries will benefit equally.[30] Many countries cannot exploit their shale deposits because of technical and infrastructure constraints. In Asia, gas importers like China and India will be big winners. Potential losers are Japan and Malaysia if their governments do not quickly put in place policies to adapt to the new global energy landscape.

How will the United States's coming energy exports shape its commercial and political interests in Asia? How will it shape a new energy mix and energy security policies for Asian countries? What are the challenges and opportunities for shale gas, the Green Economy, and renewable energy development in Asia?

These issues and the prospects for a greener economy will be discussed in chapter 8.

The Transformation of Global Trade and Financial Flows

Asia's developing countries are expected to become the world's largest trading bloc by 2030; China and India are projected to be the top world traders.[31] The transformation of global trade is anticipated. Developing countries, particularly those in Asia, will increase their share of world trade. By 2015, the trade in goods among developing countries will overtake that between developing countries and developed countries. But the developing countries' trade surpluses will disappear, notably because China is reorienting its economy toward domestic consumption—and that will progressively increase chances of financial instability. Moreover, the rise of trade interdependence among developing countries carries greater "contagion" systemic risk because developing countries are inherently more vulnerable to shocks than developed countries are.

Central to the 2008 global financial crisis is a process whereby endogenous risk is generated and amplified within the banking system and credit markets. Neither prudent administration nor responsible fiscal policies can be completely relied on to prevent such crises in the future because all financial and banking markets are interconnected. The 2008 crisis was transformed into a global economic crisis that ultimately required a global solution and an Asian regional response. With ample liquidity provided by Bank of Japan, Japanese mega-banks have been aggressively acquiring banks in Southeast Asia and building a yen-based banking network. The greater Japan's QE, the greater the future endogenous risk this network creates for the financial system. Blanket deposit insurance, Basel II compliance, Basel III implementation, and IAS 39 amendments are among the tools that need to be briefly discussed.

What risks does Asia face from the near-zero interest rate policies and the reversal of QE? Where will Asia find the next growth drivers? In both the banking/financial and manufacturing sectors, anticipating adversity must include preventive measures, business continuity plans, and crisis management. We will discuss these issues in chapter 3.

Regional Connectivity and Urbanization

In Asian countries with relatively underdeveloped infrastructure/urbanization bases, development will have multiplying effects on wealth creation. From 2013 to 2020, China leads the pack with $5 trillion in planned infrastructure investment; India is second with $1 trillion, and ASEAN collectively is close to $.5 trillion.[32] Most of the expenditures are in transportation and power.

The formation of the AEC in 2015 is driving greater regional infrastructure connectivity to support increased intra-regional trade.

Urbanization can also be shaped in at least three ways in Asia.

First, industrialization brings urbanization. Manufacturers need economies of scale and economies of scope. They need easy access to specialized services such as air and marine ports, logistics, and financial and accounting experts. Second, government policy can drive urbanization. In March 2013, China announced a new urbanization plan focused on sustainability and environmental protection in its 12th and 13th five-year plans (2011–2020). A "hub and spoke" model of cities was proposed. Third, urbanization may spring from mass transit systems and the building of infrastructure such as roads, airports, and trains. The North–South and East–West Corridors, shown in Figure 1.2, are being constructed to connect all the major cities in the Greater Mekong Subregion as a part

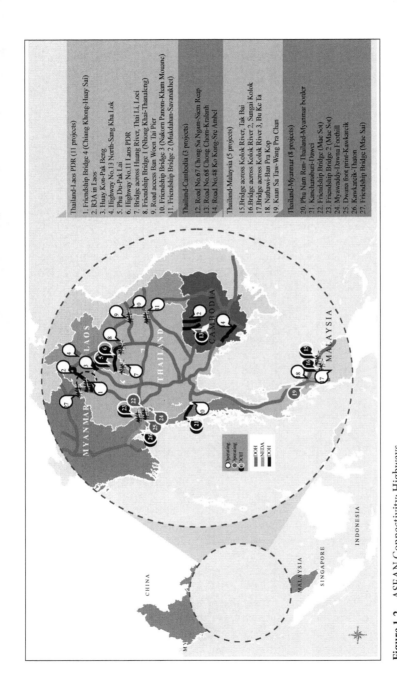

Thailand-Laos PDR (11 projects)

1. Friendship Bridge 4 (Chiang Khong-Huay Sai)
2. R3A in Laos
3. Huay Kon-Pak Beng
4. Highway No.13 North-Sang Kha Lok
5. Phu Du-Pak Lai
6. Highway No.11 Laos PDR
7. Bridge across Huang River, Thai Li, Loci
8. Friendship Bridge 1 (Nhong Khai-Thanaleng)
9. Road access Ban Woen Tai Pier
10. Friendship Bridge 3 (Nakom Panom-Kham Mouane)
11. Friendship Bridge 2 (Mukdahan-Savanakhet)

Thailand-Cambodia (3 projects)

12. Road No.67 Chong Sa Ngam-Siem Reap
13. Road No.68 Chong Chom-Kralanh
14. Road No.48 Ko Kong-Sre Ambel

Thailand-Malaysia (5 projects)

15. Bridge across Kolok River, Tak Bai
16. Bridge across Kolok River 2, Sungai Kolok
17. Bridge across Kolok River 3, Bu Ke Ta
18. Nathawi-Ban Pra Kop
19. Kuan Sa Taw-Wang Pra Chan

Thailand-Myanmar (8 projects)

20. Phu Nam Ron- Thailand-Myanmar border
21. Kanchanaburi-Dawei
22. Friendship Bridge (Mae Sot)
23. Friendship Bridge 2 (Mae Sot)
24. Myawaddy-Dawna Foothill
25. Dwana foot print-Kawkareik
26. Kawkareik-Thaton
27. Friendship Bridge (Mae Sai)

Figure 1.2   ASEAN Connectivity: Highways

Notes: DOH = Department of Highway; NEDA = Neighbouring Countries Economic Development Cooperation Agency.

Source: Dr. Chadchart Sittipunt, Thai Minister for Transport, presentation at the Thai Investor Forum, London, October 10, 2012. Copyright © 2014, Pongksak Hoontrakul.

of ASEAN connectivity projects through new highways and land bridge network.

But not all urbanization will yield more economic development. In the last two decades, Japan's urbanization ratio has risen, but the country's economic growth has slowed. India has made little advance in urbanization, but its economy has grown via liberalization. Often politics, particularly at the local level, plays a key role. A city with greater political status tends to be more urbanized as the central government puts more money into the area even though it may lack any geographic advantage.[33]

These issues will be examined in chapters 6 and 7.

Talent, Human Capital, and "the Middle-Income Trap"

Increased knowledge and technical skills are needed for a country to raise its economy to the next level. Economic development typically starts with basic endowed factors—land and labor. Of course, capital also is vital, although a policy of openness to foreign direct investment may resolve this constraint. In a simple sense, industrialization is a process of migrating low-productivity agricultural workers to higher-productivity, mass production manufacturing—in other words, the transformation from a factor-driven economy to an efficiency-driven one. China, Malaysia, and Thailand are prime examples of countries that used this method to graduate to middle-income status in the last decade.

A country falls into "the middle-income trap" when it cannot move up to higher income status. As wages and land prices rise, the country is unable to compete in export markets with low-cost manufacturers elsewhere. Economic growth stagnates and it might even decline.

Building up infrastructure and urbanization helps to create jobs and improve productivity. But generally this is not sufficient for a country to move up to high-income status. This requires a further transformation: shifting from resource-driven growth to innovation-driven growth. And that, in turn, requires upgrading both human capital and public institutional arrangements (government, laws, etc.).

Countries like Japan and Singapore have few natural resources. But they overcame this constraint and reached high-income status by developing their human capital with excellent education and training programs.

Can the new ITs help a country come out of the middle-income trap without a substantial upgrading of its formal education system?

The use of social technologies helps high-skill knowledge workers to increase their performance by 20 to 25 percent.[34] Many companies now use social media and nearly all report benefits for their employees. Monitoring and responding to social media conversations from customers help to create value and to develop innovative products.

Chapter 5 will shed some light on these issues.

Case Study

The World's Megatrends and Game Changers: What about Asia?

Pongsak Hoontrakul

This book was inspired by my extensive experience over the years as panelist, participant, or facilitator at prominent conferences in many countries. These include World Economic Forum meetings at Davos (2009), Dalian (2009), Ho Chi Minh City (2010), Jakarta (2011), and Bangkok (2012), as well as conferences organized by Asian financial institutions and universities. These conferences featured discussions of important current topics such as changing consumer patterns in developing countries, M&A trends, Myanmar's opening, and urbanization. One common theme was that Asia is gaining a dominant role on the world stage. But the discussions typically were influenced by the perspectives or the agenda of the West.

In July 2012, I organized the Sasin Bangkok Business Forum sponsored by the Sasin Graduate School of Business Administration at Chulalongkorn University, Bangkok. The theme was "Asia in Transformation." Leaders from Asia's business, political, academic, and nongovernmental sectors exchanged views with top business executives for two days. The consensus was that we were already in the Asian Century, with economic power shifting from West to East and the geopolitical relationship between the United States and Asia being reshaped by that shift. We discussed many fascinating developments such as the impact of social networks on markets, the rush toward infrastructure connectivity of the Greater Mekong Subregion countries, the Green Energy Economy, and the impacts of the 2008 global financial crisis. Yet, what was lacking was a long-term view for Asia.

After retiring from Sasin in 2013, I continued to research these themes, especially by reading the work of leading investment bankers in and outside the region. I found two fascinating papers that provided good frameworks to look into the future: "Global Trends 2030: Alternative Worlds" by the National Intelligence Council in the United States and "Game Changers: Five Opportunities for US Growth and Renewal" by McKinsey Global Institute. But they offered only a US perspective.

I came to realize that megatrends in the West—like the growing empowerment of individuals, changing demographic patterns, and the shale gas revolution—also are occurring in Asia. And that Asia's governments and businesses must deal with the same game changers like changing trade patterns, expanding infrastructure, and nurturing new talents and skills. All this presents the region with new challenges and new opportunities that will require both visionary thinking and realistic policymaking.

My colleagues at leading educational, research, and financial institutions were eager to collaborate on this book because they agreed these were indeed the crucial issues that we need to understand in order to prepare for the Asian Century.

A Thai Billionaire Tycoon Shrewdly Maneuvers to Acquire F&N

Pongsak Hoontrakul and Nisanart Thadabusapa

Fraser and Neave Limited (F&N) is a 130-year-old Singapore-based conglomerate with roots in the country's colonial era. Its highlight joint ventures include teaming up with Amsterdam-based Heineken to establish Asia Pacific Breweries (APB) to produce Tiger Beer. Thai billionaire tycoon Charoen Sirivadhanabhakdi took over F&N in February 2013 as part of his company's overseas expansion.

The seven-month takeover saga started when Charoen's Thai Beverage PLC (ThaiBev) bought a 22 percent stake in F&N from OCBC Bank of Singapore on July 18, 2012 at S$8.88/share, for a total of S$2.78 billion (US$2.2 billion). At the same time, Kindest Place Group, a vehicle linked to ThaiBev and owned by Charoen's son-in-law, acquired another 8.6 percent stake in APB for below S$50 apiece from an OCBC unit, Great Eastern Holdings. Effectively, Charoen was holding about 17.4 percent of APB shares, approximately 9 percent of which came from his 22 percent stake in F&N.

Heineken's crucial interest in APB suddenly looked insecure.

With a relatively young and large population, Southeast Asia—especially with the AEC to be formed in 2015—and other Asian markets for alcoholic beverages will grow at a higher rate in the coming decades than the European and North American markets. Charoen had his own Chang Beer brand. If he took over APB, he would add APB's well-known beer brands including Tiger, the market leader in Singapore, and Bintang, the market leader in Indonesia. ThaiBev would expand its economies of scale and scope in production and distribution in time for AEC 2015. And this would jeopardize Heineken's future growth.

Charoen knew that it was very likely that Heineken would take all necessary action to protect its interest in APB and that that would include bidding up all the shares. And that meant he stood to reap billions in disposable gains.

On August 18, 2012, Heineken countered with a final offer of S$53.00/share for the rest of APB and its intention to delist APB. F&N shareholders accepted the offer on September 28, 2012, thus leading to the privatization of APB.

Charoen certainly would not go home empty-handed. His focus now turned to the crown jewel that he really wanted: F&N, whose businesses ranged from milk to shopping malls.

During the bidding for APB, ThaiBev became a strategic shareholder in F&N with 29 percent ownership. On September 13, 2012, Charoen's company TCC Assets bid S$9 billion (S$8.88 a share) for the rest of F&N.

Then entered another Southeast Asian billionaire, the Riady family of Indonesia. The CEO of Overseas Union Enterprise (OUE), a Singapore-based company, is the son of Mochtar Riady, who controls Indonesia's Lippo Group, with businesses ranging from property and financial services to food across Asia. On November 15, 2012, OUE offered S$9.09 a share for F&N, topping Charoen's bid.

M&A fever seized the Singapore Exchange. The market speculated that Charoen would do whatever it would take to acquire F&N. It was thought that his aim was to expand in Asia after having been active in buying businesses in Thailand, and that he viewed strategic acquisitions as a shortcut to achieve his goals.

In order to end rampant daily speculation, the Singapore Exchange unprecedentedly insisted on an auction for the final offer for shareholders' consideration, if neither bidder was able to lock the deal.

On January 18, 2013, three days before the auction was to start, TCC Assets bid S$9.55 a share, topping the OUE offer. Charoen announced that ThaiBev and TCC Assets had gradually obtained shares in F&N totaling 39.94 percent from the open market. If OUE wanted to outbid Charoen, it would have to pay more than S$9.55 per share for the 39.94 percent portion that he owned.

Because of Charoen's 39.94 percent share ownership announcement, OUE did not dare to counter the bid. That cleared the path for Charoen's takeover on February 18, 2013, with a final holding of 90.32 percent of total issued shares.

The deal highlighted Charoen's ambitions to expand both within Thailand and abroad, and to diversify his investments, which included a large property portfolio throughout the region, and his revenue stream, which was mainly from alcoholic drinks. With F&N he acquired exposure to high-growth Southeast Asian markets with attractive demographics and consumer-spending trends. The takeover reflected Charoen's expansion strategy of first identifying under-valued assets and then executing a well-planned series of first acquisition moves.

Notes

1. "Global Financial Stability Report (GFSR): Responding to the Financial Crisis and Measuring Systemic Risk," *IMF*, April 2009 (http://www.imf.org/External/Pubs/FT/GFSR/ 2009/01/ and http://www.imf.org/external/pubs/ft/gfsr/2009/01/pdf/summary.pdf).

2. Xi Jinping, "The China Dream, The People's Dream," Inauguration speech at the National People's Congress, March 17, 2013 (http://cpc.people.com.cn/n/2013/0318/c64387–20819181.html) (in Chinese).

3. The four nations that President Obama visited were Japan, South Korea, Malaysia, and Philippines. More discussion at Kevin Liptak, "5 takeaways from Obama's trip to Asia," *CNN*, April 29, 2014 (http://edition.cnn.com/2014/04/29/politics/obama-asia-trip/).

4. National Intelligence Council, *Global Trends 2030: Alternative Worlds*, December 2012.

5. Adrian Mowat et al., "China 2020: 130 Million Swing," *Equity Research*, May 31, 2011.

6. Edward Teather, "ASEAN Linkages and Why They Matter," *UBS Investment Research*, June 24, 2011: 4.

7. Doron Levin, "The Real Winner in the China-Japan Row," CNN.com, November 1, 2012 (http://features.blogs.fortune.cnn.com/2012/11/01/the-real-winner-in-the-china-japan-row/?iid=HP_LN) and Masaaki Kanno and Masamichi Adachi, "Macroeconomic Impacts of Japan/China dispute," *JP Morgan*, October 6, 2012: 1–5.

8. T. Moe et al., "Asia Pacific 2014 Outlook: Back on Track," *Goldman Sachs*, November 21, 2013.

9. Ibid.

10. P. Hooper et al., "World Outlook: A Leap Back to Trend Growth," *Deutsche Bank Research*, December 11, 2013.

11. Ibid, p. 67.

12. Moe, "Asia Pacific 2014 Outlook."

13. Anantha Naraya and Sagar Rastogi, "India IT Service Sector: The SMAC pack," *Credit Suisse*, July 10, 2013.

14. Simon Kemp, "Social, Digital & Mobile in APAC in 2014," *WeAreSocial*, January 23, 2014 (http://wearesocial.net/blog/2014/01/social-digital-mobile-apac-2014/).

15. Laura He, "Facebook: Mobile Growth Take Off in Emerging Markets," *Forbes*, October 21, 2012 (http://www.forbes.com/sites/laurahe/2012/10/21/facebook-mobile-growth-takes-off-in-emerging-markets/).

16. Krittivas Mukherjee, "India's Worldfloat a challenger to Facebook," *The Straits Times*, May 10, 2013.
17. "Smartphones-The GEMs Telco Study for 2013," *CitiGroup*, November 2012.
18. Carrie Yu, "2013 Outlook for the Retail and Consumer Products Sector in Asia," *PwC*, 2013 (http://public.adequatesystems.com/pub/attachment/233 954/03521338916231161364 972452625-fr.pwc.com/PwC%20%20Etude%20 Asia%20outlook%20030413%20basse%20 def.pdf?id=882391).
19. Ibid.
20. Ebru Sener Kurumlu et al., "Asia Consumer 2014 Outlook and Strategy," *J.P. Morgan*, January 22, 2014.
21. Francis Fukuyama, "The Middle-Class Revolution," *Wall Street Journal*, June 28, 2013 (http://online.wsj.com/news/articles/SB10001424127887323873904578571472700348086).
22. Willem Buiter and Ebrahim Rahbari, "Trade Transformed: The Emerging New Corridors of Trade Power," *Citi GPS: Global Perspectives & Solutions*, October 18, 2011.
23. Hak Bin Chua et al., "Asia: Demographic Divide & Peaks," *GEM Economics— Asia, Bank of America Merril Lynch*, August 23, 2013: 1–20.
24. Ibid.
25. Amar Gill, Eric Fishwick and Anna Tantuico, "Asia Graying: Investment Implications of Rapid Ageing," *CLSA*, December 2012.
26. Mas Fisher, "How China Stays Stable Despite 500 Protests Every Day," *The Atlantic*, January 5, 2012 (http://www.theatlantic.com/international/archive/2012/01/how-china-stays-stable-despite-500-protests-every-day/250940/).
27. Jason Channell et al.," Energy Darwinism: The Evolution of the Energy Industry," *Citi GPS: Global Perspectives & Solutions*, October 2013.
28. Ibid.
29. Richard Kersley, Ed Westlake, and David Hewitt, "The Shale Revolution II," *Credit Suisse*, October 1, 2013.
30. Ibid.
31. Buiter and Rahbari, "Trade Transformed."
32. Andrew Tilton et al., "Asia Economics Analyst: ASEAN's Half a Trillion Dollar Infrastructure Opportunity," *Goldman Sachs*, Issue no: 13/18, May 30, 2013: 1–18.
33. Vincent Chan et al., "China Market Strategy: Urbanization and its Limits," *Credit Suisse Equity Research*, March 13, 2013.
34. Michael Chui et al., "The Social Economy: Unlocking Value and Productivity through Social Technologies," *McKinsey Global Institute*, July 2012: 1–184.

2

Asia's Evolving Economic Dynamism and Political Pressures

Pongsak Hoontrakul

Introduction

Politics matters. It matters even more critically in Asia because of the diversity of its political systems and levels of economic development. Businesses must understand what drives public policies that are typically determined by local values and structures.

Asia as a continent has never been conquered. There is no single Asian identity in terms of values, culture, religion, language, or most importantly, politics. Many parts of Asia were colonized by Western European powers. After World War II (WWII), countries such as India, Indonesia, Malaysia, and Vietnam gained independence and developed political structures based on the colonial models. A few countries like China, Japan, and Thailand stayed independent for hundreds if not thousands of years, and have deep roots in their ancient beliefs, religions, cultures, and political systems.

After the war, Asia has had a wide range of political systems, although many also have been dominated by single-party structures. For all these countries, governance is no longer as simple and smooth as it used to be. Increasing educational levels and use of new technology communications have empowered many citizens. The rising middle classes demand more accountability and civil liberty from politicians. In Singapore, Myanmar, Malaysia, and elsewhere, opposition groups have sprung up like never before. Political dynasty families like Gandhi in India, Park in South

Korea, and Aquino in the Philippines are being challenged amid scandals and economic slowdowns.

Yet with so many Western countries mired in debt, Asia is primed for greater leadership on the world stage.

First, economic power is shifting from West to East. China and India not only weathered the global economic crisis that began in 2008, but have actually continued growing. The ten-member Association of Southeast Asian Nations (ASEAN) will rise to global prominence as it forms a common market, the ASEAN Economic Community (AEC), in 2015.

Second, there is a geopolitical shift. The United States rose after WWII, and when the Soviet Union collapsed in 1991, it found itself the sole superpower. Now, once-regional powers like China and India are rising on the international stage.

Finally, there is Asia's transformation by the information and communications technology (ICT) revolution. Asian societies and their discontents have enthusiastically embraced mobile communications and social media networks. The Arab Spring of the Middle East was a revolution by Facebook and Twitter. How will the ICT revolution transform lives in Asia, as industrialization has done during the past five decades?

Asia's Political and Economic Landscape

Staging the Economic Boom

War and bloody conflict forged many of Asia's sovereign states and political systems. Some countries ended up in communism and poverty; others prospered through industrialization and democratization. The end of WWII brought Japan a new liberal democratic constitution in 1947. At the end of the Korean War (1950–1953), the peninsula was separated; South Korea was supported by the United States and North Korea by China. Then the Vietnam War (1955–1975) caused security alarms throughout Southeast Asia and sharpened the democracy versus communism divide.

After WWII, Asia experienced an unprecedented long economic boom (1940s–1970s). The baby boom (1946–1964) created by young males returning from the war created structural world demand. A series of technological changes—transistors, integrated circuits, personal computers, and mobile phones—significantly enhanced labor productivity. This was a golden age of capital accumulation with high output growth, low inflation, and low unemployment.

With strong support from the United States, the "Japanese miracle" (1955–1990) placed Asia back on the world business map. Japan's export-led model was followed by Taiwan and South Korea in the 1970s and then in the 1980s by some of the Southeast Asian countries. Today, China, Japan, South Korea, and Singapore are leading the pack, followed by Malaysia, Thailand, Indonesia, the Philippines, and Vietnam. But at the same time, poorer countries like India, Myanmar, Laos, and North Korea that are struggling with industrialization will suffer even wider disparity with their neighbors.

A Mélange of Political Systems

Asia has all types of political systems. Many of these systems evolved from the decolonization process after WWII and the campaign to counter the threat of communism during the Cold War (1947 to 1991) between the Western Bloc dominated by the United States against the Eastern Bloc led by the Soviet Union and China. The varieties of civil–military relations in Asia are formed.[1] In immature political systems, the military—representing unity, discipline, and authority—is generally a decisive factor during periods of political chaos.

Contemporary Asia's political systems include absolute monarchy in Brunei; constitutional monarchy in Thailand, Japan, and Malaysia; military dictatorship in North Korea; federal parliamentary state in India; unitary presidency with constitutional republic in South Korea, Indonesia, the Philippines, and Singapore; and single-party communist states in China and Vietnam.

Many Asian countries—whether democratic, authoritarian, or hybrid—have long been dominated by single parties. The Liberal Democratic Party has dominated Japanese politics since 1955. The People's Action Party has ruled Singapore uninterrupted since 1959. Suharto was Indonesian president for 31 years (1968–1998).

India has become the world's most populous democracy, with an indirectly elected prime minister as head of government. India has dispersed political power in a loose confederation to accommodate states that used to be ruled by individual Maharajah (or kings). India won its independence from Britain in 1947 through nonviolent resistance led by Mahatma Gandhi. India's first prime minister, Jawaharlal Nehru, adopted a socialist-inspired economic model that was used for the next 17 years (1947–1964). Dragged back by the inefficiency of its state-owned enterprises and government intervention and subsidies, India's economic growth stagnated at around 3.5 percent from the 1950s to the 1980s.

Nehru's grandson, Prime Minister Rajiv Gandhi, took major steps in 1985 to deregulate and to liberalize the economic structure.[2] India began enjoying growth of close to 6 percent per year from 1990.[3] Today, India's ICT sector, outsourcing back office operations, and software development services have become a major economic engine. The service sector now accounts for nearly two-thirds of Indian output. Still, despite a young and large population, India remains a low-income country. Its industrial sector is held back by red tape and regulatory burdens. And the country lacks a strong middle class, which is an essential foundation for an effective democracy.

China has a self-appointed collective leadership in a one–party system. The Communist Party of China (CPC) steers all business and economic decisions in the world's second largest economy. China has concentrated political power with high risk in succession. This reflects a more than 2,000-year-old belief in the need for a strong and centralized executive branch to unify the vast territory. China suffered civil war from 1927 to 1949. The CPC won in 1949 and its Kuomintang rivals retreated to Taiwan. The two states still are dominated by these two parties today. Taiwan has long enjoyed strong support from the United States and prospered. But the Communists headed by Chairman Mao Zedong suffered the Great Chinese Famine (1959–1962) that killed an estimated 30 million or more people. Not until 1992, after the end of Cold War, did paramount leader Deng Xiaoping launch market-style reforms that opened the way for the country to reclaim its world economic status.

Back to Basics with Aristotle

The fourth-century thinker Aristotle was a student of Plato and a teacher of Alexander the Great, and one of the founding philosophers of Western civilization. With today's world beset by ineffective governments, it is instructive to reread Aristotle's "Politics,"[4] a classic treatise on the ruler and the ruled. Aristotle wrote that there are only three types of rulers and six types of rule, as shown below:

Type	Aim: the common good	Aim: self-interest
One ruler	Kingship	Tyranny
Few rulers	Aristocracy	Oligarchy
Many rulers	Democracy	Chaos

First, if only one person rules and he works for the common good, he is a benevolent king; if he cares only about his self-interest, then the people will suffer from tyranny. If many people rule and they pursue the common good, democracy results; if they are self-interested and unethical, chaos will reign. In between is a collective leadership that can be either an aristocracy (common good) or an oligarchy (self-interest).

Alexander the Great asked Aristotle which system was best for his vast empire that consisted of many countries. Aristotle replied that it was easy: Just look at the quality of your people. If they are poor and uneducated (as in today's low-income countries), then you need a strong, single ruler to build the nation first. In that case, benevolent kingship is the most effective form of rule, Aristotle said. But if your people are sophisticated and educated citizens (as in today's high-income countries), democracy and a majority-vote system is best, he said.

But what about when today's lower-income countries are progressing toward middle-income status? In these countries, such as China, the better-off people want economic and civil liberty, the poor want social welfare and redistribution, and the powers-that-be want to maintain the status quo. This can lead to potentially explosive conflict. Would a collective leadership of well-educated people chosen in a limited voting system be best? Of course, if this collective leadership abuses its powers, oligarchy prevails. What Aristotle does not tell us is how to ensure the peaceful transition of political systems as a country moves (or down) the economic ladder.

Economic Power Shifting to the East

After WWII, industrialization brought economic prosperity to Asia. With strong support from the United States, during 1940–1980 Japan leaped from low- to high-income status, its economy second in the world behind the United States. As its labor became expensive, during 1960–1990 Japan relocated its labor-intensive and low-value-added manufacturing like textiles and assembly lines to the newly industrialized economies (NIEs): South Korea, Taiwan, Hong Kong, and Singapore. Soon the NIEs caught up with Japan by deepening their value-added products and sophisticated services. From 1975 onward, Japan started to relocate its manufacturing bases to Southeast Asian countries like Thailand, Malaysia, Indonesia, and the Philippines.

By the 2000s, Thailand and Malaysia had developed into middle-income countries; Indonesia and the Philippines are likely to follow soon. Table 2.1 shows the remarkable growth driven by factor accumulation (labor and capital) for Asian emerging markets during the 1970s–2010s. The table illustrates that early on all these countries from Korea to

Singapore, from Thailand to China, from Indonesia to India were initially driven by cheap labor inputs in the 1970s and the 1980s and then by capital accumulation in the 1990s–2011.[5] In East Asia, unlike in Latin America, capital accumulation increased labor productivity and generated growth over the decades.[6] It is important to note the slowing down in "total factor productivity" (TFP—the measure of the efficiency of all inputs in production) in the majority of Asian emerging markets. The Philippines, Thailand, and Malaysia can still boost their TFP by capital accumulation because they have high domestic savings and excess capacity.[7] But they and the other NIEs may not enjoy growth like in previous decades unless they upgrade to the new knowledge-based economy.

Facing economic slowdown and rising inflation, in 1992 China's Deng Xiaoping launched the "socialist market economy." In 1994, a new company law was promulgated. Foreign direct investment poured into China to leverage on the new policies and to capitalize on the vast pool of labor and emerging consumer market. China's agricultural and industrial output grew an average of 10 percent a year from 1990 to 2011. Because of its large population and success in industrialization and urbanization, China has become the center of Asia's production network and factory of the world.

China has to reduce its accelerated speed of capital accumulation[8] (see Table 2.1). The wide-ranging reforms that President Xi launched at the Communist Party's Third Plenum in November 2013 to rebalance the economy and achieve "China's Dream" should help China avoid a near-term hard landing and unleash its long-term growth potential. China's economic surge has exacerbated many social problems such as environmental degradation and income disparity, notably in the rural inland areas.

India further liberalized its market in 1991. "License Raj"—investment, industrial, and import licensing—was coming to an end. In this digital age, India's large population of young English-speaking workers has become dominant in global business processing outsourcing, enabled services, software development, and financial research. More than 23 percent of the workforce is employed in the business services sector, which is growing at an average of more than 7.5 percent per year. Foreign exchange reserves rose from US$5.8 billion in March 1991 to $277 billion in September 2013. After the general election in 2014, further market reform is expected. Like Indonesia and Vietnam, India can accelerate industrialization by adding more input, but is holding back on capital expenditure due to low domestic savings apart from a heavy regulatory burden.[9]

According to the International Monetary Fund (IMF), China's nominal gross domestic product (GDP) in 2012 was $16.24 trillion, the second

Table 2.1 Emerging Market Asia (EMA)—Historical look at a growth accounting exercise

		1970s	1980s	1990s	2000–2011
CHN	Real GDP	6.67	9.74	10.00	10.20
	Labor	1.83	1.64	0.75	0.41
	Capital	3.47	3.31	4.35	6.25
	TFP	1.37	4.79	4.90	3.54
HKG	Real GDP	9.02	7.44	3.58	4.49
	Labor	1.81	1.41	0.70	0.46
	Capital	3.81	3.72	3.39	1.76
	TFP	3.40	2.30	-0.51	2.28
IDN	Real GDP	7.76	3.27	4.79	5.81
	Labor	1.30	1.76	0.81	0.71
	Capital	3.45	4.41	2.91	2.76
	TFP	3.01	0.22	-0.66	1.69
IND	Real GDP	2.94	5.58	5.84	7.30
	Labor	2.09	1.87	1.20	1.09
	Capital	1.12	1.42	2.16	4.34
	TFP	-0.26	2.30	2.48	1.87
KOR	Real GDP	10.08	8.62	6.68	4.51
	Labor	2.51	1.62	0.74	0.85
	Capital	4.11	4.36	4.81	2.58
	TFP	3.45	2.64	1.13	1.08
MYS	Real GDP	9.43	3.27	4.79	5.81
	Labor	2.14	1.84	1.78	1.39
	Capital	3.77	4.04	4.76	2.21
	TFP	3.52	-0.11	0.71	1.41
PHL*	Real GDP	5.78	3.27	4.79	5.81
	Labor	2.68	2.32	1.74	1.54
	Capital	1.90	1.63	1.26	1.24
	TFP	1.20	-1.93	-0.25	1.67
LKA*	Real GDP	4.59	3.27	4.79	5.81
	Labor	1.09	0.53	1.20	1.20
	Capital	1.52	1.44	1.13	1.71
	TFP	1.99	2.27	2.95	2.22
SGP	Real GDP	9.44	7.81	7.31	5.93
	Labor	1.79	1.40	1.86	1.60
	Capital	7.08	5.11	4.57	2.99
	TFP	0.56	1.30	0.88	1.34
THA	Real GDP	10.12	7.26	5.35	4.19
	Labor	0.97	1.34	0.35	0.84
	Capital	5.00	4.19	5.42	1.53
	TFP	4.15	1.73	-0.42	1.82
TWN	Real GDP	10.12	7.70	6.35	4.09
	Labor	2.13	1.44	0.69	0.45
	Capital	6.23	4.48	4.58	2.29
	TFP	1.75	1.78	1.08	1.35
VNM*	Real GDP	4.76	4.73	7.42	7.11
	Labor	1.42	1.62	1.54	1.89
	Capital	0.70	1.13	3.32	3.20
	TFP	2.65	1.97	2.56	2.08

Note: 1. CHN=China; HKG=Hong Kong; IDN=Indonesia; IND=India; KOR=Korea; MYS=Malaysia; PHL=Philippines; LKA=Sri Lanka; SGP=Singapore; THA=Thailand; TWN=Taiwan; VNM=Vietnam; GDP=gross domestic product; TFP=total-factor productivity.

2. We use actual labor share of income compiled in PWT8.0 which is not assumed to be constant, except for countries with (*) where data are unavailable or looks inaccurate, in which case we assume labor share of income is 70% as in Gollin, 2002.

Source: Chua et al., 2013. Copyright © 2013, Johanna Chua, Citi.

largest in the world, followed by Japan's $5.96 trillion. That compared with the ASEAN-4's combined $1.82 trillion, and India's $1.84 trillion. (ASEAN-4 comprises countries at broadly similar levels of development—Indonesia, the Philippines, Thailand, and Malaysia.) By 2030, the nominal GDP of China, India, and ASEAN combined will equal more than half of the world GDP.[10] China's foreign exchange reserves are the highest in the world, well over $3.56 trillion as of June 2013, followed by Japan's $1.27 trillion, the ASEAN 4's $654 billion, and India's $277 billion. Indeed, Asia now holds more than 60 percent of world reserves.

The Next Growth Engine: The Knowledge-Based Economy

The ICT revolution that started in the United States in the 1980s has brought a new business and social paradigm to the world. The first stage, Web 1.0, was the digital revolution to create the "knowledge-based" or "new" economy, a completely different business model, as shown in Table 2.2. The old economy is mainly based on tangible assets like land, buildings, and equipment. The new economy is mainly based on human capital and intellectual property like software and informational content. The industries of the last two centuries were built on fossil fuels. The new economy firms of the twenty-first century are built on data. This has brought higher productivity, more value creation, and significant upside in utility, efficacy, and monetization. The next stage, Web 2.0, started in 1999 and brought social media to the world.

The "social economy" value is estimated to be more than $1 trillion annually across the value chain as more than a billion people have adopted

Table 2.2 Key factor comparison between old and new economies

Business model	Old economy	New economy
	Asset-based model	Intellectual-based model
Product	Goods/service	Innovation
Production	Mass	Customerized
Asset Factor	Capital and Land	Digital and Human Capital
Asset Form	Tangible	Intangible
Fixed Cost	Land and Machinery	R&D
Variable Cost	Labor/Material/Factor Cost	Almost Zero
Distribution Process	Physical	Virtual
Economics	Scarcity	Abundance
Profitability	Marginal Cost = Marginal Benefit	Value Proposition × Networking Effect

Source: Pongsak Hoontrakul. Copyright © 2014, Pongsak Hoontrakul.

new behaviors using social media.[11] The new technology is a seismic shift in information content from physical to digital—displacing supply chains in discs/disc players/disc drives—and mobile Internet use with smartphones and tablets.[12] The high value is typically generated in software and content applications and somewhat in high-tech components (e.g., the iPhone and iPad). It has been very challenging for traditional electronics and electronics components exporters like Thailand, Malaysia, Taiwan, Singapore, and Japan to upgrade to the new value chain. One exception seems to be South Korea.

Industrialization and Democratization

Along with urbanization, industrialization fosters a middle class as the foundation for an effective democracy. India and Indonesia lack strong middle classes; so while the countries are relatively high in the Democracy Index (DI) 2012,[13] they remain economically underdeveloped. It is intriguing to note that some low-income nations that have trouble to manage its economy have a high DI ranking; for instance, India has a DI ranking of 38 compared to medium- to high-income nations with lower DI countries like Thailand (58), Malaysia (64), Singapore (81), and China (142). In Asia's lower-income countries, elites play politics with the poor. They use populist policies like fuel and crop subsidies to bribe voters.[14] To finance these policies, they tax corporations, the rich, and the middle class, borrow money from future generations, and privatize public assets such as land and natural resources.

In high-income countries like Japan, South Korea, and Singapore, citizens desire better quality of life and more civil liberty. Economic growth can no longer be easily derived solely through adding factor inputs, especially in an aging society. Upgrading to the new economy by reforming public institutions and deepening digital innovation is a necessity.

In middle-income countries like Malaysia and Thailand, the *nouveau riche* and the middle classes are challenging the established institutions and elites. Thailand has essentially a dual economy, both urban/industrialized and rural/agricultural. As Thailand progressed to middle-income status in the last two decades, the rural mass did not enjoy the fruits. So here, too, populist policies dominated electoral politics. The *nouveau riche* that made its wealth from telecommunications, the new economy and the media have managed to win votes from the poor with promises of "free universal health care," "40 percent increase in the minimum wage," and "40 percent increase in prices for your rice." The middle class and the old elite rebel against this time and again, but the nouveau riche uses its electoral might to quash challenges.

Thailand has gone through 19 coups and 17 constitutional changes since becoming a constitutional monarchy in 1932. Thailand has managed to stay independent and has progressed steadily. It took the United States more than 200 years to become a stable democracy, and the first half was filled with civil war and unrest.

It is important to note that democratic systems may suffer subtle failures like poor-quality public education and hospital services, but authoritarian systems can and will suffer grand failures like famine or military miscalculation. China has more effective policy implementation than the democratic countries due to its tight control of the media and suppression of opponents. But history has taught us that this may one day lead to grand failures and/or violent regime change.

However, the 2008 global economic crisis has set back the global democratization process, causing political and social dysfunctions to democratic countries both advanced and developing. There has been, for example, a government shutdown in the United States and a systemic crisis of unity in the eurozone accompanied by riots in "peripheral" countries like Spain and Portugal.

Moreover, although the number of "democratic" countries in the world has tripled to more than 120 from 1974 to 2005, actual political freedom has declined globally.[15] Modern strongman regimes have adapted adroitly to today's more open social ethos. They have learned to disguise themselves in democratic dress and to replace open brutality with subtle forms of coercion. They use advertising money to control and manipulate the mass media so that opposition voices are suppressed. They pass laws that selectively benefit their own clique. They practice giveaway populist policies to bribe the poor in elections.[16]

Geopolitics Centering around the United States–China Rivalry

When US President Barack Obama announced the "pivot to Asia" in security and economic policy in late 2011, he was recognizing the growing importance of Asia, notably China.[17] The shift also came at a time when China was refocusing its foreign policy on Asia again after not-so-successful ventures in Africa and Latin America.

The Asia pivot policy is a transformational shift. It gives the United States more flexibility to promote its interests and to counterbalance China's rising influence. Under this policy, for instance, the United States has engaged in more troop deployments and rotations to Australia and

Singapore, led attempts to secure the Trans-Pacific Strategic Economic Partnership (TPP, a free trade agreement), and joined the East Asia Summit (EAS).

Asia is now home to the world's largest navies, including some of the most sophisticated warships in the world.[18] The sea-lanes of communication are central to regional and global trade and will remain a central factor in Asian defense planning. The US's shale gas revolution and its imminent rise as a major gas exporter will further reshape geopolitics in the sea-lanes from the Middle East to Asia.[19] These export routes feed energy-hungry Asian countries including China, which will soon become the world's largest energy importer.

China's worst fear is that the US navy's 7th Fleet will blockade the string of islands from Japan to Taiwan adjacent to China's coastline. About 90 percent of Chinese oil use is imported by sea,[20] while Chinese good trade, especially export, depends heavily on the sea-lanes.[21] This is one reason for China's increasingly aggressive confrontations over its disputed territorial claims on islands (called the *Daoyu* by the Chinese, the *Senkaku* by the Japanese) in the East China Sea and the Spratly Islands in the South China Sea. These islands are reportedly rich in energy resources. On November 23, 2013, China unilaterally declared its East China Sea Air Defense Identification Zone in the airspace over the *Daoyu/Senkaku*. The United States, Japan, and South Korea rejected the declaration by flying military aircraft over the airspace. China then deployed its first aircraft carrier, the *Liaoning*, to the South China Sea on November 26.

China's biggest dream is to take back Taiwan for strategic security and political unity reasons. A forcible takeover is unlikely as both the United States and China have too much to lose in any possible conflict.[22] Nevertheless, China's navy has been modernizing at an "alarming" rate starting in the 1990s.[23]

Aside from the United States, China's other big rival in the region is India. China has the highest number of active duty military in the world, followed by India, North Korea, and South Korea. China has a large army for internal security, with long borders with India and Russia. Having unresolved border issues and war experience (1962) with China and an unstable neighbor in Pakistan, India has no choice but to develop its minimum deterrent capability. India has been the largest arms purchaser in the world during the last five years.[24] In the space race, on November 5, 2013, India outdid China by launching its first spacecraft to Mars. The technological implications are far-reaching—from the telecom satellite business to the capability to launch missiles with a range of 5,000 kilometers (3,100 miles) to reach most parts of China. India's military conducts joint exercises with the United States many times per year. As fellow democracies, it is logical for the United States to pair up with India to deter China.

Food and water shortages could cause tensions between China and its neighbors.[25] China's land surface is comparable to the United States but it is not sufficient for its billion-plus population. About 65 percent of Chinese land consists of deserts in the north and west and mountains in the south. Only 12 percent is arable. So, China already is under water stress—and hence food stress—in many areas.[26] As former Chinese Prime Minister Wen Jiabao once said, water shortages threaten the very survival of the country. Shortages could cause explosive conflicts between China and India and between China and the Greater Mekong Subregion with which it shares the Mekong River—Myanmar, Thailand, Laos, Cambodia, and Vietnam. It is vital to note that there have been more than 30 wars or armed conflicts in Asia after WWII (see Figure 2.1).

Elites under Challenge and a New Paradigm

As Asian countries find their proper alignment in the region's new geo-politics, at home political establishments are facing increasing opposition from groups including rising middle classes frustrated by the old politics and energized by the networking tools of the new technology.

It is a time of big changes in Asian leadership. In a period of less than four months, from November 2012 to February 2013, three of the largest economies in Asia all changed their top leaders.[27] All are part of political dynastic families. On November 15, 2012, Xi Jingping became China's president. Xi's father is Xi Zhongxun, a former vice premier and the first generation of communist revolutionaries who gave refuge to Chairman Mao and the party base in the Long March in 1935.[28] (See Chinese Princeling case study.) On December 26, 2012, Shinzo Abe won a general election in a landslide and returned as prime minister for the second time in five years. Abe is the grandson and grandnephew of two former prime ministers and the son of a former foreign minister. On February 25, 2013, Park Geun-hye became the first female president of South Korea. She is the daughter of former President Park Chung-hee, who seized power in a military coup in 1963 and ruled with an iron fist before he was assassinated in 1979.

Figure 2.2 shows the many political dynastic families in Asia. Asian societies are more receptive to dynastic succession than the West.[29] Having a famous political family name boosts political careers. But it is no guarantee of success. For example, the former Philippine President Gloria Macapagal-Arroyo, who ruled from 1998 to 2010, is remembered

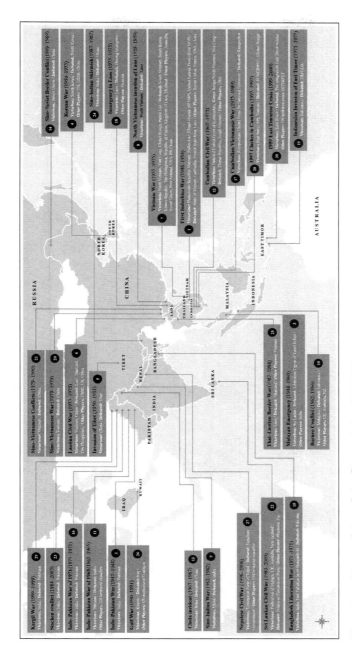

Figure 2.1 Wars and Armed Conflicts in Asia, 1946–2000

Sources: 1. Macquarie Research Aug 2010.

2. Norman Friedman (1999).

3. Author.

Copyright © 2014, Pongksak Hoontrakul.

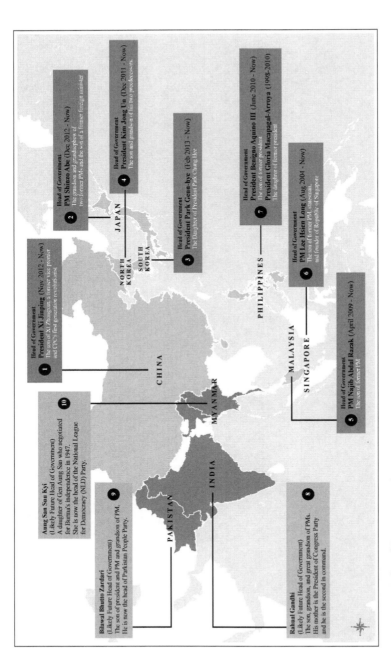

Figure 2.2 Political Dynasties in Asia

Note: Last update is on December 1, 2013.

Sources: 1. Mahbubani; 2. Korea; 3. Ved; 4. Stratfor. Copyright © 2014, Pongksak Hoontrakul.

as one of the country's most corrupt leaders even though her father was a respected president.[30]

In the uncertain world after the 2008 economic crisis, one geopolitical risk is the vulnerability of elites.[31] Localization—adjusting political priorities to be more accommodating to local agendas—is increasingly visible as the United Nations (UN), the IMF, the World Bank, the World Trade Organization (WTO), and other international institutions established by the West after WWII are being criticized by all sides. The legitimacy of elites is being eroded by their failure to effectively lead and to deliver what society's diverse interest groups expect. Citizens are demanding more from their leaders on issues ranging from environmental degradation to widening inequality to corruption. Rapid news cycles and social media have enabled opposition movements to create new, abrupt, and continuous challenges.[32]

In Southeast Asia, Malaysia presents an illustration of the growing challenges to the establishment. In 2013, opposition leader Anwar Ibrahim fiercely protested what he called a fraudulent general election that returned to power as Prime Minister Najib Razak, the head of the United Malays National Organization (UMNO). After failing to win over ethnic Chinese and other minorities, UMNO—the longest continuing ruling party in the world—lost the popular vote, with 5.24 million votes to the opposition's 5.62 million. But it managed to stay in power because its coalition, the National Front, captured 133 of Parliament's 222 seats. The more inclusive style of politics that Najib tried in order to lure minority voters did not work. So he returned to the old race-based politics to shore up his traditional Malay base.[33]

Rising Middle-Class Demands

The ever-rising middle classes will increasingly raise pressure on the authorities who fail to meet their rising expectations.[34] These expectations include not just security and basic services, such as health and education, but also freedom of speech and civil liberty. By 2030, some two billion people of the world's new middle classes will be in Asia, notably China and India. Since they are the ones who pay the most taxes, they are demanding more accountability on how their money is spent. They will surely engage in more political activism and mass street protests like in Thailand starting in late 2013, forcing once-dominant parties to make more compromises.

One clear danger is that vulnerable leaders are likely to search for distractions and scapegoats in order to maintain their grip on power. That includes the leaders of China, where the new middle class is voicing rising discontent with the status quo. After announcing an ambitious economic and social reform plan at the Communist Party's Third Plenum during November 9–12, 2013, President Xi chose to play the nationalist card.[35] On November 23, 2013, China unilaterally declared an air defense zone over the *Daoyu/Senkaku* islands that both China and Japan claim as their territory. The United States, Japan, and South Korea rejected the declaration by flying military aircraft over the airspace. Three days after declaring the air defense zone, Xi deployed China's first aircraft carrier to the South China Sea, where China's claims to the Spratly Islands are disputed by several Southeast Asian countries.[36] Indeed, geopolitical risk in Southern China Sea is persistently one of the top five global risks according to World Economic Forum.[37]

The ICT Challenge—A New Paradigm

Elites are also being strongly pressured by the growing use of mobile communications, the Internet, and especially social media by the middle classes and other discontents. In 2013, more than one billion people were using Facebook and about 200 million people were using Twitter around the world. Asia is now the top social networks user in the world. Indonesia has the second-largest number of social media networks users, after the United States; India, the Philippines, and Thailand are among the top seven.[38] Facebook is a vivid example of social media as a game-changing tool for people to collectively pressure political regimes, as in the 2010–2012 Arab Spring. The phenomenon was repeated to some degree in the "Bersih 3.0" rally in Malaysia for free and fair election in 2012, Cambodian protests against corruption and election fraud in 2013, and mass street demonstrations against the government in Thailand starting in late 2013 (see "Thailand's 'Great Mass Uprising': The Digital Spark" case study).

Mindful of popular discontent, China has long controlled TV, radio, and newspapers. In cyberspace, China's Great Firewall blocks access to any material considered subversive or obscene. Facebook, Twitter, and Google are all blocked in favor of local-made social media sites like Qzone, Weibo, and Baidu, which can all be easily monitored. But the rise of the middle class and the explosion of social media have refined China's social and political discourse. The number of Chinese Internet users has been growing at 20 percent per year; most connect via mobile devices.

Xi has cracked down on antistate comments on social media and threatened jail for "online rumors" and "disturbing public order."[39] On

September 13, 2013, for exemplar, Wang Gongquan, a wealthy venture capitalist, was arrested on such charges; he had more than 1.4 million social network followers who shared his interest in political reform. But there is no sign that social media will bring about a legitimacy crisis in China like in the Arab Spring.[40] In China, social media mostly enable people to vent frustration over localized issues such as land disputes, environmental degradation, and labor conflicts.

India is an open society that likes to debate philosophical and political issues. Yet out of 1.2 billion people, the country had only 165 million Internet users as of March 2013.[41] Coupled with the country's loose federation and diffused electoral constituencies in different states, this means social media will not be a game changer in Indian politics anytime soon. Though he had close to 1.9 million Twitter followers in 2013, Congress Party Minister Shashi Tharoor has been unable to convince Raul Gandhi, a possible future prime minister, to try a Twitter campaign.

In a country with tightly control media like China, the explosion of social network users is a challenge, but manageable in the near term. In low-income countries like India and Indonesia, the interplay of social media with politics is still limited. In middle-income countries like Thailand and Malaysia, people are increasingly going online to express political discontent.

The Agenda Ahead

Given all these changing dynamics and complexities, what fundamentals should political and business leaders keep in mind when they make policies and plans?

Institutions Matter More Than Elections

First, decision makers should understand that elections do not matter much. Institutions matter more. Holding an election is easy.[42] Creating and maintaining permanent public institutions—an independent central bank, an impartial judicial system, a high-quality educational system, a unified military security and law enforcement system, etc.—that function well on a day-to-day basis is difficult. It takes decades to develop such institutions because, among other things, a middle-class culture is an essential building block. Even though Asia's elites themselves may be increasingly vulnerable, the countries' robust meritocratic institutions carry on most of the burden of administration.

General elections in India[43] and Indonesia[44] such as those in 2014 matter less than perceived. First, elections in both countries are not contested on macroeconomic ideology even though incumbent ruling parties are expected to lose in a weak economy. Typical election debates are likely to be on local issues like land reclamation for infrastructure building, corruption, ethnicity, and religion. On May 26, 2014, Mr Narendra Modi, the head of Bharatiya Janata Party (BJP), became the first Indian prime minister in the last three decades to command an absolute majority in Indian parliament by his highly personalized campaign and inclusive outreach approach. Despite the initial hype in short-term positive stock market movement to reflect his tall mandate, PM Modi may not meet the huge expectation in terms of the country's economic direction as suggested by Indian history. Basically, Modi may be forced to compromise on policy decision making with states and bureaucratic system.[45] Second, India's weak central government makes the policy, but it is typically the states that implement it, and implementation takes a long time (average 6–8 years). Thus, what the states do matters more. Indonesia has a relatively strong presidency, but it is retarded by a fragmented legislative branch. External shocks like inflation and currency depreciation will shape policymaking regardless of the elections outcome.

The implication for businesses is that they should focus more on long-term trends and less on day-to-day politics, and track institutions, not personalities. The more or less open the economy in countries like India and Thailand, the more or less it will be prone to external shocks that will drive policymaking. The more centralized the executive in countries like China, Vietnam, and Indonesia, the more important the government policy.

Planners also need to keep in mind that despite the scary headlines, political turmoil has little impact on Asia's economies in the medium to long run. Thailand's recent political unrest and the coup in May 2014 have had negligible shocks on consumption and business investment in the country and the Thai stock index depends more on the broader economic context.[46] Moreover, contrary to the belief that the political turbulence drives away tourists, passenger growth has been resilient at Thai airports.[47]

In a nutshell, the biggest mistake one can make is to judge local politics based on one's narrow foreign experience. Primary political processes are always driven by the underlining economic structure and interests of the powers-that-be. There is no single political system that best fits all Asian nations. In fact, the variety of political systems and stages of economic development in Asia offer great productive opportunities for business and political leaders.

A Brave New World under a New Paradigm

Another key risk to watch out for is the very real possibility of massive cyberattacks[48] knocking out critical infrastructure or hacking into government secrets. Asian countries already have seen how digital leaks of government secrets and intergovernment electronic espionage can damage diplomacy and relations among erstwhile allies.

In November 2010, Julian Assange, the Australian founder of WikiLeaks, publicly revealed more than a quarter million confidential US embassy cables. In 2013, Edward Snowden, an American national intelligence contractor, exposed how the US-led Five Eyes (the United States, Britain, Australia, Canada, and New Zealand) electronic intelligence network spied on Asian leaders. That caused resentment across the Pacific. Snowden alleged that Singapore helped tap undersea cables for the program.[49] This inflamed mistrust among Asian leaders. After learning his personal phone and emails had been tapped by the United States in collaboration with Australia, Indonesian President Susilo Bambang Yudhoyono recalled his ambassador to Australia in November 2013.[50]

It is hard to imagine how severe the damage would be particularly in more authoritarian regimes. What if China had his own version of WikiLeaks incident? Snowden's revelations raised mistrust among key Asian allies. In a world of vulnerable elites, the use (or abuse) of electronic surveillance may have far-reaching geopolitical, economic, or security fallout.

None of this should deter citizens and leaders from reaping the benefits of the digital revolution.

The technological advances from the Agricultural to the Industrial Revolutions ruptured social fabrics and political traditions. Now, social media has helped bring down governments in the Arab world and in Asia, notably Thailand.

Whether in a more feudal or a more democratic system, hierarchical structures are found across Asian leadership institutions. Many citizens have little chance to have their voices heard. Social networks can help flatten these hierarchical structures. The shift in values due to increased connections, openness, and cynicism forces leaders to be more transparent and accountable. It is fascinating to learn that after the Arab Spring, half of tweets in the Arab world were from Saudi Arabia. King Abdullah recently created the Arabic hash tags "#If I met the King, I would tell him" and "#What would you like to say to the Minister of Health?" while this may not exactly be democratic, it works.[51] If leaders in business or politics can learn to intelligently filter and to listen to these voices and respond, they may earn legitimacy and trust from the citizens. They can also themselves use social media to interact with and get closer to the citizens.

While it is premature to conclude how this third wave will ultimately transform Asia, we definitely must prepare for what could be a seismic shift in economic, social, and political relations.

The United States–China Paradigm and the Regional Agenda

Asia is now witnessing the emergence of a bipolar relationship centered on the rivalry between the United States and China. This new geopolitics is dynamically shaping the region; a new equilibrium has not yet emerged.

China is engaging in a "Marching West" food supply strategy as a counterweight to the US pivot to Asia.[52] It is diversifying away from the United States as a major source of food supply. For example, China has direct investments in the vast untapped agricultural resources of Central Asia. In 2012, China's CAMC Engineering Co. signed up with Ukraine UkrLand Farming to build $4-billion facilities to annually produce 400,000 tons of pork and 600,000 tons of chicken and a five-million-ton-capacity grain-handling terminal. China has secured more than 100,000 hectares (247,000 acres) of land from Tajikistan.[53] In November 2013, China signed a memorandum with the European Union (EU) for cooperation in food, agriculture, and biotechnology; China's clear intention was to move forward on the global food governance issues raised by the Group of 20 (G-20) and the WTO in the Doha round negotiations.[54]

ASEAN stands in the middle of this rivalry. ASEAN's weakness is that it is an intergovernmental institution, not a supranational body. Its strength is that it also is a neutral and nonthreatening platform for dialogue and cooperation. How will the United States–China rivalry reshape ASEAN?

Case Study

China: A Party Dominated by Mysterious "Princelings"

Pongsak Hoontrakul

The world's second-largest economy is steered by the CPC in a one-party system. At the apex of CPC is the general secretary. The core of the collective leadership is the 25-member Politburo; it is like the inner circle of the old imperial court. First among equals is the Standing Committee, whose seven members hold top party, military, and government posts.

The Politburo normally convenes once a year. The Standing Committee discharges most of the duties and responsibilities vested in the Politburo. The party's National Congress convenes every five years to set long-term policy.

The 18th National Congress in November 2012 brought a once-in-a-decade change to the Chinese leadership. Power was handed over to the "fifth generation"[55] of leaders who can barely remember the events of the foundation of the People's Republic of China in 1949. Xi Jinping was elected the party general secretary, the chairman of the Central Military Commission, the country's president, and the first-ranked member of the Standing Committee. Li Keqiang became the second-ranked member and the country's premier.

Many members of the Politburo are "princelings"—members of elite families that descended from the party's founding revolutionaries. At least three of the powerful members of standing committee relate to previous administrators. Mr Xi Jinping is a son of a famous general Xi Zhongxun, vice-premier (1959–1962); Mr Wang Qishan is a son-in-law of Mr Yao Yilin, first vice-premier (1988–1993)[56]; and Mr Yu Zhengsheng reportedly was good friends with the paramount leader Deng Xiaoping and his family.[57] To many Chinese, "princelings" connotes nepotism and cronyism, analogous to that of the hereditary monarchies of other countries. Actually, the princelings have seen their power much reduced since the 1980s.[58] China's nouveau riche and rising middle class have been demanding fair play and protection for their property and other rights. Corruption and other scandals also have weakened the princelings' reign, particularly as many of the scandals have been uncovered by "citizen journalists" and popular resentment has been amplified by social media postings.

Thailand's "Great Mass Uprising": The Digital Spark

Pongsak Hoontrakul

Over several months starting in November 2013, former Deputy Prime Minister Suthep Thaugsuban and his "People's Democratic Reform Committee" led many thousands of people onto the streets to try to oust the Thai government. The demonstrators accused Prime Minister Yingluck Shinawatra of corruption and mismanagement and of being a puppet of her brother Thaksin, who is in self-exile abroad to escape a corruption jail sentence. The almost-daily rallies, dubbed *Muan Maha Prachachon*—the Great Mass Uprising, provide an intriguing example of the widespread use of social media to press for political change in a still-developing democracy.

The protestors zealously used Facebook, Twitter, and other networks to voice dissent and to organize demonstrations, marches, and occupations of government offices. They uploaded onto YouTube video clippings of political speeches and entertainment performances on the stages they had erected on the streets. During the last quarter of the year, leading up to the mass demonstrations at Democracy Monument in Bangkok, the number of Thais using social media grew by 30 percent, to 24 million users; they posted 7.1 billion Facebook "likes" and sent 5.5 billion messages. About 70 percent of these users accessed social platforms via their mobile devices. About 2.5 million users followed Twitter.[59] In less than two weeks, more than half a million people registered at the petition platform change.org to protest the government's attempt to pass a bill that would grant amnesty to Thaksin.[60]

When hundreds of thousands gathered at Democracy Monument on November 24, it was claimed that more than 12 million social media users posted more than 30 million messages on a single day. The telecommunications companies had to install two additional mobile network stations and upgrade six existing stations in order to cope with the demand.[61]

Thai satellite TV channels that broadcast pro-government views (Asia Update Channel group) as well as those that broadcast antigovernment views (e.g., the Blue Sky Channel group) enjoyed rating booms.[62] For the first time, Thais watched live 24-hour telecasts of demonstrations in multiple locations. These included bloody clashes, from December 1–4, when police used tear gas and rubber bullets against protesters who tried to seize police headquarters. A tactical truce was called to observe the King's birthday on December 5. When the protests resumed, the government was forced to dissolve parliament on December 9 and call new elections.

The digital divide was real, reflecting Thailand's general social divide. The antigovernment demonstrators using Facebook were mainly high- to middle-income people, while the pro-government people were primarily from the poor countryside.[63]

Some people expressed concern that such overwhelming use of social media controlled by Western companies could one day open the door to outside interference in Thai affairs.

A Chronology of Thailand's Recent Turmoil

- **September 2006:** Army overthrows Thaksin's government
- **August 2008:** Thaksin flees abroad to avoid jail sentence for corruption
- **December 2008:** Mass anti-Thaksin street protests; opposition leader Abhisit Vejjajiva becomes prime minister
- **March–May 2010: Mass** pro-Thaksin street demonstrations; dozens killed in military clearing operations

- **July 2011:** Thaksin's sister, Yingluck Shinawatra, leads pro-Thaksin party to general election win and becomes prime minister
- **November 2013:** Outraged by an attempt to pardon Thaksin, anti-government protesters begin a new round of mass street rallies
- **December 2013:** Yingluck dissolves the parliament and calls new elections

Notes

1. For more discussion see Croissant et al., *Democratization and Civilian Control in Asia* (Basingstoke: Palgrave Macmillan), 2013.
2. Philippe Aghion et al., "The Unequal Effects of Liberalization: Evidence from Dismantling the License Raj in India," *American Economic Review*, 2008, 98:4, 1397–1412 (http://www.aeaweb.org/articles.php?doi=10.1257/aer.98.4.1397).
3. T.N. Srinivasan, "China and India: Growth and Poverty, 1980–2000," discussion paper, Standford Center for International Development, September 2003: Table 3: p. 14 (http://web.stanford.edu/group/siepr/cgi-bin/siepr/?q=system/files/shared/pubs/papers/ pdf/credpr182.pdf).
4. Aristotle (b. 384–d. 322 BC), "Aristotle's Political Theory." See more details at http://plato.stanford.edu/ entries/aristotle-politics/.
5. Johanna Chua et al., "Asia Macro and Strategy Outlook: Is the Emerging Asia Growth Story Losing Its Luster?," *Citi*, October 25, 2013 (https://ir.citi.com/0IT%2b%2f%2b72H6 ZhDTjLeX790kvKO49%2f3Ca5M6r3pS7cXlM2 Pw045N0%2fbpf5nkwRBLdJKrKUKv1dScY%3d).
6. Ibid.
7. Ibid.
8. Ibid.
9. Ibid.
10. T. N. Srinivasan, "The Shift in the Balance of Power," *Standard Chartered*, January 2011.
11. M.Chuietal.,"TheSocialEconomy:UnlockingValueandProductivityThrough Social Technologies," McKinsey Global Institute, July 2012 (http://www.mckinsey.com/insights/high_tech_telecoms_internet/the_social_economy).
12. Johanna Chua et al., "Asia Macro Flash: Disruptive Techonology and Asia's Changing Export 'Beta'," *Citi*, November 18, 2013 (https://ir.citi.com/QHN7s%2B5xiA76Rgw8dBenZyfy GaVQqG8yu7AZS%2B4bFBxLgiq3FZj%2FGVat0OCc2AAW).
13. "Democracy Index 2012: Democracy is at a Standstill," *The Economist's Intelligence Unit*, January 2013 (https://www.eiu.com/public/topical_report.aspx? campaignid=Democracy Index12).
14. More discussion by Pongsak Hoontrakul, "Globalization and Trilemma," *Journal of Review of Pacific Basin Financial Markets and Policies* (Singapore: World Scientific), December 1999, 2:4, 471–514 (http://http://www.worldscientific.com/doi/abs/10. 1142/S0219091599000266).

15. William Dobson, *The Dictator's Learning Curve: Inside the Global Battle for Democracy* (Doubleday) (New York: Anchor Book), 2012.

16. Ibid.

17. M.E. Manyin et al., "Pivot to the Pacific? The Obama Administration's 'Rebalancing' Toward Asia," *CRS*, March 28, 2012 (http://www.fas.org/sgp/crs/natsec/R42448.pdf).

18. In military sense, United States has the largest naval fleets with 11 aircraft carriers and followed by the distant second—China. See more discussion at Hackett (ed.), *The Military Balance 2010* (The International Institute for Strategic Studies, Oxfordshire: Routledge Journals), 2010.

19. Kaplan, Robert D., "The Geopolitics of Shale," *Stratfor*, December 19, 2012 (http://http://www.stratfor.com/weekly/geopolitics-shale).

20. Chirstopher J. Pehrson, "String of Pearls: Meeting the Challenges of China's Rising Power Across the Asian Littoral" (www.StrategicStudiesInstitute. army.mil), the US Government, July 2006, pp. 6–8 (http://www.strategic-studiesinstitute.army.mil/pdffiles/ pub721.pdf).

21. George Friedman, "The Geopolitics of China: A Great Power Enclosed," *Stratfor*, June 15, 2008: 1–11.

22. Ronal O'Rourke, "China Naval Modernization: Implications for US Navy Capacities- Background and Issues for Congress," *CRS*, September 5, 2013 (http://www.fas.org/sgp/crs/row/RL33153.pdf).

23. Ibid.

24. "India as a Great Power: Know Your Own Strength," *The Economist*, March 30, 2013 (http://http://www.economist.com/news/briefing/21574458-india-poised-become-one-four-largest-military-powers-world-end).

25. It is critically important to note that both food and water crises are among the top greatest threats facing the world in 2014. See more discussion at "Global Risk Report 2012," Nineth Edition, *The Risk Response Network* [World Economic Forum (WEF), Geneva], February 2014 (http://www3.weforum. org/docs/WEF_GlobalRisks_Report_2014.pdf).

26. "Water in China: Desperate Measures," *The Economist*, October 12, 2013 (http://http://www.economist.com/news/leaders/21587789-desperate-measures).

27. According to IMF statistics on world economic status ranking in total GDP in USD in 2012, The United States was ranked No.1 with regard to total GDP (USD16.2 trillions), no. 2 China (8.2), no. 3 Japan (6.0), and no. 15 South Korea (1.2). Note that India is no. 10 (1.84), [http://en. wikipedia.org/wiki/List_of_countries_by_GDP_(nominal)].

28. CPC's red army headed by Mao made a strategic military retreat from KMT's army to rural area. This was later named as the Long March (Oct 1934–Oct 1935).

29. Kishore Mahbubani, "Dynastic Asia," *Project Syndicate*, January 3, 2013 (http:// www. http://www.project-syndicate.org/commentary/asia-s-children-of-the-powerful-come-to-power-by-kishore-mahbubani).

30. Ibid.

31. "The Vulnerability of Elites: Geopolitical Risk in 2013," *The Global Agenda Council on Geopolitical Risk* (World Economic Forum in Dubai), November 2012 (http://www3.weforum.org/docs/WEF_GAC_GeopoliticalRisk_2013.pdf).

32. Ibid.
33. "Politics in Malaysia: Bumi, not Booming," *The Economist*, September 28, 2013 (http://http://www.economist.com/news/asia/21586864-ruling-party-returns-its-old-habits-race-based-handouts-bumi-not-booming).
34. Francis Fukuyama, "The Middle-Class Revolution," *Wall Street Journal*, June 28, 2013 (http://online.wsj.com/news/articles/SB10001424127887323873904578571472700 348086).
35. William Pesek, "China's Xi Jingping Pumped Up on Political Testosterone," *Bangkok Post*, November 30, 2013.
36. See more discussion by R.A. Bitzinger, "China's ADIZ: South China Sea Next?," *RSIS Commentaries non 219/2013,* December 2, 2013 (S. Rajaratnam School of International Studies, Nanyang Technological University, Singapore.), (http://www.rsis.edu.sg/publications/ Perspective/RSIS2192013.pdf).
37. Identified as the one of the top five global risks by "Global Risk Report 2012," 7th Edition, *The Risk Response Network* [World Economic Forum (WEF), Geneva], March 2012 (http://www3.weforum.org/docs/WEF_GlobalRisks_Report_2012.pdf, and again as the top global technological risk by "Global Risk Report 2014," 9th Edition, *The Risk Response Network* [World Economic Forum (WEF), Geneva], February 2014 (http://www3.weforum.org/ docs/WEF_GlobalRisks_Report_2014.pdf).
38. Simon Kemp, "Social, Digital & Mobile in APAC in 2014," *WeAreSocial,* January 23, 2014 (http://wearesocial.net/blog/2014/01/social-digital-mobile-apac-2014/).
39. See more discussion of "China's New Leadership Declares War on Social Media," *Freedom House,* September 23, 2013 (http://www.freedomhouse.org/blog/chinas-new-leadership-declares-war-social-media).
40. C. Goble and L.H. Ong, "Social Unrest in China," *London: Europe China Research and Advice Network*, 2013 (http://www.euecran.eu/Long%20Papers/ECRAN%20Social% 20Unrest%20in%20China_%20Christian%20Gobel%20and%20Lynette%20H.%20Ong.pdf).
41. A. Kalra and D. Lalmalsawma, "Social Media Not a Game Changer in 2013 Election," *Reuters*, September 25, 2013 (http://blogs.reuters.com/india/2013/09/25/social-media-not-a-game-changer-in-2014-elections/).
42. See more discussion at Robert D. Kaplan, "Elections Don't Matter, Institutions Do," *Stratfor*, January 15, 2014 (http://www.stratfor.com/weekly/elections-dont-matter-institutions-do).
43. See more discussion by Neelkanth Mishra and Ravi Shankar, "India Market Strategy: 2014 Outlook," *Credit Suise*, December 2, 2013.
44. See more discussion by Helmi Arman "Indonesia Macro View—Prospects 2014: How Does Macro Stabilitization Mix With Elections?," *Citi*, December 9, 2013.
45. See more discussion by Rohini Malkani and Anrag Jha, "India Macroscope: Modiscope: Mandate, Mantra and More," *Citi*, June 6, 2014 and Neelkanth Mishra and Ravi Shankar, "India Market Strategy: 2014 Outlook," *Credit Suise*, December 2, 2013.
46. Dan Fineman and Siriporn Sothikul, "Thailand Market Strategy: Profiting from Early Elections," *Credit Suisse*, December 6, 2013.
47. I. Sethi, L. Kong, and M.C. Koh, "ASEAN: Transportation & Airports," *Goldman Sachs*, December 9, 2013.

48. Massive cyber attacks risk, which was identified as one of the top global risks in 2013, was described as possible digital wildfires in a hyper-connected world. More discussion at "Global Risk Report 2013," Eighth Edition, *The Risk Response Network* [World Economic Forum (WEF), Geneva], February 2013, pp. 6 and 23–27 (http://www3.weforum.org/docs/ WEF_GAC_Geopolit icalRisk_2013.pdf).

49. "Singapore coy on Asia spying claims," *Bangkok Post*, November 30, 2013: 5. More discussion see Glenn Greenwald, Ewen MacAskill, and Laura Potras, "Edward Snowden: The Whistleblower Behind the NSA Surveillance Revelations," *Gaurdian*, June 10, 2013 (http://www. theguardian.com/ world/2013/jun/09/edward-snowden-nsa-whistleblower-surveillance), see also Pongsak Hoontrakul, "Lessons from Wikileaks: Is This the World Turning Point?" *Matichon Daily Newspaper*, January 25, 2011 [Thai].

50. "Australia spied on Indonesia President Yudhoyono," *BBC*, November 18, 2013 (http://www.bbc.co.uk/news/world-asia-24952229).

51. Thomas L. Friedman, "The Lesser-Known Arab Wakening," *Bangkok Post*, December 2, 2013.

52. More discussion at Zhang Hongzhou, "China is Marching West for Food," *RSIS Commentaries No.023/2014*, Feb. 4, 2014 (S. Rajaratnam School of International Studies, Nanyang Technological University, Singapore).

53. Ibid.

54. Ibid.

55. The founding leader was Mao Zedong and succeeded by Deng Xiaoping. The third generation leader was Jiang Zemin and followed by Hu Jintao.

56. Coh Sui Noi, "Princelings Still Rule Despite Bo's Ouster," April 22, 2012 (http:// guanyu9.blogspot.com/2012/04/princelings-still-rule-despite-bos.html).

57. Benajamin Kang Lim, "China Princeling Emerges from Defection Scandal," *Reuters*, June 19, 2007 (http://www.reuters.com/article/2007/06/19/us-china-party-yu-idUSPEK15174020070619).

58. "Princelings," Wikipedia (http://en.wikipedia.org/wiki/Princelings).

59. Saiyai Sakawee, "Thailand Grew by 33% in 3 Months to 24 Million Users," *Tech in Asia*. September 6, 2013 (http://www.techinasia.com/facebookthailand-grows-to-24-million-users-infographic/).

60. Piyaporn Wongruang, "545,00 Sign Web Petition to Stop Bill," *Bangkok Post*, November 6, 2013f (http://www.bangkokpost.com/ breakingnews/378353/545000-sign-web-petition-to-stop-bill). More discussion see Asina Pornwasin, "Many Facebook Users Protest Against Amnesty Bill," *The Nation*, November 4, 2013 (http://www.nationmultimedia.com/ politics/Many-Facebook-users-protest-against-amnesty-bill-30218651.html).

61. Jon Fernquest, "News makes up larger piece of online pie," *Bangkok Post*, November 26, 2013.

62. Saengwit Kewaleewongsatorn, "Ratings boom for political TV," *Bangkok Post*, November 14, 2013. (http://www.bangkokpost.com/news/politics/379713/ ratings-boom-for-political-tv).

63. Ibid.

3

Life after QEs

Pongsak Hoontrakul

Introduction

The collapse of Lehman Brothers in 2008 opened a new era of monetary policy. The world's major central banks—the US Federal Reserve Bank (the Fed), the Bank of England (BOE), the European Central Bank (ECB), and the Bank of Japan (BOJ)—embraced the unconventional measure of quantitative easing (QE) to inject an unprecedented scale of liquidity into the financial system. In addition to the more than $5.8 trillion injection from 2007 to the end of 2013,[1] the banks cut short- term policy rates to near zero. Their aim was to prevent the endogenous risk generated within the banking system and credit markets from escalating into a global catastrophe.[2] Though the goal was achieved, this strategy risked major unintended consequences on an unprecedented scale.[3] And it remains to be seen how long it will take for the reversal of QE to normalize the financial conditions affecting credit and how much collateral damage to the real economy will occur. Certainly the transition will profoundly impact businesses and everyone exposed to borrowing, lending and inflation, potentially for decades.

QE essentially works through (1) asset prices and (2) exchange rates.

By the end of 2013, the Fed alone had injected a total of more than $3 trillion in three series of QEs.[4] QE's immediate effect was to increase the value and reduce the yield of financial assets. Investors searched globally for higher yield, pouring tremendous liquidity into Asian emerging markets on the expectation of their strong growth potential. This caused rapid strengthening of their currencies and surges in prices of all asset classes—bonds, equities, and real estate.[5] Hong Kong housing prices, for instance, rose more than 100 percent from 2009 to 2013.[6] Critics identified the potential for asset price bubbles.

QE's other unintended consequence is on exchange rates. Extraordinarily loose monetary policy by one country causes its currency to weaken against other currencies. This simply diverts disinflationary or even deflationary pressures from one country to other countries via international trade.[7] One legacy of the global financial crisis is an inflation level in most countries well below the comfort level.[8] The temptation arises for countries to use currency devaluation to fuel export growth, dubbed as "currency war."[9]

Moreover, the zero interest rate policy distorted financial market mechanisms. QE lifted asset prices but failed to foster a sustainable economic recovery. Investors have pursued equities because of the low return on bonds. The result is a mispricing of the risk-adjusted market mechanism. While the Fed was injecting liquidity into the system, commercial banks were tightening up credit standards, thereby promoting economic contraction and counteracting the Fed's inflationary efforts. The stalemate between these two forces produced subpar and fragile growth as the excess capacity and overhanging debts of companies, households, and governments are gradually unwound.[10] In other words, without the discipline of a properly functioning risk-adjusted rate of return, the clearing process is very slow and displays overly optimistic prices. Liquidity ends up producing the wrong types of economic growth such as speculative investment, luxury consumption, and unfeasible projects. This results in misallocation of capital, in contrast to investment in socially beneficial infrastructure.

QE-induced capital allocation to Asia had distinctive attributes. The capital inflows to Asia ex-Japan were estimated to be at least $1.3 trillion during 2010 to 2012 alone.[11] About two-thirds ($0.8 trillion) was for cross-border loans, especially from Japan, while the rest ($0.5 trillion) was split between equity (55%) mainly from the United States and bond investment (45%) from others. This is quite worrisome since this flow represented about 10 percent of total gross domestic product (GDP) for Asia ex-Japan. If the Asian equity market correction of 30 percent after the Fed's first warning in May 2013 about the possibility of "tapering" QE was any indication, the impact of debt contraction—more for loans and less for bonds—could be catastrophic.

The Fed's tapering, through a reduction in its bond-buying, began in January 2014; the purchases were likely to end completely by year-end.[12] The tapering is intended to be a gradual, global regime shift from high liquidity and low growth to low liquidity and high growth. Because the world is not synchronously recovering, the central banks' policy rate adjustment and QE tapering and eventual exit will be unevenly normalized. It is hoped that a strong US recovery with tame inflation and manageable fiscal drag will support the Fed's tapering and policy interest rate normalization. The Fed may gradually begin its balance sheet shrinkage and policy rate increase in 2015.[13] After cutting its deposit rate to negative territory for the first time with a large number of liquidity injection measures in June 2014, ECB may, however, eventually begin QE in 2015 if the macro outlook deteriorates significantly.[14] And despite staying on hold for the monetary easing in May 2014, BOJ remains dovish with additional QE possible given any worsening signs of economic environment.[15] It will be interesting to see what will be the net effect across Asia of the counteracting US and Japanese actions, along with Europe's easing bias.

In the near future, a number of patterns will change. The historical trade between developed and emerging markets will be pushed to second place by increased trade among the emerging markets themselves.[16] With their surplus in trade with the developed countries shrinking, a number of Southeast Asian countries will experience much slower trade volumes. This will also be influenced by China's shift toward greater reliance on domestic consumption rather than exports or fixed asset creation.[17] However, trade will be enhanced by the formation of the Association of Southeast Asian Nations (ASEAN) Economic Community (AEC) in 2015, by increased lending within Asia, particularly from Japan, and by two proposed major trade treaties: the Regional Comprehensive Economic Partnership (RCEP) and the Trans-Pacific Partnership Agreement (TPP).[18] Mergers and acquisitions (M&A), especially in the banking industry, will be a feature of the increased trade, facilitated by the surplus of funds generated by Japan's zero interest rate policy and QE.

Both East and West must adjust to a new world of lowered growth and disinflation. The old formula of exporting commodities and assembling goods with cheap labor will no longer suffice to drive growth in emerging markets. Urbanization and building essential infrastructure will better serve to boost Asian economies. Financing these needs will require improved risk–reward sharing systems such as public–private partnerships.

Money Matters

It is estimated that between 2008 and 2012, QE boosted GDP in the United States and UK between 1 and 3 percent, reduced unemployment by 1 percent, and prevented deflation.[19] During 2009 to 2011, the Fed's QE gave economic benefits equivalent to a 80–120-basis point reduction in the ten-year Treasury bill yield, creating more than two million jobs and nearly 3 percent higher output.[20] In the United States, investors reaped $8 trillion of wealth gains from the stock market in 2013.[21] This powerful wealth effect stimulated demand, as evidenced by record-high automobile sales in the United States. The global incentive to consume was also enhanced.

Still, many say that QE merely amounts to printing new money to repay old debt, and that it creates a "wealth illusion" that will be recognized as such when inflation ensues. Indeed, lavish spending and speculative investment from "easy money" has been seen everywhere, especially in Asia. Citigroup recommended a "maximum bullish" position for equity investment in the global gambling industry in 2014.[22] (See also the case study of Prada Spa.) Critics compared the situation with the Japanese government's preservation of "zombie companies," as QE keeps afloat unviable companies—and that will prove costly in the long run, especially with banking and finance companies.

Critics of QE say the better approach may be the opposite: higher interest rates and a liquidity squeeze, requiring "work-outs" or bankruptcies of failing companies, as in Thailand after the 1997 financial crisis.[23] This debate will continue since it is a time-proven process. What matters now for Asian countries are how to live with QE tapering and its end after years of plentiful liquidity and zero interest rate policy.

The Fed's QE succeeded in restarting the economy, but it has not led materially to new credit creation in banking system. Most of the private sector—both corporate and household—is still de-leveraging overhanging debt, while banks are rebuilding balance sheets and, in so doing, denying credit to firms. Large corporations have issued long-term debt at low rates, but smaller firms have been denied this vehicle. It remains to be seen how robust the US economy will be as interest rates begin to rise as expected in 2015.

In Europe, fiscal austerity imposed on southern countries slowly was replaced by more tolerance and signs of more QE to nurture a continental economy characterized by moderate growth in the less profligate north and more contraction around the Mediterranean. Creating a more resilient European banking system and other structural issues will take time to resolve. The ECB is likely to maintain an accommodative monetary bias for the next few years, in the absence of inflation threats.

In Japan, on April 4, 2013, new BOJ governor Haruhiko Kuroda pledged to end two decades of deflation by implementing a "2–2–2–2 policy": to double the bank's monetary base and holdings of Japanese government debt and to achieve a 2 percent inflation rate within two years. As a result, the yen devalued by almost 30 percent in a matter of weeks. This was followed by monetary easing by the ECB and the central banks of 14 other countries like a "silent" currency war.[24] Specifically after ECB cut its policy rate by 0.25 percent on May 2, 2013, other central banks in Asia followed suit, for example, India by −0.25 percent on May 3, South Korea by 0.25 percent on May 8, Vietnam by −1 percent on May 13, and Thailand by −0.25 percent on May 23.[25] Then the Fed's tapering talk in May 2013 caused a panicked plunge in stock exchanges and currency depreciation in emerging Asia, as capital began to flow back to North America in anticipation of higher yields.

We can examine the most likely near-term scenarios. The United States should enjoy robust GDP growth rate of around 3 percent and subdued inflation of around 2.5 percent from 2014 to 2016, as shown in Table 3.1[26]. With an end to QE, the Fed's policy rate will rise to 1.75 percent in 2015 and 3.75 percent in 2016, and will peak at 4.5 percent in 2017.[27] Correspondingly, the Treasury's ten-year bond yield is forecast gradually to increase by 1 percent per year.[28] During 2014 to 2016, GDP growth for Europe and Japan are likely to remain subpar at 1 to 1.5 percent and at 0.7 to 1.2 percent, respectively, with inflation below the world average at 2 percent.[29] Both Europe and Japan are likely to keep their key official rates relatively low until 2017, while their ten-year bond rates will steadily increase. Because of an unsynchronized recovery in the United States, the UK, the eurozone, and Japan, their rate normalization process is conjectured to be uneven, as mentioned earlier. The common factor for the developed economies is an enormous public debt that can be lowered only by solid growth or inflation.

Asia's three most populous countries—China, India, and Indonesia—are conjectured to maintain a priority on macroeconomic stability, with GDP, inflation, policy rates, and bond yields having small variations, as indicated in Table 3.1[30]. China's current account surplus will cause its currency to appreciate from 2014 onward, while the deficits of India and Indonesia will cause their currencies to depreciate. The sustainability of a current account surplus, being the sum of balance of trade, net foreign direct investment (FDI), and net capital flow, is the crucial issue.[31] If the current account deterioration results from consumption, the saving–investment gap is worrisome. The converse is true for productive investment.

China stands in direct contrast to the other two countries in most ways. With immense foreign reserves and a current account surplus, China must rebalance its economy away from dependence on exports. Comprehensive structural reforms announced at the Third Plenum of the Communist Party in November 2013 included liberalizing interest rates as another step to internationalize the *renminbi*, abolishing the one-child policy to counter a graying population trend, and reforming the *hukou*,

Table 3.1 Long-term forecast from 2012 to 2018 for selected countries

	GDP, CPI Inflation, Key Official Interest Rate, Ten-Year Bond Yield and Exchange Rate													
	GDP growth, % yoy							*CPI inflation, % yoy*						
	2012	2013F	2014F	2015F	2016F	2017F	2018F	2012	2013F	2014F	2015F	2016F	2017F	2018F
Industrial countries														
United States	2.8	1.8	3.2	3.8	3.0	2.8	2.7	2.1	1.6	2.5	2.3	2.5	2.6	2.3
Japan	1.4	1.6	0.7	1.3	1.2	1.3	1.3	0.0	0.3	2.7	1.5	1.2	0.7	0.7
Euroland	−0.6	−0.4	1.0	1.4	1.5	1.6	1.7	2.5	1.4	1.0	1.4	1.7	2.0	2.0
United Kingdom	0.1	1.5	2.7	2.0	2.3	2.3	2.3	2.8	2.6	2.1	1.9	2.0	2.0	2.0
Emerging Markets in Asia (EMA)														
China	7.8	7.8	8.6	8.2	8.0	7.5	7.5	2.6	2.5	3.5	3.2	3.0	3.0	3.0
India	4.1	4.3	5.5	6.0	6.5	7.0	7.0	7.5	6.3	5.5	6.3	6.0	6.5	6.5
Indonesia	6.2	5.5	5.2	5.5	5.5	5.5	6.0	4.3	7.0	6.7	6.3	6.0	6.0	6.0

	Key official interest rate, % (eop)							*10Y Bond Yields (eop)*						
	2012	2013F	2014F	2015F	2016F	2017F	201BF	2012	2013F	2014F	201BF	2016F	2017F	201BF
Industrial countries														
United States	0.13	0.13	0.13	1.75	3.75	4.50	4.50	2.00	2.50	3.00	4.00	5.00	5.00	5.00
Japan	0.08	0.07	0.07	0.08	0.08	0.50	0.75	0.75	0.70	0.80	0.90	1.00	1.20	1.40
Euroland	0.75	0.25	0.25	0.75	1.75	2.75	3.50	1.32	2.20	2.25	3.00	3.50	4.25	4.25
United Kingdom	0.50	0.50	0.50	0.75	1.75	2.75	3.75	1.83	3.00	3.25	4.00	5.25	5.50	5.75
Emerging Markets in Asia (EMA)														
China	3.00	3.00	3.25	3.25	3.25	3.25	3.25	n.a.	n.a.	n.a.	n.a.	n.a.	n.a.	n.a.
India	8.00	7.75	7.00	7.50	7.50	7.50	7.50	n.a.	n.a.	n.a.	n.a.	n.a.	n.a.	n.a.
Indonesia	5.80	7.50	7.50	7.00	7.00	7.00	7.00	n.a.	n.a.	n.a.	n.a.	n.a.	n.a.	n.a.

FX rate vs. USD (eop)

	2012	2013F	2014F	2015F	2016F	2017F	2018F
Industrial countries							
United States	1.00	1.00	1.00	1.00	1.00	1.00	1.00
Japan	82	103	115	120	115	110	107
Euroland	1.32	1.30	1.15	1.10	1.05	1.00	1.10
United Kingdom	1.63	1.55	1.40	1.38	1.44	1.44	1.44
Emerging Markets in Asia (EMA)							
China	6.28	6.12	6.00	5.90	5.82	5.75	5.70
India	54.80	63.00	60.00	62.00	64.00	65.00	64.50
Indonesia	9646	11800	11700	12000	11500	11000	11000

Note: 1. GDP = gross domestic product; CPI = consumer price index; yoy = year over year; eop = end of period; FX = foreign exchange.
    2. US DY forecast by US Fixed Income team.

Source: Hooper et al., 2013, p. 67. Copyright © 2013, National Authorities, Deutsche Bank Research.

or household registration system, to stimulate domestic consumption. The aim is to spur domestic consumption and thus balance the reliance on exports and often misdirected infrastructure development.

India and Indonesia, on the other hand, suffer from rising external debt, persistent current account deficits, large fiscal gaps, and poor economic outlook. All this has made them vulnerable to reduced foreign capital flows, as shown when the Fed in May 2013 hinted at the start of tapering. India's short-term measures to reduce market pressure included restricting capital outflows, limiting gold bullion imports, and increasing the policy rate. Table 3.2 compares the measures taken by Indonesia and India. Macroeconomic stability is the top priority for both. The shortlist of sensible measures includes expediting badly needed infrastructure, opening up to more FDI, and lessening regulations.

In Japan, since the end of 2012, Prime Minister Shinzo Abe has aggressively pursued the four arrows of Abenomics. On the monetary front, as the first arrow, the BOJ in mid-2013 unleashed QE to reinflate the economy. On the fiscal front, as the second arrow, a 10-trillion yen stimulus package was passed to address long-term structural issues. It included creating strategic economic zones, increasing the value-added tax (VAT; on consumption) from 3 percent to 8 percent, and removing a 3 percent corporate tax surcharge. The stock market index (Tokyo Stock Price Index, TOPIX) soared 44 percent in 2013.

Abe's third arrow is the most important: structural reform for sustainable growth. Domestically these include deregulation of markets, labor mobility and relaxation in the immigration law to counter Japan's aging population problem. Japan aims to double its Asian business footprint by increasing FDI to the region—particularly Southeast Asia—by 35 trillion yen ($350 billion) by 2020. Thailand may benefit the most; Japan is the largest single source of FDI in Thailand (40%).[32] In effect, the BOJ is printing more yen for Japanese firms to acquire overseas assets; this is analogous to monetizing Japanese debt for its neighbors. Finally, Abenomics' fourth arrow is aimed at restoring fiscal-financial sustainability, given the immense amount of national debt that Japanese citizens have bought. VAT hike to 8 percent from 5 percent was, for example, implemented in April 2014.

QE also induced capital allocation to Asia in other ways. The capital inflow to Asia ex-Japan was estimated to be at $1.3 trillion from 2010 to 2012.[33] About two-thirds (or $.8 trillion) was predominantly in the form of cross-border loans, mostly from Japan.[34] Loans received by India ($89 billion), Indonesia ($46 billion), and China ($257 billion) constituted nearly half of the total loans, and in terms of GDP, amounted to 3 percent for China and 5 percent for both India and Indonesia.[35] These loans grew by up to 20

Table 3.2 ID and IN authorities have taken several measures to deal with market pressures

India	Indonesia
Measures to improve the current account	
Banned gold coin/bullion imports	To reduce fuel imports by raising the level of biodiesel composition in diesel fuel to 10%
Hiked import duty on gold, silver, and platinum to 10%	Improving mineral exports by lifting export quota related to mineral fuels
Sale of gold by importers to jewelers/bullion traders/banks only on upfront cash payment	Raise luxury tax for imported luxury goods from around 75% to 125%–150%
20% of imported gold required to be exported	Boost exports by giving additional tax deduction to labor-intensive sectors
Measures to aid monetary and exchange rate stability	
Overnight call money rate increased to 10.25%	BI hiked the policy rate by 50 bps to 7.00%
Capping overall amount that banks could withdraw from the repo window to 0.5% of their deposits	Raised overnight deposit facility rate to 5.25% and lending facility to 7.00%
Raised daily amount banks need to keep as CRR to 99% from 70% of the required CRR	Announced a signing of an extended US$12 bn bilateral swap agreement with the Bank of Japan
Reported RBI interventions to contain sharp volatility in FX move	BI extended the tenors of FX term deposits
FIIs need mandate of P-note holder in order to hedge the latter's INR exposure	Eased FX purchasing requirements for exporters that are selling FX proceeds from exports
	Adjusted the FX swap requirements to banks
	Eased the regulation on foreign debt
	Issued Bank Indonesia Deposit Certificates (SDBI) to manage IDR liquidity
Measures to boost investments/to maintain economic growth momentum	
Cabinet Committee on Investment (CCI) has cleared infrastructure projects worth US$28 bn in 2013	Expediting and simplifying investment permits in the resources sector
Eased FDI norms in multi-brand retail; increased FDI limits in telecom and defense sector	Ensuring government infrastructure investment projects are on track
	Tax holidays and tax allowances in a various commodity sector

Note: 1. B I= Bank Sentral Republik Indonesia; bps = basis point; CRR = cash reserve ratio; RBI = Reserve Bank of India; FX = foreign exchange; FII = foreign institutional investor; INR = Indian rupee; IDR = Indonesian rupiah.

2. Measures in italics are proposed, others are implemented.

Source: Press Information Bureau. Reserve Bank of India, Bank Indonesia, Indonesian Ministry of Finance. Copyright © 2013, Press Information Bureau Reserve Bank of India, Bank of Indonesia, Indonesia Ministry of Finance.

percent in Asian countries during 2010 to 2012.[36] As financial centers for China and Southeast Asia, about one-third ($277 billion) of all cross-border loans passed through Hong Kong and Singapore, representing a striking 64 percent and 40 percent of their GDP, respectively.[37] One hundred percent of inflows were received by Singapore in the form of offshore loans, compared to 70 percent for Hong Kong. Effectively, Japan extended massive credit to Singapore and Hong Kong as indirect lending to China and Southeast Asia. Despite their efforts to funnel that money to the region, both Singapore and Hong Kong instead experienced an overheating of property markets. In Southeast Asia, Malaysia was the biggest beneficiary of the capital infusion, receiving $124 billion, or 40 percent of its GDP, split equally between loans and capital markets.[38] At this level, Malaysia's ability to absorb more capital inflow prudentially is limited. On the other hand, the inflows were only about 10 percent of GDP for the lowest recipients of funds, Thailand with $64 billion and the Philippines with $29 billion.[39]

The remaining third of the capital inflow to Asia ex-Japan during 2010 to 2012 was split about 55–45 between equity (mainly from the United States) and bonds (from others).[40] South Korea ($63 billion) and ASEAN, particularly Malaysia ($35 billion), Indonesia ($22 billion), and Thailand ($20 billion), were the top capital recipients for bonds.[41] Despite a negative inflow to the Chinese bond market during 2010 to 2012, 16 percent (or $10 billion) of total new bond issuance in Asia in the first nine months in 2013 was for the Chinese property bond market, fueling an already roaring real estate market.[42] On average, Chinese high-yield property bonds provided a 221 percent cumulative return (or 11.4 percent annualized) from 2005 to 2013 with no defaults. The capital inflow to Asian bond markets, except in the high-yield Chinese market, subsided significantly in 2013.

In the Asia-Pacific region, Australia had the highest level of inflow to its bond market—$222 billion, or 28 percent of the regional total.[43] Given the commodities boom, Australian miners and corporations probably took advantage of ultralow rates to issue long-term bonds in order to finance new investment opportunities or to replace credit such as bank loans and commercial paper, thereby minimizing refinancing risk for future liquidity squeezes. Investment in metals and mining projects take at least five to ten years from start-up to realize the first output potential, while oil and gas projects take even longer. Thus, overinvestment in supply could backfire in the coming years with flat or lower commodities prices.[44] Perhaps concerns for Asian debt market bubbles are concentrated in a few localized bond markets where the inflows represent a considerable percentage of their total size: Australia (39%), New Zealand (26%), Hong Kong (27%), Malaysia (18%), and Indonesia (18%).[45]

Equities dominated the securities flow to Asia at $239 billion, mainly from the United States.[46] But this represented less than 10 percent of aggregate market totals. Indeed, Asia's equity markets have far greater breadth and depth than its bond markets for absorbing these enormous inflows. The risk of future withdrawals from the markets, as foreshadowed by the response to the Fed's May 2013 tapering suggestion, is mitigated by the BOJ's QE, which will pump in massive liquidity well into 2014. And the chance that Japanese banks will withdraw their large cross-border loans will remain low in the near future. At the same time, stock markets across Asia have already priced in QE's tapering, as evidenced by their marginal reaction to the actual tapering announcement in December 2013. One has to wait and see how Asia's bond markets respond when the US policy rate starts to rise in 2015.

The rebalancing situation for emerging Asia in 2013 to 2014 is nothing like during the Asian financial crisis of 1997.[47] Today, foreign exchange reserves in emerging Asia exceed external debts in every country except Indonesia, and none of the ASEAN countries has its external debts above 50 percent.[48] Besides falling commodities prices, rising investment in infrastructure is the main cause of the gaps of Indonesia and Malaysia. From the perspective of a sustainable balance, and ignoring financial considerations, Indonesia's current account deficit has the most urgent need to be addressed. Thailand's deficit is tolerable in the short run.[49] Malaysia's is in between, although the fast pace of deterioration there needs to be addressed with fiscal tightening and financial regulation to reduce systemic risk.[50]

In summary, the world will remain awash with liquidity for the foreseeable future. QE has not wrecked financial values and market structure, but has brought the global economic system closer to a phase of subpar growth and subdued inflation. However, QE did transform relative valuation, making assets overvalued in the long term. Although the Fed aimed to eliminate QE in 2014, the BOJ's QE was just accelerating, and the ECB was easing its bias to accommodate structural reforms. Collapsing the Fed's balance sheet will be a very long, slow process that will depend on the realized macroeconomic data. The Fed is likely to commence policy rate normalization perhaps in 2015 or later, as it reduces its balance sheet. In financial markets, this should be very bearish for Treasury bills and very bullish for the dollar against Asian currencies, notably the yen with its divergent monetary policy. Similarly, the BOE, ECB, and BOJ, in that order, must undergo the same tapering process. Developed economies will be saddled with a high level of public debt for an uncomfortably long period.

Slow Trade in Goods and Services

It is estimated that China will surpass the United States with the world's biggest share of international trade by 2015, and India is expected to join China at the top by 2050. Similarly, by 2030, Asia's emerging economies will overtake the European Union (EU) in total exports and imports. The core of the world trade regime is shifting from trade between the emerging and the developed economies to trade among the emerging economies themselves.[51] This transformation is being driven by rising incomes and consumer growth in emerging economies as the result of industrialization, urbanization, and regional integration. There is a general rising trend in emerging markets intra-trade, notably in Asia. The formation of the AEC and the two major trade pacts under negotiation (the TPP and the RCEP) will further catalyze this trend.

In Europe, the economic crisis had subsided by 2014, but many challenges such as high youth unemployment and banking restructuring remained. Hence, much of the economic recovery demand in Europe is import substitution, yielding few benefits for Asia's exporters. Those exporters will be relying on the United States to provide real demand recovery. Benefiting the most will be East Asian businesses such as the auto sectors of South Korea and Japan, and new-tech device producers and knowledge-intensive services of South Korea, Japan, and Taiwan. Thailand, which makes auto parts, may be the only Southeast Asian country to benefit from the revival of imports in the West. China is shifting to a more domestically oriented economy with more structural reform and urbanization, so it will become a greater importer.[52]

The declining trade surplus with the developed countries will leave Southeast Asia with a shortage of capital inflow. (Fortunately, the region is cushioned by its accumulated foreign reserves and by Japanese capital inflows.) Hence, their financial markets will be subject to downward shock. An economic slowdown will spread across Asia, and currencies will have little prospect of appreciation in the short run. Asian policymakers may attempt to manipulate their currencies for competitive devaluation, at least until their economies are restructured to focus more on domestic or regional demand.[53] Generally, the trend of Southeast Asian currencies against the dollar and the yen will be a bumpy decline depending on the aggressiveness of the BOJ's QE. The *renminbi* should appreciate gradually as China tries to contain inflation and maintain 7.5 percent growth.[54] The volatile Indian and Indonesian currencies will tend to sink in response to measures to stabilize their economies.

The primary concern for currency markets is the BOJ's actions. The BOJ has attempted to manage its currency since 1992, and first formally introduced a zero interest rate policy in 1999 and then QE in 2001.[55] For each instance of QE, the yen initially depreciated but later appreciated again due to the persistence of Japan's growing trade surplus.[56] The main problem was Japan's failure to shift from heavy dependence on manufacturing exports to a more advanced service-oriented and knowledge-based economy. (See Sony case study.) Abenomics aims to create inflation to stimulate growth; critics see this as manipulating the currency to keep Japan's old industrial-based paradigm afloat. What if China and/or Korea follow this currency manipulation policy?

Japan is drowning in sovereign debt equivalent to more than 200 percent of GDP—the highest proportion in the world. And it faces declining potential growth as a mature economy with an aging population. The initial drastic yen devaluation may result in Japan exporting not just goods but also some of its structural problems like deflation.

The yen was forecast to continue weakening to 120 against the dollar (a 20% devaluation) in 2014.[57] This competitive devaluation will yield windfall profits for many Japanese exporters, especially in sectors where Japan already has a strong global market share, as shown in Table 3.3. Protective polarized film for liquid-crystal displays (LCDs), automobile continuously variable transmissions (CVTs), aluminum capacitors, game software, and memory testers are five top high-knowledge-intensive products monopolized or nearly monopolized by Japan. Japan also commands oligopolistic global market share in large manufacturing sectors like automobiles, digital video disk (DVD) players, and electronic components and equipment. Although sales volume will increase, profits may be mixed from a weakening yen because these manufacturers have relocated plants to Southeast Asia during recent decades. Key traditional industrials such as automobiles, steel, and electronics may have mixed reactions to yen depreciation due to global supply chain reallocation. (See Japan's automakers case study.) Japanese steel makers and airlines will face adverse effects, while their regional competitors will gain.[58] Japanese electronics and technology firms like Sony, Sharp, and SanDisk will benefit while their foreign competitors like Samsung and Nokia will partially lose out. These sectors directly challenge rival manufacturers, particularly from South Korea and Europe. Faced with this challenge from Japan, countries may launch another round of competitive devaluation.

The conclusion of the TPP may spur services and agriculture sector deregulation because of TPP requirement for higher standards (e.g., regulatory coherence, safety standards, fair competition rules, intellectual property right, etc.). Together with Vietnam and Malaysia, Japan will be among the biggest winners from exporting merchandise to the United

Table 3.3   Japan's global market share in different product categories

Category	Japan's market share (% global)
Protective polarizer film for LCDs	100
Automobile CVTs	92
Aluminum capacitors	89
Game software	87
Memory testers	83
Electrode materials for Li-ion batteries	78
MLCCs	78
DSCs	75
Car navigation systems	74
Silicon wafers	72
MFPs/MFCs	69
Polarizers	64
Wire harnesses	58
Small motors for automobiles	47
Li-ion batteries for mobile phones	46
LCD TVs	44
Semiconductor lithography equipment	43
Electronic components	43
DVD players/records	41
Mobile-phone camera modules	36
HDDs	34
Multilayer PCBs	32
Automobiles	32
Silicon-based solar cells	27
Display devices	25
Semiconductors	22
Electronic equipment	22
Computers and data terminals	16

Note: Auto CVT = automobile with continuously variable transmission; MFPs/MFCs = multifunction printers/copiers; MLCC = Micro Leadframe Chip Carrier; LCD = liquid-crystal display; DVD = digital video disk; HDDs = hard disk drive; PCBs = printed circuit boards.

Source: Credit Suisse Equity Research—Kersley et al., 2013. Copyright © 2013, Richard Kersley, Credit Suisse.

States in relative income gains, while Thailand, the Philippines, and China will suffer minor losses.[59] Otherwise, if Abenomics' third arrow fails to restructure the economy, this QE attempt will only create a historic asset bubble, as the surge in asset prices in 2013 to 2014 would not be backed up by a fundamental change in the economy.

Much of our discussion has focused on the monetary stimulus on the demand side and the possibility of a global economic recovery. This global fillip does not help to resolve a supply-side gap, even though the transition to self-sustaining global expansion may be in sight.[60] A prolonged habit of filling existing demand with innovation-less production may lead to a permanent loss in output—lowering the capacity to grow in both developed markets and Asian emerging markets. The current sluggishness in emerging economies' potential growth is a symptom of the unwinding of the excess production built up during a decade-long credit boom.[61] Since the financial crisis, consumers in developed countries have changed their lifestyles and preferences, especially in rapidly evolving new-tech devices. One can only hope that this will lead to a supply-side dividend in addition to stronger demand.

Asia's opportunity for growth lies in shifting to economies that are both more domestically oriented and more regionally integrated, notably in ASEAN. South Korea, Japan, and Taiwan can show their emerging neighbors, notably China and the middle-tier "ASEAN-4" countries—Indonesia, Malaysia, Thailand, and the Philippines—how to move up into the higher-value-added areas of the industrial chain. But they themselves have climbed up to the new economy's digital innovation and high-tech services.

Fast Transformation in the Financial and Banking Industry

While QE and the zero interest rate policy act slowly in transforming the real economy, their impact on the financial services and banking industry is fast and direct. Together, they provided fresh capital and lower costs to nurse the banks back to health, to enable a write-off of bad debts and a boost in asset prices. The zero interest rate policy encouraged individuals and financial institutions to move money from safe to risky assets to obtain yield and cash flow. Thus, the policies have induced speculation and created asset price bubbles, exposing markets to the same risks that in previous periods have led to sharp corrections.

In fact, there is no complete understanding of the mechanisms linking QE to financial markets and banking,[62] and policymakers must keep a sharp eye out for any unforeseen consequences.[63] These unconventional measures have not been taken before on such a scale. The closest precedent would be the period immediately following World War II.[64] During the war, price stability was obtained by statutory imposition of wage and price controls. The net result was a high-inflation world before wage and price controls were abolished and the value of the debt subsequently declined. Will the removal of QE have a similar effect? It seems unlikely. After World War II, economic growth was driven by rebuilding war-torn countries. What will drive growth after the financial crisis? The United States cannot afford to drive growth by investing the countless billions in infrastructure needed for the future. In addition, in the circumstances created by QE, there is plenty of money and credit but not enough assets and productive projects to pursue.

Banks in Asian emerging markets have channelled their abundant liquidity and cheap funding inflows into real sectors. As a result, Asian companies have aggressively increased capital expenditure and gone cross-border to expand and to acquire businesses. As QE slowly disappears, the impacts will vary across countries and industries. East Asia will fare better than Southeast Asia due to their diverging economic performances.[65] With commodity prices expected to be flat for the near future and strapped by funding pressures, Indonesia and India, both low-income and resource- and agriculture-based countries, will continue to raise policy rates and tighten monetary bases.

Once a country passes the threshold of $3,000 in GDP per capita, it reaches middle-income status, typically at the first stage of industrialization. Banking credit then becomes significant enough to expand the economy via consumer credit and capital expenditure. Singapore, Malaysia, Thailand, and China reached the $3,000 threshold in 1978, 1992, 2006, and 2008, respectively.[66] Thailand's domestic private credit as a percentage of the GDP has changed the most, nearly 50 percent in year seven of the cycle, in contrast to Indonesia's 5 percent in year two.[67] Note as well that on aggregate, Thai and Malaysian household debts are relatively high, more than 80 percent and far above the trend line; yet, Thailand's credit without special finance institutions is much lower—a little over 40 percent.[68] This implies that it is not Thailand's middle class but its rural population, with household debt close to 30 percent of GDP, which is feeding the high debt ratio. (The implication is that the more the Thai government offers populist programs and easy credit to the rural population, the more indebted they become.)[69] India, Indonesia, the Philippines, and China are still below trend with respect to household debt.[70]

On the corporate level, a QE tapering framework may impact differently across countries and sectors.[71] Improving growth rates in developed markets, notably the United States, will lead to rising interest rates. The impact will be mixed—nonlinear and specific to different sectors.[72] Potentially benefitting from recovery in the developed economies will be East Asian exporters—South Korea, Taiwan, and China—that sell automobiles or preferred electronic products to the United States. However, higher interest rates would mean a higher cost of funding, with yield compression, valuation compression, and a steepening yield curve.[73] Capital-intensive sectors like transportation, utilities, and telecommunications will be hurt, while Australia, the Philippines, and Thailand will bear a considerably higher cost of credit.[74] This would also put heavy pressure on multinational banks, regional insurers, and the property sector, through mortgages and project financing. Hong Kong and Singapore will likely face consolidation in property markets. Finally, the dollar will potentially strengthen to the benefit of Asian exporters to the United States. In Asia, multinational firms that report their books in dollars will be at a disadvantage. Countries like India and Indonesia that have current account deficits will become more financially distressed.

On the industry sector level, capacity expansions are seen across Asia in 2014, with perhaps some market consolidation in 2015.[75] Outstanding external corporate debt varies by country and sector.[76] For the steel and aluminum sector, for example, Australia, China, and India with severe margin contractions −183 percent, −177 percent, and −41 percent from 2008 to 2013 respectively, increased debt–equity (D/E) ratios 84 percent, 182 percent, and 140 percent, respectively, and potential change in their capacity in upstream business.[77] It is highly likely that steel and aluminum will face a further margin squeeze and restructuring in both countries, pressured by rising interest rates in the post–QE world.[78] In the oil and gas sector, Thailand and South Korea, for another instance, may continue to enjoy good margin expansion with low D/E ratios and with a bias to refining capacity reduction. Moreover, the oil and gas sectors of Thailand and South Korea, respectively, have $6.438 billion and $8.980 billion in external dollar corporate debt outstanding, or 52.7 percent and 11.1 percent of total external debt in dollars for the sector.[79] Thailand's oil and gas industry may seem to have high dollar loan value outstanding, but it is merely 1.1 percent of the country's total external debt. As a matter of fact, it is sensible for oil and gas industries to obtain dollar loans to match their assets and income streams valued mainly on a dollar basis.

China's real estate has the highest share of debt at 35 percent, equivalent to $33.864 billion debt outstanding, or 8.9 percent of total Chinese external debt. China's real estate sector is using dollar loans to generate income in *renminbi*. This is a classic case of unhedged funding (sometimes in maturity, sometimes in currency), which, history shows, can have disastrous results. Apart from speculating in real estate prices, China's real estate investors are also speculating on yuan appreciation. This is indeed a very risky venture. Chinese central bank and authorities engineered series macro prudential measures to cool down real estate price in the last few years and yuan depreciation in 2014.

M&A trends have been strong in Asia in recent years as QE gave firms easy access to cheap capital and credit. M&A inbound to Asia exceeded outbound in 2012—principally with Europe on both sides.[80] One exception is Japan, its outbound M&A exceeding inbound. Asian countries, notably China and Thailand, regularly hunted for commodity-based (typically energy and basic materials) ventures offshore; foreign firms focused on the financial and consumer sectors in Asia. One focus of interest, especially from Japan, is the fast-moving banking industry.

By the end of 2013, the world's top 15 banks based on total assets included four Chinese and three Japanese banks.[81] For two consecutive years, Industrial & Commercial Bank of China (ICBC) and Mitsubishi UFJ Financial Group, (MUFG), Japan, were ranked the no. 1 and no. 5 banks, respectively. For our discussion, the Chinese banks are less significant than the Japanese banks. Chinese banks have high concentration risk in the domestic market, notably in real estate and fixed-asset-related lending, while Japanese banks have more regional (and somewhat global) exposure, especially in project finance. As the BOJ accelerated its QE "money printing," Japanese banks have become less vulnerable to the Fed's tapering. They also have fully complied with Basel III capital requirements and leverage ratio obligations and are ready for expansion to boost their equity return.[82]

Japan's banks and corporations appear ready to fill the gaps opened by the reversal of capital to the United States. Its mega-banks have been on overseas shopping sprees to acquire banks, as shown in Table 3.4. MUFG took over seven banks between March 2012 and July 2013 for total deals of 1.14 trillion yen. Four deals were in the United States, mostly for retail- and real estate-related exposure; two were in ASEAN, namely Thailand and Vietnam; and one was in Australia. The largest deal was to acquire Bank of Ayudhya in Thailand from GE Capital for 560 billion yen. Two other top Japanese banks also have been active in acquisitions, as shown in Table 3.10 (see Table 3.4).

The biggest lesson from the global financial crisis is the presence of endogenous risk generated by and amplified within the banking system and credit markets, from the fall of Lehman Brothers in 2008 to the bailout of Spanish banks in 2012. When the turmoil spread from the United States to Europe, all major financial centers were caught up until the global credit system was frozen. It is worth noting how, before the crisis, hot money flooded into European peripheral countries like Spain and Portugal, which appeared to have high growth potential, and later rushed out again after the crisis revealed otherwise. Similarly, it appears that on the back of QE, Japanese banks have been aggressively and simultaneously pouring cheap and abundant yen credits into regional banking hubs in Hong Kong, Singapore, and other locations as discussed earlier. They have been buying ASEAN's banking franchise assets to gain more direct exposure and are supporting Japanese manufacturers in establishing footholds in ASEAN countries.

This yen-based banking network is being driven by the BOJ's policy. The greater the QE, the more interconnected the balance sheets will be. This is constructing a future endogenous risk that may explode when QE is reversed and credit tightened. The BOJ has become ASEAN's "central bank" to some degree. Unfortunately, ASEAN has no own bank regulator for this fast-evolving and potentially gigantic network. Policymakers must seriously consider too-big-too-fail issues, financial safety nets, and banking supervision for the region, especially with the formation of the AEC.[83]

Both West and East Must Rebalance Priorities

Before the financial crisis, the West's current account was chronically in deficit to the East's account.[84] The slump in demand caused by the crisis sharply narrowed this imbalance. QE gave birth to cheap dollar financing from the West, with too much hot money pursuing too little productive investment in the East. Similar stories can be found in the eurozone crisis. The long-term picture is still rosy for the East's emerging countries, which have young populations and growing consumer markets. But the reversal of QE may cause hardship to some of these countries, particularly those with weak balance of payments. In rebalancing their economies, Asian leaders must focus on (1) moving up the industrialization pecking order, (2) building cities for the growing population, (3) developing infrastructure to enhance competitiveness, and (4) increasing regional economic integration to expand consumer markets. Every new business cycle requires new risk-taking behavior and new financing to correspond to new fundamentals.

This development requires long-term financing and large pools of savings and capital at a time of tapering US QE. In the post–QE world, capital outflow risks will vary across in Asia. Cheap and abundant liquidity has fueled domestic growth such that many Asian countries' leverage has reached a historical high. Much of this can be explained by capital expenditure.[85] East Asia will fare better than Southeast Asia due to the shift in capital expenditure.[86] From 2008 to 2012, Indonesia and Malaysia enjoyed a construction boom fueled by easy credit, boosting their GDP by 4 to 6 percent, while Thailand's populist policies like car purchase subsidies and a personal credit boom lifted the automobile sector. The reversal of QE will create drags in all these cases. In addition, the easy credit enabled Indonesia, Malaysia, and Thailand to reach their highest capital expenditure levels in a decade, with the nominal fixed asset

Table 3.4 Investment statistics for the three major banks

8306 MUFG

	Type	Country	Company	Amount	Summary
Jul 2013	Acquisition	Thailand	Bank of Ayudhya	Max ¥560bn	Plan to subscribe for 75% of total issued shares by TOB
May 2013	Acquisition	United States	Services to homeowners associations and community management companies		Union Bank (consolidated subsidiary of BTMU) to acquire First Bank association bank services
Apr 2013	Acquisition	United States	Commercial real estate portfolio	Approx ¥360bn	Union Bank to acquire from PB Capital which is owned subsidiary of Deutsche Bank
Dec 2012	Investment	Vietnam	Vietnam Joint Stock Commercial Bank for Industry and Trade (VietinBank)	Approx ¥63.1bn	Acquisition of 20% of ordinary shares and VietinBank became an equity method affiliate of BTMU
May 2012	Acquisition	United States	Services to homeowners associations and community management companies	Approx ¥10bn	Union Bank to acquire from PNC Bank
Mar 2012	Acquisition	United States	Pacific Capital Bancorp	Approx ¥120 bn	UnionBanCal Corporation and Union Bank to acquire Pacific Capital Bancorp
Mar 2012	Investment	Australia	AMP Capital Holdings	Over ¥30 bn	Acquisition of 15% equity interest and AMP Capital Holdings became an equity method affiliate of MUTB
Jul 2011	Investment	United States	Morgan Stanley		Conversion of convertible preferred stock into common stock. MUFG holds 22.4% of the voting rights and MS becomes an equity method affiliate of MUFG
Apr-11	Investment	China	SWS MU Fund Management	Approx ¥9bn	Acquisition of 33% of the voting rights from BNP Panbas and SWS MU became an equity method affiliate of MUTB

8316 SMFG

	Type	Country	Company	Amount	Summary
Jul 2013	Acquisition	France	Societe Generale Private Banking	Over ¥10bn	Acquisition of 100% shares
May 2013	Acquisition	Indonesia	PT Bank Tabungan Pensiunan National	Approx ¥150bn	To become a significant minority owner of up to 40%
Dec 2012	Investment	Hong Kong	Bank of East Asia	Approx ¥35bn	To increase its investment to 9.5% from 4.73%
Apr 2012	Investment	United States	China Post & Capital Fund Management	Approx ¥10bn	Acquisition of 24% equity interest
Mar-13	Investment	Indonesia	PT Indonesia Infrastructure Finance		Subscription for 14.9% of total issued shares
Jan-11	Acquisition	UK	Aircraft leasing business	Approx ¥550 bn	SMFG, Sumitomo Mitsui Finance and Leasing and Sumitomo Corp acquire RBS's aircraft leasing business

8411 Mizuho FG

	Type	Country	Company	Amount	Summary
May-12	Acquisition	Brazil	Banco WestLB do Brasil	Approx ¥30 bn	Acquisition of 100% shares by Mizuho Corporate Bank
Sep-11	Investment	Vietnam	Vietcombank	Approx ¥45 bn	Subscription for 15% (after dilution) of total issued shares by Mizuho Corporate Bank

Note: MUFG = Mistubishi UFJ Financial Group; SMFG = Sumitomo Mitsui Financial Group; Mizuho FG = Mizuho Financial Group.
Source: Yamanaka and Muranaka, 2013. Copyright © 2013, Takehito Yamanaka and Ryuta Muranaka Credit Suisse.

investment (FAI) to GDP ratio reaching 33 percent, 27 percent, and 28 percent, respectively.[87] This is in contrast to East Asia, which in aggregate cut back domestic investment to the lowest level in a decade.[88] FAI is intrinsically capital-intensive and sensitive to interest rate levels and funding availability. If FAI generates productivity gains, inflation will be restrained and re-leveraging will be prolonged. If not, nominal GDP will decelerate and nonperforming loans will rise.

Also, from 2008 to 2013, the ratio of private credit to GDP for Hong Kong, Thailand, China, and Singapore increased significantly to more than 73 percent, 34 percent, 27 percent, and 22 percent, respectively.[89] In the post–QE era, tighter liquidity and rising real rates could destabilize Asia and hurt growth potential, especially for China and fiscal deficit countries like Indonesia and India. More restrictive credit means lower growth. Indonesia, Malaysia, Thailand, and the Philippines together need more than half a trillion dollars to build their infrastructure alone through 2020.[90] (Details will be discussed in chapter 7.)

Banks must adapt their business models to the new conditions. New regulations like Basel III and more stringent accounting standards require banks to hold more capital and to limit their leverage. Disintermediation in banking has been going on over the last few decades. Securitization, equitization, and mutualization are prime examples of this trend. At the onset of the financial crisis, there was approximately $8.7 trillion of assets funded via securitization issued mainly by Western banks.[91] Much of this is still on the banking books. It is naive to believe that commercial banks can go back to their traditional basic reliance on taking deposits and making loans to creditworthy borrowers for a profitable yield. It is particularly noteworthy that banks in Europe severely shrank their balance sheets (by 3.5 trillion euros) between May 2012 and September 2013, for about 10 percent of their total balance sheets.[92] A contraction of derivative books, notably securitized financial products, is the biggest driver. Only 900 billion euros is on account of European peripheral banks and the rest (2.6 trillion euros) is due to core banking caused mainly by weak economic growth and new regulations. Asia's banks have not uniformly implemented Basel III. This implies that many banks in Asia, except in Japan, are not ready for major expansion. Because there are variations in these frameworks and because even banks in the same country are in different stages of following these regulations, there is an almost "risk-free" money-making opportunity from using cheap capital sourced from looser regulatory locations to lend to the tighter regulatory locations.

Instead of offering hot money rushing in and out and doing financial trading for quick profiteering, the West can be the East's partner as the East seeks new ways to propel growth. The West can share its long experience and expertise in long-term risk and reward sharing finance such as securitization and public–private partnerships, as well as in technology and management. And the prosperity from East's supply-side-related growth can be shared for mutual benefit. The new global financial system should be diversified, not concentrated, and built on highly interlinked confidence, not interlocking banking balance sheets.

Conclusion

The global economy needs the stimulus of QE in order to guard against the risk of deflation. Yet, it cannot rely indefinitely on QE, which ultimately can promise only resurgent inflation. The loss of confidence in central banks and their ability to control economies through monetary policy would be catastrophic for business; the stagflation of the 1970s indicates the mildest potential scenario.

Intimations of tapering had marked effects on interest rates in the United States and globally in 2013, and in selected emerging markets in 2014. The burden on the Fed to smoothly manage the gradual withdrawal of stimulus is huge.

The influence of QE on economic development and trade flows will become less important as the underlying pressures build. Less-developed economies must add capacity in industries and infrastructure, with or without cheap financing. At the same time, developed economies such as Japan must rationalize their industries to avoid the wasteful consequences of regulations protecting old, unsustainable industries. A Chinese industrial policy that has created a huge buildup in select industries also has to mature to a more market-oriented as opposed to a central planning approach.

Trade liberalization would further help to rationalize industrial development, preferably based on comparative advantage. But progress has been hamstrung by local interests that seek to protect established oligopolies or employment in inefficient industries. Here, the natural Chinese entrepreneurial spirit is counteracting the central planning tendencies that have fostered the state-owned enterprises dominating the Chinese economy. Official pronouncements may indicate a faster transition to a more open economy, which would heavily influence Chinese trade policies, and by extension Asia's and the world's.

Much of Asia's capital formation is hampered by an excessive reliance on bank funding rather than through bond and equity financing. Basel III's insistence on higher capital ratios has diminished the supply of bank capital and induced savers to channel their funds to equity or higher yield bond instruments. Europe, a developed market, has seen its growth slowed by the traditional domination of banks. Asia must expand its poorly developed capital markets, and create a more liquid debt market to aid the capital expansion of its industries. QE's reversal will act against this process if investors feel that equity markets are threatened by a rise in interest rates. Yet, equities will benefit most from a rational interest rate environment that is both expansionary enough for growth and tight enough to limit inflation. Nothing is new here, but investors must respond rationally.

It is probably much too soon for Asia to contemplate development of an active industry in securitization. The recriminations about excessive securitization in the United States have largely subsided, with a call for a renewed issuance of derivatives that will help to ease balance sheet restrictions and permit increased bank lending to industry (especially smaller firms). This time, let's hope that the root of the problem can be controlled by controlling the moral hazard in the primary issue of debt. For the market to develop in Asia, it will be similarly essential to provide confidence in these instruments. Presumably, this stage will follow a greater development of traditional financial markets.

The United States has started to eliminate QE, the UK will follow, the eurozone never really embraced it, and Japan cannot afford much of it, given its massive national debt. In time, the gradual removal of QE from the world's banking systems will allow the traditional forces of financial market expansion, industrial rationalization, and mutually beneficial trade to drive global economic growth.

Case Study

"Japan's Automakers Are Reclaiming Its Prosperity"

Pongsak Hoontrakul

The yen's competitive devaluation generally has created a virtuous cycle for Japan's automakers. The short-term windfall profit and long-term volume growth potential will help them comfortably adjust their business strategies to increase shareholders' value. However, the benefits have been unevenly felt for each automaker, varying according to its geographic exposure and products.

In 2013, the yen dropped roughly 30 percent against the US dollar and the top ten Japanese auto and auto parts producers made record profits. All the producers benefitted from the yen depreciation to some degree. Toyota, Honda, and Nissan benefitted the most for the top three, for example, as every yen weakening against the dollar gave the company an additional 40,000, 14,000, and 15,000 yen per million yen of transactional value, respectively.[93] On the other hand, Suzuki and Isuzu benefit the least below 650 yen per million yen of the transactional value.[94] Every yen weakening against the euro added only one-tenth of that, however.[95] The euro appreciation did not provide as much benefit for the Japanese producers because they are nearly at full production capacity in the United States but not in Europe, and market demand in the United States is much stronger than in Europe. Thus, Japanese automakers operating in the United States can readily increase the level of Japanese-made content in their vehicles and reap profits, whereas in Europe they have to be content with increasing production efficiency.

European and Japanese original equipment manufacturers (OEMs) or auto parts manufacturers command about a quarter of global supply each, followed by the US Big Three at 20 percent.[96] Furthermore, Japan has 37 percent of the US market, its largest market outside Japan, followed the Big Three at a distant second.[97] But in Europe, all Japanese OEMs except Nissan have been constantly losing market share due to their excess capacity built up prior to 2008.[98] Europe remains the least profitable market for Japan and has been subjected to streamlining and cost cutting. Hence, European OEMs face a limited threat from the Japanese devaluation.

Another interesting case is the Indian market. The yen declined faster than the rupee against the dollar in 2013 but among the Japanese automakers, only Suzuki reaped net benefits.[99] The Indian market is quite protectionist on foreign imported content/OEM products or final products. Although Japanese makers have more than half of India's auto market, they cannot benefit much from the weak yen because India's very high import duties result in almost the entire car being produced locally. Suzuki is the only Japanese automaker with a joint venture in India; Maruti Suzuki (India) dominates nearly half of the industry. The joint venture has its exposure in yen at about 21 percent of net sales via royalty charges, and direct import of parts from Japan and indirect components from its US and European subsidiaries.[100] India is expected to soon ease its protective tariffs; when that happens, the other Japanese auto producers also will benefit from the yen weakening.

South Korea OEMs are in intense competition with Japan's. But despite the nosedive in Korean automakers' stock prices in high correlation with the yen depreciation, Korean sales and profits remained satisfactory in 2013. It turns out that product cycle is also an important driver in the auto and auto parts business. There were 15 new car models introduced in the United States during 2008–2012, and manufacturers offer price deductions ranging from 30 percent to 70 percent in periods between the release of new models.[101] This cycle may be distorting the impact of the dollar appreciation on sales and profits.

In short, the yen devaluation is one factor in the auto industry's competition, but market structure, geographical capacity planning, OEM product cycles, and institutional constraints like local tariff barriers also matter.

"Prada and Emerging Asian Nouveau Riche"

Pongsak Hoontrakul and Nisanart Thadabusapa

Prada, the Milan-based luxury goods group, is a case study in using business acumen to navigate difficult global market conditions. While other luxury fashion businesses have struggled financially in recent years, Prada has outperformed its competitors in developing products and in exploiting changing market trends. And it has made a strategic decision to stake a place in the heart of the Asian luxury market.

Asia is the future of the luxury market because of its dynamic economies. The region has always been a priority for Prada. Two-thirds of the 91 stores that Prada opened in 2010 were in Asia; Singapore and Shanghai were among the key locations.

On June 24, 2011, Prada launched its first initial public offering (IPO) on the Hong Kong Stock Exchange; it was the first Italian company to float in Hong Kong. The IPO received strong support, raising US $2.6 billion that Prada used to cut its debt and to finance the expansion of its directly operated stores.

Prada is not just opening stores across China, a key growth market for the luxury sector, but also increasingly manufacturing its high-end fashion there.

Prada said in June 2011 that about 20 percent of its collections, including bags, shoes, and clothes, were being made in China (*The Wall Street Journal*, June 24, 2011). So far, it appears that the "Made in China" label—a label that luxury buyers presumably do not want—has not hurt sales. Prada posted a remarkable net profit increase of 46 percent in 2012, mostly from Chinese and Asia markets. But will consumers continue to accept the China label?

China's luxury market has been slowed by a weaker overall economy and a government crackdown, starting in 2012, on the corrupt practice of giving expensive gifts to officials.

Luxury buyers also prize uniqueness, and so far Prada has benefitted from the fact that it does not have as big a profile and as many stores in China as say, Louis Vuitton. Prada also has a more diverse product mix. It is not built around dominant signifiers like Louis Vuitton's monogram bags. As a result, Prada is better positioned than many other luxury brands to tackle the rapid maturation of the market.

Manufacturing in China reflects the new reality for luxury brands. They can no longer grow and increase profits by simply increasing retail prices. In the traditional luxury business model, raising prices was a way to keep the brand positioned for the wealthy and for those consumers who wanted to live the lifestyle of the wealthy. Now, cost reduction is the only way to survive.

In recent years, luxury goods companies have shifted their main distribution from wholesale to retail, which commands higher margins and offers more control over store locations and customers' buying experiences. As of October 2013, Prada had 516 directly operated stores, up from 211 in 2008.[102] It had 27 such stores in China.

While most brands still run with only two collections per year, Prada has pioneered higher-margin "flash collections" that it uses to supplement its main collections. The flash collections allow Prada to respond quickly to changes in fashion trends; it takes only four to six weeks from product design to placement in the stores.

In 2014, Prada is estimated to have an annual revenue of 4 billion euros with a net profit of over 700 million euros with next year growth rate of over 10 percent for both numbers.[103] Almost half of these figures are derived from Asia and are growing.[104] Prada has been outperforming its competitors on brand momentum supported by a focus on fashion, a shift to direct retail channels, and an increasing global presence. What would happen if any of these factors were to start to disappoint?

Notes

1. Nathan Sheets and Robert A. Scokin, "Perspectives: Our Global Top 10- A Tour of the Post-Crisis World Economy in 10 Easy Charts," *Citi Research*, July 5, 2013: 1–20.
2. Pongsak Hoontrakul, David Walker, and Julapa Jagtiani, "The Global Financial Crisis and Implications for Thailand," discussion paper, IADI, BIS, Basel, June 20, 2012.
3. Klaus Schwab, "2014 Will Make or Break the Economy," *Bangkok Post*, January 13, 2014 (http://www.bangkokpost.com/opinion/opinion/389247/2014-will-make-or-break-the-economy).
4. QE 1 from Nov 2008 to Aug 2010 equated to about USD2.1trl securities (mainly MBS and T-Bill) purchased by Fed. QE 2 from Nov 2010 to June 2011 equated to USD600 billion of purchases in T-Bill only. Finally in QE 3 from

Sept 2012 until further notice, Fed decided to perpetually buy USD85 billion per month of both T-bill and MBS. The last and final QE 3 is popularly
known as "QE-Infinity."

5. Richard Iley et al., "Asia Ex-Japan: Key Macro Themes For 2014," *BNP
Paribas*, January 2014: 24. For more discussion see R. Dobbs, S. Lund, T.
Koller, and A. Shwayder, "QE and Ultra-Low Interest Rates: Distributional
Effects and Risks," McKinsey Global Institute, November 2013: 1–72.

6. Ibid., pp. 19–22.

7. Stephen King, Karen Ward, and James Pomeroy, "Global Economics—
Deflation: The Hidden Threat," *HSBC Global Research, Macro Global
Economics Q1 2014*, January 2014: 1–2, 8 (Table 2) and 10–12.

8. Ibid. on pp. 1–2, 8 (Table 2) and 10–12.

9. According to Brazilian Finance Minister Mr. Guido Mantega, competitive
devaluation or currency war broke out in 2010. Many states imposed capital
controls and tax on short-term capital flow. See more discussion by James
Mackintosh, "Currency War," *The Financial Times*, September 28, 2010.

10. Bob Prince and Amit Srivastava, "Bridgewater Daily Observations," May 20,
2009: 1.

11. Andrew Tilton et al., "Asia Economics Analyst: A Deep Dive Into Regional
Financial Flows: Possible Impact of US Fed Tapering," *Goldman Sachs*, issue
no: 13/32, September 6, 2013: 1–25.

12. On December 18, 2013, the Fed board resolved to modestly reduce the rate
of asset purchase from USD85 billion to USD75 billion. It also implied that
additional USD10 billion per month cutback will be considered in each subsequent meeting at their discretion subjected to its forecast macro data. It is
conjectured the two main conditions are the inflation and unemployment
rates to be below 2 percent and 6.5 percent rate, respectively. The Fed also
stressed for more "enhanced forward guidance" in keeping the interest rate
low, perhaps beyond 2015.

13. William Buiter et al., "2014 Investment Themes: A World in Transition:
Tapering, Restructuring and Reform." *Citi GPS: Global Perspectives &
Solutions*, January 13, 2014: 24–25 (https://www.citivelocity.com/citigps/
ReportSeries.action?recordId=23). More discussion see Joyce et al., "The
Great Unwind: The Implications of Bernanke Taper Delay," Presentation in
Bangkok, *Deutsche Bank Research*, September, 2013.

14. Laurence Boone et al., "ECB: Almost Like QE, But Not There Yet", *Bank of
America Merrill Lynch*, June 3, 2013: 1–12.

15. Masayuki Kichikawa et al., "BOJ: Optimistic But Dovish", *Bank of America
Merrill Lynch*, May 21, 2014: 1–7.

16. First examined by Willem Buiter and Ebrahim Rahbari, "Trade Transformed:
The Emerging New Corridors of Trade Power," *Citi Research*, October 18,
2011: 1–80; and reviewed by Ebrahim Rahbari and Deimante Kupciuniene,
"Global Economic View: Slow Trade, Fast Trade Transformation," *Citi
Research*, March 11, 2013: 1–20.

17. Ebrahim Rahbari and Deimante Kupciuniene, "Global Economic View: Slow
Trade, Fast Trade Transformation," *Citi Research*, March 11, 2013:1–20.

18. Izumi Devalier and Rupali Sarkar, "A Pretty Big Deal: Everything You Need to Know About the Trans-Pacific Partnership," *HSBC Global Research*, December 18, 2013.

19. Ben Bernanke, "Monetary Policy since the Onset of the Crisis," speech delivered at the Federal Reserve Bank of Kansas City Economic Symposium, Jackson Hole, Wyoming, August 31, 2012.

20. Ibid.

21. Bruce Kasman, David Hensley, and Joseph Lupton, "Global Data Watch: The Global Consumer is Lifting," *J.P. Morgan*, December 20, 2013: 1–4.

22. Anil Daswani et al., "Global Gaming: Maximum Bullish in 2014: A Watershed Year for Macau and the US," *Citi Research Equities,* January 6, 2014: 1–236.

23. Pongsak Hoontrakul, "Thailand's 1997 Banking Crisis: Recoveries from Assets of Troubled Banks," discussion paper, International Association of Deposit Insurers (IADI), BIS, Basel, September 8, 2013.

24. .Jimmy Koh et al., "Global Macro Outlook 2H2013: US QE Tapering Dynamic & China Interbank Cash Crunch," *UOB Banking Group*, July 10, 2013.

25. Ibid.

26. P. Hooper et al., "World Outlook: A Leap Back to Trend Growth," *Deutsche Bank Research*, December 11, 2013: 1–71.

27. Ibid., pp. 17 and 67.

28. Ibid., p. 67.

29. Ibid. for Europe p. 22 and 67 and for Japan on p. 32 and 67.

30. Ibid. for pp. 34–35 and 67.

31. Fiona Lake et al., "Not Your Older Brother's Asia Financial Crisis," *Goldman Sachs, Portfolio Strategy Research*, 2013: 18–19.

32. Anthaporn Arayasantiparb, "1H'14 Thai Strategy: The Magic of Abenomics," *UOBKayhian*, January 11, 2014 (http://research.uobkayhian.com/content_download.jsp?id= 19512&h=7487db4b18866f75529483d51e31fd49).

33. Tilton et al., "Asia Economics Analyst: Deep Dive Into Regional Financial Flows."

34. Ibid.

35. Ibid.

36. Ibid.

37. Ibid.

38. Ibid.

39. Ibid.

40. Ibid.

41. Ibid.

42. Soo Chong Lim et al., "China Property Sector: A Credit Primer," *J.P. Morgan*, May 9, 2013; Lucia Kwong and Ryan Li, "Asia Real Estate Handbook," Part 1, *J.P. Morgan*, June 12, 2012 (https://markets.jpmorgan.com/#research.article_page&action=open&doc= GPS-872705 -0).

43. Tilton et al., "Asia Economics Analyst: Deep Dive Into Regional Financial Flows."

44. William Buiter and Edward L. Morse, "2014 Investment Themes: A World in Transition: Tapering, Restructuring and Reform," *Citi GPS*, January 2014:

24–25 (https://ir.citi.com/TLJ9swWrFlvEyRXLHyZ%2BzjZfN%2F8dm2TH MASZIBiQp1LMOdJtmxp2CA%3D%3D).

45. Paul J. Davies, "Asian Debt: Beware of Bubbles," *Financial Time*, May 22, 2013 (http://www.ft.com/intl/cms/s/0/acd43be0-bec9-11e2-87ff-00144feab 7de.html#axzz2nY0pjd9z).

46. Tilton et al., "Asia Economics Analyst: Deep Dive Into Regional Financial Flows."

47. Zheng Kit Wei, Helmi Arman, and Jun Trinidad, "ASEAN Macro View: Chartbook: Current Accounts – A Saving-Investment Perspective," *Citi Research*, August 27, 2013: 1–12.

48. Josh Klaczek and Joy Wu, "Asia Banks & Corporate Credit: Cycles of Foreign Bank Lending: Pre-97 vs Pre-2013," *J.P. Morgan*, September 10, 2013: 4.

49. Wei et al., "ASEAN Macro View," pp. 3 and 11.

50. Ibid.

51. First examined by Willem Buiter and Ebrahim Rahbari, "Trade Transformed: The Emerging New Corridors of Trade Power," *Citi Research*, October 18, 2011: 1–80; and reviewed by Ebrahim Rahbari and Deimante Kupciuniene, "Global Economic View: Slow Trade, Fast Trade transformation," *Citi Research*, March 11, 2013: 1–20.

52. Sheets and Scokin, "Perspectives," pp. 13–14.

53. Jeremy Hale, Maya Bhandari, and Maximilian Moldachi, "Foreign Exchange Forecasts: November 2013," *Citi Research*, November 21, 2013: 1.

54. Ibid.

55. John Normand, "JP Morgan Currency Timelines: From the Brentton Woods Breakup to the EMU Crisis," *J.P. Morgan*, August 14, 2013: 3.

56. Ibid.

57. Richard Kersley et al., "Yen and You: The Competitive Edge", *Credit Suisse*, July 1, 2013: 1–121; Tim Shanagher and Daisuke Takato, "Japan Outlook 2014: The Year to Deliver on Expectations," *Credit Suisse*, December 16, 2013: 1–30.

58. Ibid. for steel, pp. 59–73 and for airlines, p. 97.

59. Peter A. Petri, Michael G. Plummer, and Fan Zai, "The Trans-Pacific Partnership and Asia-Pacific Integration: A Quantitative Assessment," *Policy Analyses in International Economics*, issue no. 98, October 2011 (Washington: Peterson Institute for International Economics); Izumi Devalier and Rupali Sarkar, "A Pretty Big Deal: Everything You Need to Know About the Trans-Pacific Partnership," HSBC Global Research, December 18, 2013.

60. Bruce Kasman, David Hensley, and Joseph Lupton, "Global Data Watch: The Supply slide," *J.P. Morgan,* December 13, 2013: pp. 1–4.

61. Ibid.

62. Hans Lorenzen, "Too Much Money, Not Enough Assets to Buy: Inside the Global Supply–Demand Imbalance," *Citi Research*, April 25, 2013: 1–15.

63. Sheets and Scokin, "Perspectives," p. 11.

64. Ibid., p. 8.

65. Andrew Tilton et al., "Asia Economics Analyst: Diverging Fortunes—the Emerging Asia Outlook for 2014," *Goldman Sachs, Economics Research*. Issue no: 13/43, November. 21, 2013: 1–25.

66. Ibid., pp. 1–12.
67. Ibid.
68. Melissa Kuang et al., "Thailand: Banks: Correction Overdone, Valuation Attractive," *Goldman Sachs*, January 16, 2014: 11.
69. Ibid.
70. Ibid.
71. T. Moe et al., "Asia Pacific 2014 Outlook: Back on Track." *Goldman Sachs, Economics Research*, November 21, 2013.
72. Ibid.
73. Ibid.
74. Ibid.
75. Tilton et al., "Asia Economics Analyst: Deep Dive Into Regional Financial Flows."
76. Andrian Mowat et al., "Battered by Bonds: Perspectives and Portfolios-Lite," *J.P. Morgan*, June 10, 2013: 1–48.
77. Tilton et al., "Asia Economics Analyst: Deep Dive Into Regional Financial Flows."
78. Ibid.
79. Mowat, "Battered by Bonds."
80. Markus Rosgen and Yue Hin Pong, "M&A: Asia Buys Commodities, Foreigners Buy Financial and Consumer," *Citi Research*, November 12, 2012: pp. 1–14.
81. (http://www.relbanks.com/worlds-top-banks/assets).
82. T. Yamanaka and R. Muranaka, "Japanese Major Banks: In initial phase of medium-term rally," *Credit Suisse*, September 9, 2013: 1–35.
83. See more discussion by Hoontrakul et al., "The Global Financial Crisis.".
84. Stephen King, "Reversal of Fortune: From Excess Liquidity to Financial Drought in the Emerging World," *HSBC Global research*, September 4, 2013: 1–12.
85. Josh Klaczek, "An Inflection Point on Leverage and Growth," *J.P. Morgan*, June 10, 2013: 11.
86. Josh Klaczek and Joy Wu, "Asia Banks & Corporate Credit: Looking for a Shift in the Capex Cycle," *J.P. Morgan*, September 29, 2013: 1–10.
87. Ibid.
88. Ibid.
89. Klaczek, Josh, and Joy Wu, "Asia Banks: Looking Beyond 2q: Growth Correction vs Credit Crisis," *J.P. Morgan*, August 25, 2013: 5.
90. Andrew Tilton et al., "Asia Economics Analyst: ASEAN's Half a Trillion Dollar Infrastructure Opportunity," *Goldman Sachs, Economics Research*, issue no: 13/18, May 30, 2013(a): 1–18 (http://www.btinvest.com.sg/system/assets/14801/ASEAN%20infras %20opportunity.pdf).
91. D. Wheeler et al., "Does the World Need Securitization?," *Citi Research*, December 12, 2008, pp. 1–12.
92. N. Panigirtzoglou, M. Lehmann, and J. Vakharia, "Flow & Liquidity: Severe Balance Sheet Shringkage,"*J.P. Morgan*, November 22, 2013: 3–4.
93. Chris Ceraso et al., "Yen and You: The Competitive Edge: Global Autos," *Credit Suisse*, July 01, 2013: 43–58.

94. Ibid.
95. Ibid.
96. Ibid.
97. Ibid.
98. Ibid.
99. Ibid.
100. Ibid.
101. Ibid.
102. (http://www.pradagroup.com/documents/press/Profile_PRADA_Group_ April_ 2013.pdf).
103. Ebru Sener Kurumlu, Shen Li, and Henry Tan. "Prada S.P.A", *P. Morgan*, April 3, 2014: 1–21.
104. Ibid.

4

Fast Track to Regionalization and Internationalization

Christopher Balding and David Garcia

Introduction

Financial and economic market integration with neighbors are hallmarks of sound development strategies. However, regional competition within the Association of Southeast Asian Nations (ASEAN) countries blocks the latter change from transpiring, specifically because foreign and domestic politics are conflicting in member nations. Such discord encountered by policymakers strains regional development and impedes long-term growth of the world's most populous trading bloc. Even as Southeast Asian countries have been regarded as development miracles, much is left to be desired: the number of intra-ASEAN financial transactions, in the form of mergers and acquisitions (M&A), remains low (Chakravarty and Ghee, 2012); poor coordination between fiscal and monetary policy that may cause buildup of risks when coupled with high capital inflows (Balakrishnan et al., 2012); and stifled region-wide trade continues through increased dependence on Chinese manufactured products (Kalra, 2010). By both fostering growth and regional stability, opened financial markets will stabilize cross-border partnerships by dislodging domestic interest groups and shifting regional concerns to region-wide growth vis-à-vis other trading blocks.

The megatrends driving Asian regionalization move on parallel tracks but closer examination provides a diversity of experiences within each country. China the autocratic dragon has grown rapidly but faces large risks in the future due to a variety of factors such as a declining population while others like India, the chaotic democracy, is enjoying a demographic dividend that looks to continue as its population continues to grow.[1] In fact, with the exclusion of China, a recent study by the International Monetary Fund (IMF) concluded that "demographic factors will be much more supportive in India and some ASEAN economies" to long-term growth (Anand et al., 2014). Despite the opportunity for regional or bilateral cooperation in a variety of areas, Asian regionalization remains a relatively elusive objective beset by conflicts over sea rights, territorial conflicts, market access for investors and companies, and historical antagonisms that predate World War II. Given the range of issues over which Asian countries maintain disputes, it is no surprise that this mutual distrust spills over into areas which present great opportunity for cooperation.

Cross-Border Investment

Despite the rapid growth of ASEAN economies, there remains significant barriers to cross-border investment and specifically M&A activity. Investment into China is tightly controlled with most foreign firms remaining junior partners. Foreign direct investment (FDI) into China frequently requires technology transfer to Chinese joint-venture (JV) partners, and acquisitions or mergers of Chinese companies are rare. While Chinese firms have started investing outside of China, it remains a relatively limited portfolio focused on strategic sectors such as natural resources and technology. Portfolio investment activity is strictly limited with tight control over both investment levels and the ability to repatriate capital or profits. Despite significant demand for *renminbi* (RMB) assets by both companies to invest in China or portfolio investors seeking greater access to the RMB, China has limited the use of the RMB in onshore or offshore uses (Maziad and Kang, 2012). Even the offshore RMB exchange market suffers from asymmetries that prevent China from increasing its influence through greater use of the RMB in trade settlement both regionally and internationally (Craig et al., 2013). China has little appetite to use its increased economic influence to promote the RMB, despite significant demand. In short, the Chinese market is generally not hospitable to foreign investors.

China is rapidly expanding its international investment levels. There remains however, significant distrust of Chinese investors given the close links with the state or their financing arms and the strategic assets these companies target. Internationally minded Chinese firms have targeted natural resources, high tech, and flagship acquisitions. A small number of Indian firms have been quick to seize opportunity and move beyond their home market. The business process outsourcing (BPO) firms are well known, but Indian firms like Tata Motors and Arcelor Mittal are industrial firms expanding outside of India into developed markets. Interestingly, Indian firms have not expanded into regional neighbors like China, Thailand, or Pakistan but rather focused on purchasing distressed assets as strategic investments. The internationalization of Indian national champions focuses on acquisition of managerial expertise.

Only more developed centers like Singapore and Hong Kong have engaged in significant regional integration through either increasing trade flows or cross-border investment. This may stem from their financial center status or as an attractor of talent, capital, and productive firms that prompt them to increase their regional influence. However, even Singapore and Hong Kong have become global centers of finance in their own right. These financial hubs attract talent from around the world to work in their international market place; they draw corporate listings and capital raising activities globally; their world-class universities act as magnets regionally for talented young students from throughout the region. Cross-border investment within Southeast Asia flows through Singapore and Hong Kong given their financial and economic influence. However, over the long run, their position is threatened. China is seeking to increase the role of Shanghai, while Bangkok, Kuala Lumpur, and Mumbai seek to transform themselves into financial centers creating a financial services industry to serve national and regional clients. Despite concern that financial market liberalization yields to a lack of strong regulation, research on ASEAN stock markets finds "idiosyncratic" influences on asset pricing that would benefit from strong regulation and increase liquidity and investor sentiment (Lipinsky and Ong, 2014). Given the role of financial services in a growing affluent class and in credit creation, states actively seek to nurture this valued industry. Singapore and Hong Kong, however, remain directors of capital and not regional integrators in stature of the potential of China or India. Their markets open to trade, finance, and labor do not have the ability to impact the regional economy and integration the way China or India can.

However, it is not purely regulatory barriers that constrain cross-border investment within the ASEAN region. Maybe most importantly, many of the ASEAN economies have similar industries, similar levels of economic development, similar levels of technology, and similar objectives. Despite the potential for a pan–ASEAN bond market, studies have indicated that significant hurdles on such basic factors as infrastructure to realize the potential (Felman et al., 2011; Gray et al., 2011). In another instance, potential resource constraints are a primary concern of economic planners and businesses across ASEAN, limiting potential cooperation in extractive industries. In other cases, ASEAN companies are direct competitors with Bangladeshi garment manufacturers directly competing with Chinese firms for export markets. Furthermore, ASEAN economies are still rapidly accumulating capital that they prefer to direct into domestic economies rather than use for international acquisitions.

Trade Relations

Research on trade over the last 30 years has reshaped theory. Krugman first integrated preferences into his research, observing consumption bundles alter as foreign goods enter a market as a result of a change in preferences. This assumption halted the belief that changes from trade were purely monetary and galvanized others[2] to develop imperfect competition models aimed at demystifying trade-related economic changes; simply put, much of the research observes the economic effects of trade. Trade, however, implies countries swap relatively cost-advantageous goods and services, leading to increased utility. Such simplifications preclude the possibility of protectionism that typifies many developing countries' growth strategies. Maximizing utility in a developing country obliges the social planner to apprise the negative impact such trade relationships have on domestic firms. Realizing this fact prompted two primary development strategies: the import-substitution and export-oriented models. Given the export focus of economies in Asia, there is significant competition for the same industries and firms.[3] This competitions leads to a cannibalization of the available markets where countries maintain high regional barriers. Thai, Vietnamese, and Bangladeshi firms are competing for the same low-wage garment-processing jobs that prompt the state to maintain high trade barriers in a misguided attempt to compete with each other. Regionalization will remain minimal as long as the state believes that high trade barriers and suspicion leave their states better off than low trade barriers and cooperation. Internationalization has prompted states to more closely link their economies with developed economies in Europe, Japan, and the United States rather than regional partners. Even now, many ASEAN economies remain closely linked to developed economies through trade channels that impact domestic economies (Isnawangshi et al., 2013). This is both a challenge and an opportunity to improve regional linkages in trade.

On the surface, ASEAN countries follow classical export-led development strategies: They received foreign capital, developed local businesses, and expanded outward. Under this exterior, however, a different story emerges finding deep regional divides among member states in which antagonistic stances stem from cultural and religious differences throughout history. Although Japan and China's contentious relationship garners much attention, in the larger economic sense, the rivalry between ASEAN member nations and China is the bigger concern within the region.

Export-oriented models are inherently more open than import-substitution ones and thrive as closed economies open up. East and South Asia's growth represents the superiority of this model which has shown to have not only long-term advantages (sustainable growth) but also short-term ones (higher access to foreign investment). The export-oriented model, nevertheless, challenges the exporting nation to offset rising domestic costs with rapidly increasing productivity; thus, identifying and generating trade agreements with new markets remain vital. Burgeoning costs weaken competitiveness, forcing a transition from export to domestic-oriented production and from labor- to capital-intensive goods. This implies rising levels of capital and reduced levels of consumption to drive an export-oriented economy. While the long-run outlook may be positive, it causes trade frictions and nations see their interest in short-term zero-sum game, restricting opportunities for cooperation between regional neighbors.

ASEAN's Transformation

Creating Substitute Markets

In classic trade arrangements, developed and developing countries' markets act as complements, generating wealth for both nations. The political economic framework led to factionalizing among nations as strategic allies were designated "favored nations"; this unique division demarcated distinct groups, originally based on political ideology, which has grown into recognition of states that abide by specified trade agreements. Japan and the Asian Tigers, most notably, presented a staunch anticommunist stance, justifying America's and Western Europe's partnership with them. These politically based economic groups bracketed countries into de facto trading blocs and foreshadowed eventual bilateral and trading bloc free-trade agreements. As trading blocs formed, import tariffs receded to accommodate partners in a "win–win" setting but failed to account for the growth strategies of the member states. While political alliances deter military conflict, competition between ASEAN neighbors strips trade agreements of mutual benefit through cooperation as proposed in the traditional Edgeworth box.

Frictions from Development
Traditional export-led development strategy asserts that the social planner first increases manufacturing-based foreign investment, implying limited technological know-how. To correct this weakness, the government invests significantly in the development of human capital, allowing domestic firms to find knowledgeable employees and expand outward. Firms first migrate to large cities (products and services) or rural areas (manufacturing and mining) in border countries. In doing so, cultural differences are mitigated while deficiencies in international expansion strategies are phased out. However, simultaneous development among regional neighbors does not ensure the emergence of resource grabs as firms compete for increasingly scarce investment.

The term "climbing the ladder" is synonymous with the IMF and World Bank strategy of development and is useful for describing regional conflict. As one might expect, meaningful trade agreements between export-oriented nations seldom occur due to the similarity of the member countries' trade growth strategies, epitomizing the conflict between countries on the same rung of the ladder. For example, a coffee-producing nation need not trade with other coffee-producing nations, while two countries exporting lumber rarely swap goods. Much in the same fashion, ASEAN member states—on paper—represent one of the largest and important trading blocs. However, the face value of the agreement fails to deliver tenable trading alliances among the member states.[4] Currently, much trade from middle- and low-income countries in Asia would be considered substitute goods rather than complementary products. In other words, where high-income countries may trade similar but not identical products, such as Lexus and BMWs, which increase aggregate trade between themselves, middle- and low-income countries trade substitute products that are not differentiated and therefore compete directly with products from other middle- and low-income states. By climbing the value ladder, countries hope to create brand value that differentiates their products from pure substitute products.

Shifting Trade Dynamics

Generally though, much of the economic groundwork for broader ASEAN growth stems from the Japanese experience in which the country gradually developed to rival the United States economically in the 1980s; however, competition—rarely encountered by the Japanese during their development cycle—remains the sticking point of ASEAN countries today, primarily since much competition for new markets comes from within the trading bloc. Sluggish trade growth among ASEAN originates from the inherent weakness of the export-based strategy as member nations export components for firms based in developed countries. Profits spring from the comparative advantage in wages of these developing countries rather than their innovative capabilities; thus, trade frictions and economic disputes relate more to the position in the value chain since little product differentiation exists. Foreign investment, in this respect, is restricted by availability of choices rather than quantity.

As these nations have developed, these markets are increasingly demanding advanced technology, reducing firms' need for low-skilled workers through automation. The resulting situation pressures governments and industries to increase performance, highlighting one fact: more output is needed for the same amount of workers. While industries must produce at lower costs, governments must cultivate the economic environment to ensure domestic firms remain competitive. Trade blocs, which consist of partners with similar strategies—such as ASEAN—are developed under the auspices of bilateral and multilateral trade expansion that will create jobs, when in fact, these policies require substantially greater time.

As politicians become increasingly concerned with maintaining gains from development while expanding into new markets, an inward focus inevitably takes hold of government policy; ASEAN countries are no different. In other words, as trade develops, actors shift from obtaining investment to obsessing over the implications associated with it. For this reason, regimes routinely pacify interested parties through a variety of protectionist measures that reduce the level of openness in the economy. While FDI has tapered somewhat in the last decade, a significant amount can be related to exogenous shocks and long-term outlook rather than protectionism. In fact, this supports the fact that ASEAN nations have embraced internationalization by promoting direct competition with foreign countries, integrating their market with China, and transforming markets into complementary markets, rather than competing ones.

Direct Competition with Developed Markets

Over the long term, foreign capital—enjoyed at initial stages of development—loses appeal as domestic firms shift from strict manufacturing to domestic branding, directly conflicting with Western firms and changing local producers from complement firms to direct substitutes. Akin to Japan in the 1970s and Korea in the 1990s and 2000s, ASEAN markets will continue to move up the supply ladder. Initial competition between government-led research institutes and foreign firms focused on developing science and technology will be short-lived as state–private partnerships alleviate competition and cultivate an entrepreneurial business environment. One indicator highlighting this trend can be seen in the Malay government's direct investment in science and technology, which has increased the number of engineers and formed strategic partnerships with large, research-oriented firms (i.e., General Electric and Siemens).[5]

The China Effect

China has directly influenced trade in a number ways, specifically, through opening its economy. The unfettered access to Western markets by ASEAN countries undoubtedly allowed companies to misallocate resources to some degree. China's opening, consequently, led to a glut of cheap labor that still pushes costs down in ASEAN countries today. Undoubtedly, one reason for slower growth in countries such as Malaysia and Thailand has been more connected to China's appeal for investment and consumption, but the effect is negligible.[6] Moreover, Chinese strict capital policy ensures that FDI remains within the country, limiting investors' ability to quickly withdraw from the market as was experienced in the Asian financial crisis. China's comparative advantage, however, is slowly eroding as internal inflation reduces overall competitiveness, allowing ASEAN countries (namely Vietnam and Cambodia) to thrive.[7]

Moreover, the China–ASEAN free-trade agreement, which lowered 90 percent of tariffs to near-zero percent in 2010, can be seen as ASEAN's crowning achievement. The short term might benefit Chinese merchants, who still benefit from generous government subsidies, but the long-term gross domestic product (GDP) outlook for ASEAN firms is positive: they have high access to a large pool of Chinese consumers, relatively cheaper goods, and significantly higher integration into the global community. Singapore (1), Thailand (18), and Malaysia (6) are ranked higher than China (99) on the Ease of Doing Business Index released by the International Finance Corporation (IFC). Malaysia and Thailand will act as conduits to China for investors looking at broader trade and economic opportunities in Southeast and East Asia over the next 15 years.[8]

The largest ASEAN nations are already shifting their merchandise exports away from developing countries. Since 1990, these exports have declined 15–20 percent, indicating a shift to developing countries—specifically, China. Moreover, the seemingly endless failures of ASEAN since its inception will finally bear fruit, as member nations will have a fully developed trade bloc where industries in one country complement the preferences of the markets in another one. China's emergence as a viable trade partner shifted attention from Indonesia—the largest market in

ASEAN—because of Indonesia's inability to develop infrastructure and eliminate corruption[9] (see Figure 4.1).

Creating Complementary Member Markets
Fixation on trade and investment agreements pinpoints little in terms of intrinsic economic factors related to growth, which is ultimately determined by factors of productivity and demand; in this sense, ASEAN countries have outpaced other developing countries. From both the top-down and bottom-up, ASEAN countries abstained from excessively protectionist behavior. Both economically and culturally, Southeast Asian countries remain foreign friendly: Ease of doing business in many ASEAN nations is high (or improving), while tourism remains a strong sector of commerce. Perpetual receptiveness initially hindered growth, but unquestionably acted as a blueprint for future domestic governance.[10] Today, ASEAN countries are thriving vis-à-vis other members of regional trading blocs.[11] Far from these obvious reasons, their economies skipped regionalization for direct integration into the global economy—unlike that found in *Mercado Común del Sur* (Mercosur).

Mercosur, the largest and most comparable trading bloc to which ASEAN is often compared, takes advantage of member states' competitive strengths through economic stratification; clear boundaries identify the export-oriented agricultural nations (i.e., Columbia, and Bolivia), manufacturing-oriented countries (i.e., Chile and Brazil), and petro-economies (i.e., Ecuador and Venezuela). In doing so, the nations develop long-term trading agreements that fosters an overall leverage unforeseen by ASEAN nations. Furthermore, the economic goodwill fosters partnerships—rather than conflict—among regional neighbors. Comparing ASEAN to Mercosur,

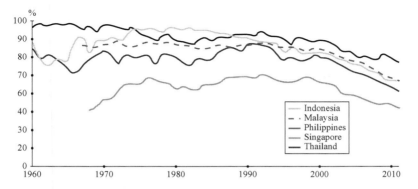

Figure 4.1 Percentage of Merchandise Exports to Developed Countries

Source: Worldbank (http://data.worldbank.org/) and Author's Calculation.
Copyright © 2014, Christpher Balding and David Garcia.

however useful, is limited partly because the member nations of both blocs have historical influences that must be accounted for in sound trade policy.

Despite the frictions in the regionalization of trade, Asian countries have continued to rapidly expand their internationalization efforts. Even after the global financial crisis, merchandise exports from Asian countries to the rest of the world continued to increase rapidly, though intraregional trade did not experience similar levels of growth.

The dysfunction, however, remains politically motivated, as East Asian and Pacific trade has thrived. Figure 4.2 shows a clear growth in trade among developing nations in East Asia and the Pacific. While the data fail to indicate to which country exports flow, the overall trend is clear: future demand will come from developing countries. Furthermore, these statistics exclude, Japan, Korea, Australia, and New Zealand as trade destinations, expressing rapid growth in trade between Southeast Asia and China[12] (see Figure 4.2).

Domestic Demand

Worker quality is typically the major reason nations remain stuck in the middle-income trap; simply, innovation fails to be a key driver of the economy. ASEAN countries—having invested heavily in education over the last 30 years—experience quite the opposite problem: a shortage of investment for their highly skilled workers. As engineers, designers, and other highly skilled workers enter the market at increasing rates, employment demand for their skills will continue to rise, suggesting domestic firms will attain services, previously considered foreign, in their home

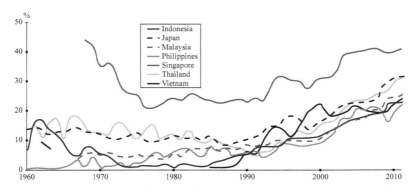

Figure 4.2   Percentage of Merchandise Exports to Developing Nations in East Asia and Pacific

Source: Worldbank (http://data.worldbank.org/) and Author's Calculation.
Copyright © 2014, Christpher Balding and David Garcia.

countries. Thus, firms are looking inward—rather than outward—to solve their employment problem, while the newly developed economies seek foreign investment. China, the largest economy with some of the most well-developed firms, has a stable of brands that remain virtually unknown, if not distrusted, outside of China (Millward Brown, 2013). Thus, these two dilemmas play a significant role in trade and cross-border deals.

Inward Shifting Perspective as a Transaction Friction

Over the course of any growth cycle arbitrage begins to emerge, as profit-seeking domestic firms encounter growing domestic demand that provides pecuniary and nonpecuniary compensation: transaction costs decline as one common language is used, jobs provided to nationals strengthen purchasing power, and governments obtain higher tax revenue. In economics terms, income rises, tax revenues increase, and supply-side costs decline—beneficial to all parties. However, the domestic benefit reduces international benefits to some degree as large cross-border deals become irrelevant: the cash is accessible, the desire is not. In Figure 4.3, we plot the number of foreign listings on Asian stock markets since 1980.

Asian indexes, generally, have been more inward looking since 1990, the number of firms in Japan has steadily declined, while Singapore experienced tremendous growth. This trend supports the notion Singapore is outward looking. Typically, domestic consolidation precedes international acquisitions by firms, giving the firm know-how and a solid base

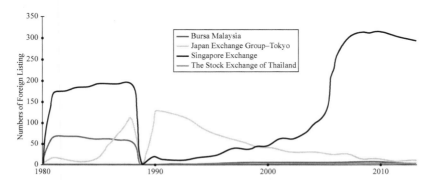

Figure 4.3 Number of Foreign Listings in Japan, Malaysia, Thailand, and Singapore Exchanges

Source: Worldbank (http://data.worldbank.org/) and Author's Calculation.
Copyright © 2014, Christpher Balding and David Garcia.

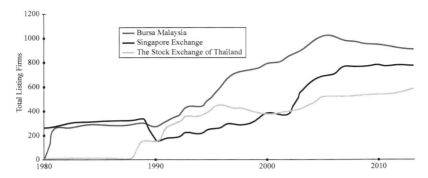

Figure 4.4   Total Listings on Malaysia, Singapore, and Thailand Stock Exchanges

Source: Worldbank (http://data.worldbank.org/) and Author's Calculation.
Copyright © 2014, Christpher Balding and David Garcia.

upon which to develop. The number of listings however has continued to increase as economic growth has been steady, if not spectacular, throughout developing Asia. In Figure 4.4, we plot stock listings for major economies.

Since 1990, the number of listed companies on the Bursa Malaysia Stock Exchange has increased fourfold, representing strong growth throughout the economy. Nearly 99 percent of listings on the Bursa Malaysia Stock Exchange are domestic, significantly higher than Singapore (roughly 40% of the market) and similar to Thailand. The increase in the number of listings is expected to continue to rapidly climb as firms raise capital, seek to expand their investor, and benefit from steady economic growth. This implies a growing demand for trained financial service professionals regionally and increased use of English if markets hope to attract foreign listings or even increase their internationalization.

Employment as a Trade Friction

ASEAN nations have shifted toward a services-oriented economy, allocating an increasing number of workers to services. This trend is more appropriately seen in Figure 4.5, which shows a growing trend by all ASEAN members in services. Some major sources of employment have been tourism, financial services, and research, all of which specialize in highly skilled workers (see Figure 4.5). As overall growth patterns over the last 20 years have shown a decline in merchandise to developing countries, Figure 4.5 highlights the growth of domestic demand as a form of growth since service-related jobs typically enjoy higher levels of income.

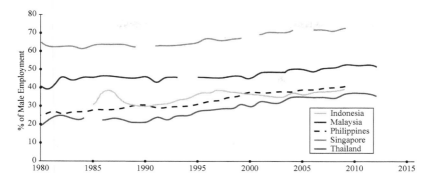

Figure 4.5   Percent of Male Employment in the Services Sector from 1980

Source: Worldbank (http://data.worldbank.org/) and Author's Calculation.
Copyright © 2014, Christpher Balding and David Garcia.

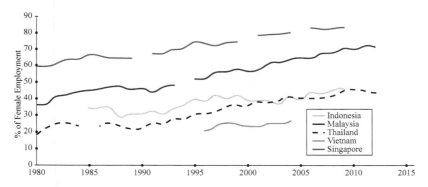

Figure 4.6   Percent of Female Employment in the Services Sector from 1980

Source: Worldbank (http://data.worldbank.org/) and Author's Calculation.
Copyright © 2014, Christpher Balding and Jame Garcia.

If economic growth remains steady, the increase in the service sector economy should continue to draw increasing numbers into higher-income service sector jobs and raise the number of women in the workforce. Income is rising for both men and women in ASEAN countries, especially as working conditions for women have liberalized. This betterment in conditions is highlighted in Figure 4.6, which shows the percentage of female employment in the services sector in relation to other sectors of the economy. Much development theory highlights the positive externalities of an educated, working female workforce (see Figure 4.6); namely, the increase in human capital stabilizes society by transferring to the following generation. In the largest ASEAN countries, this growing trend nevertheless stresses competition for jobs and minimizes the need for outsourcing.

Tremendous growth in both the services sector and the stock markets is driving ASEAN, particularly Malaysia and Thailand. As Malaysia shifts to an advanced economy, much of the domestic manufacturing will go to other ASEAN nations. Thailand remains a viable alternative, but the lack of stability in the country undermines successful transition to an upper-income economy and causing an increased pessimism regarding outsourcing jobs to Thailand; the largest competitor for these products is Vietnam because of the cheap labor costs and proximity to the Indo-China region.

FDI in ASEAN

FDI is often seen as a zero-sum scenario since finances are limited. The overall desire by firms to gain access to this capital inevitably increases as expectations to expand increase. Despite a slowdown in investment in the non-traded sector of the economy after the 2008 financial crisis, the long-term outlook for investment, especially in the traded sector, remains positive and strong (Zhou, 2013). Typically, sustained FDI is dependent upon the market conditions of the country, although limited bursts can occur from exuberance. Overall, China has absorbed significant total dollars of FDI, totaling more than US$250 billion in 2012, while exporting roughly US$440 billion—a nearly US$200 billion difference, almost 1.9 percent of GDP. Combined, ASEAN nations received significantly less FDI in absolute terms, but were equivalent as a percentage of GDP. However, these absolute terms are merely dollar values[13] (see Figure 4.7).

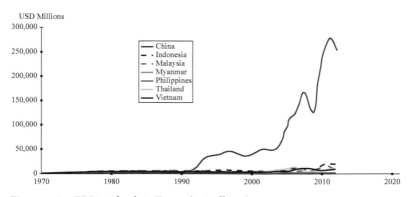

Figure 4.7   FDI in Absolute Terms (in Millions)

Source: Worldbank (http://data.worldbank.org/) and Author's Calculation.
Copyright © 2014, Christpher Balding and David Garcia.

Transformation in Malaysia

Malaysia (and Thailand) will become the regional leader of Southeast Asia for two reasons: political stability and advantageous location. The first indicator is the ease of doing business in the country that attracts FDI away from its neighbors. Furthermore, policy, implemented from the top-down, created infrastructure, maintained economic stability, and projected confidence to international leaders. Although the dual-track legal system impedes transactions to some degree, foreigners and foreign businesses, alike, are quickly developing Kuala Lumpur (KL) into Singapore's rival. Moreover, Malaysia's population is four times that of Singapore and consists of significant Chinese and Indian minority groups (25% and 7%, respectively).

Much of the competitive advantage enjoyed by Singapore is common in Malaysia, as well. Statistically, the Chinese Malay population is larger than the whole of Singapore (6.44 to 5.4 million). Furthermore, it is a regional transport hub and is quickly becoming a regional financial hub. Prior to the Asian financial crisis, market capitalization in Malaysia was 300 percent of GDP, but has stabilized to roughly 125 percent of GDP, similar to levels seen in the United States and Singapore. Moreover, this stable percentage indicates that the financial market has been growing at the same speed as the economy (roughly 6.5% year on end). To the dismay of the Singaporeans, Malaysia's long-term outlook is increasingly optimistic as more cross-border transactions will be diverted away from Singapore to KL. While the amount fluctuates, at times significantly, we show in Figure 4.8 that the stock market moves in close correlation to GDP growth over a long-run average.

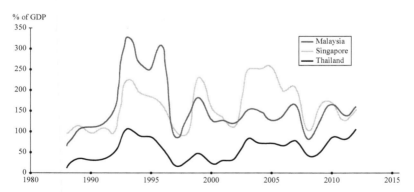

Figure 4.8   Market Capitalization of All Listed Companies as a Percentage of GDP

Source: Worldbank (http://data.worldbank.org/) and Author's Calculation.

The growth of funding in KL begs the question: Can Southeast Asia support three or more financial hubs when we consider Hong Kong? When one finds the source of the funds, the answer is yes. Finances in KL are coming from both traditional and nontraditional forms of finance, specifically Islamic financing; the predominantly Muslim Malaysian community has unfettered access to capital from other Islamic countries since the tumult found in other Muslim countries drives increasing investor confidence in Malaysia, which has remained at peace since its transition from colony to sovereign nation-state.

Transformation in Thailand

Thailand shares many characteristics of Malaysia—robust growth, dynamic economy, and a relatively foreign-friendly environment. Many of Thailand's current problems stem from the urban–rural divide: rural poverty remains a development issue with 88 percent of Thailand's 5.4 million poor living in rural areas, investment focusing on large cities, and education in the north and northeastern provinces lags behind other provinces. Also, significant ethnic tension exists in southern Thailand where Malay Muslims have fought for independence for years.

These issues are more a hindrance than a drag on the overall state of the economy: ease of doing business is high, investment continues to grow, and domestic companies are capitalizing at a breakneck pace. Optimism can also be drawn from the Thai population—which is three times that of the Malay population—indicating domestic demand will continue to grow for a number of years. Thai GDP (in nominal terms) must double roughly three times to reach levels comparable to California, which can be achieved between 25 and 30 years if current growth rates maintain; this scenario must be considered, given the growth in the Thai economy since 1980.

Is India the Answer?

As the largest provider of outsourcing services, India presents a unique dichotomy: an inward-looking workforce for an outward-focused economy. Large Indian firms are more integrated into the global economy; Indian elites use English in daily communication[14]; and the system of governance and law is directly drawn from the Westminster experience. Contrarily, Indians from lower social strata are xenophobic, increasingly hostile to foreign influence, and weary of seemingly unequal legal and political systems. These conflicts are increasing class hostility during a period of volatile growth. On the one hand, India's large population, a history of Western interaction and a large English-speaking population, presents distinct advantages over the Chinese economy; on the other

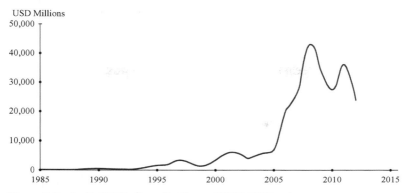

Figure 4.9   India FDI Inflows (in Current USD Millions)

Source: Worldbank (http://data.worldbank.org/) and Author's Calculation.
Copyright © 2014, Christpher Balding and David Garcia.

hand, these advantages have been unfairly distributed among the higher rungs of society.

The late 1980s presented India with a significant problem: capital reserves were quickly drying up as its payments were coming due. From this moment, Manmohan Singh, the then finance minister, opened up Indian's flagging economy to foreign investment, inducing tremendous private sector growth. This watershed point brought FDI to Mumbai, Bangalore, and other large cities, opening the Indian economy in a vastly different way from the state-led opening China experienced. Entrepreneurs marketing India as a services hub took advantage of the Indian economy in vastly different ways than previously thought. Nevertheless, India, however, failed to attract the investment found in China[15] (see Figure 4.9).

As a large open economy with a democratically elected government apparatus, India is notorious for its red tape and bureaucratic hurdles that deprive the country of efficient macroeconomic stabilization policy and competent regulatory framework for investors[16]; this sluggishness can be seen in India's response to shocks where the country's inside lag is woefully large. In many ways, India's economy thrives when the government removes itself from the economy, akin to the deregulation of key industries through privatization of state-owned enterprises (SOEs) and reduction in red tape.

Indian Development

Internationally recognized names, such as TATA group, Reliance Capital, the Times Group, and Wipro, present India as forward thinking, innovative, and outward looking. Furthermore, these companies generally engage foreign competition through conforming to international norms and practices. Thus, Indian firms represent fully competitive firms capable of forging strategic partnerships with international actors; in a sense, a pragmatic outward thinking epitomizes India's elites which Chinese elites lack. Despite large well-known internationally competitive firms, the Indian economy remains relatively closed with a relative distrust of liberal policies. In some respects, internationalization can appear as cultural retrenchment that weakens cultural norms through propagating global institutions and practices. This results in a policy uncertainty that appears to impact declines in investment that prevent the Indian economy from meeting its potential and realizing Chinese rates of growth (Anand and Tulin, 2014).

India is well known as an outsourcing destination, but numerous service industries beyond information technology (IT) and telecommunications exist in the country; these opportunities are the often-neglected component of Indian development and represent an authentic prospect for rural Indians to grow. One such place is Gujarat where roughly 90 percent of diamonds are cut, high-quality textiles (such as silks and denims) are manufactured, and solar energy is utilized. Cities such as Ahmedabad and Surat are driving long-term industrial growth, which allows smaller companies to thrive. Unfortunately, these cities are microcosm in the greater Indian economy: recent financial trends highlight India's vulnerability and lack of quality leadership at the highest levels of the federal and state governments. The Indian economy will recover as the government continues to reduce poverty and upgrade telecommunication systems.[17]

India needs not have domestic megadeals and M&A to drive growth since its large firms cater to international industry more than found domestically. In fact, India by 2025 will represent the largest and most competitive free market on earth with microenterprises stimulating growth rather than clunky SOEs. While fear of financial market liberalization is used to defend strict financial controls, there is no evidence that foreign investors, regional or international, prompt financial market instability in India (Patnaik et al., 2013). Declining advertisement costs driven by social networking, increased computer use at all levels of Indian society, and wider access to resources complement the already inventive domestic populace. Moreover, wider access to Internet-based and formal education will also provide additional boosts to total factor productivity—the intangibles in the economy.

Is China the Answer?
China has touted exceptional growth for 30 years, shifting the question from "Can China overtake America as the largest GDP?" to "When will

China overtake America as the largest GDP?" The Chinese model, truthfully, represents a unique hybrid dissimilar to the American one, in that much growth has come as the economy has simultaneously transitioned from communism and capitalism. These factors are far from disparate goals since much of the transition has centered on the development of a market-oriented economy, causing unsupportive institutions to readjust in order to adequately satisfy the elements of a market-oriented economy: competent administration selecting key industries to develop and practical regulation fostering competition and profit-seeking entrepreneurs.

China's rapid growth, in many respects, makes most industries important to the success; traditionally, the export-oriented industries located in the south were uniquely different from the natural resource-based ones in the north and the agrarian ones found throughout the country. Specifically, since the initial thought process in opening and reform was founded on gaining sufficiently large foreign financial capital, and then develop domestic brands, most northern industries centered on raw materials are disproportionately used for domestic consumption and feeding manufacturing in the south; thus, in many respects, China's internal vertical supply chain provided distinct advantage similar to that in America. Consequently, the export-led growth ultimately reverts to a rung of the ladder that ignores domestic innovation but spurs imitation. Product imitation, while detrimental to foreign companies, provides a useful spark for domestic manufacturing.

Two main drivers of China's early engines are the Special Economic Zones (SEZs) and credit cooperatives, which halted the growth of defeatist attitude evinced by Chinese nationals post cultural revolution. Much of the credit cooperatives, which were used in China's early development, represent the government's bridge between the capitalist and communist theory, whereas the SEZs marked a clear break from communist ideology. In doing so, profit-seeking ambitions reshaped the Chinese workforce into one covetous of future wealth and acquisitive of personal development, thus starting the manufacturing hub of the world. China's export hubs—the Pearl River delta (PRD) and Zhejiang province—host thousands of micro- and small and medium-sized enterprises (SMEs), which need not merge, but merely leave the market when their profit-making potential expires. Such seemingly easy entrance and exit from the market could be one reason that M&A have remained relatively small.

Partnerships, as a form of strategic knowledge transfer, remain a major source of China's development whereby international and domestic Chinese firms partner on a local project. (Siemens high-speed rail is one clear example.) In doing so, the Chinese firm gains expertise that is used for both domestic and international projects. Advocacy of this approach by the Chinese government reduces the need for the cross-border acquisition for knowledge (as discussed in Vermeulen and Barkema, 2001). A major incentive in FDI agreements is some form of technology development or transfer to continue the buildup of Chinese human capital and managerial expertise. However, foreign firms have become increasingly wary of providing specialized technology or intellectual property to Chinese firms or JVs due to both declining competitiveness and a long history of misuse of these assets.

China however, while enjoying strong and sustained economic growth, seems unwilling to globalize and has been criticized by many in the region for their policies. Their economically protectionist policies and territorial expansionist policies have increased suspicions from neighbors already concerned about China's rapid rise to prominence. Even among regional bodies like ASEAN, China remains a relatively disconnected participant preferring bilateral action where it can put its overwhelming size against other countries to secure its position. There are, however, no countries of comparable size or economic importance prepared to provide regional leadership on a range of issues. China is both indispensable and an irritant in promoting regional cooperation. Regional cooperation depends on China but regional partners do not necessarily want China to be the regional leader. The future increase in regional cooperation and internationalization of the economies and firms will depend heavily on Chinese willingness to use its influence to drive this process.

Conclusion

The long-term outlook for regionalization and internationalization of Asian economies remains bright. There are, however, significant risks and caveats. Given the expected growth in the region's economies and their export focus, it remains quite likely that regionalization and internationalization will continue to proliferate. It is not going to be a straightforward path for the region's players. There is significant distrust across a range of issues between the major states in the regions and with smaller countries. Markets remain far from open and there is only slow movement on breaking down regional economic and financial frictions that prevent increased integration. Despite evidence that countries do not divert investment capital away from other countries, many remain locked in a zero-sum game mind-set that dictates a winner only at the expense of another. Many states have preferred to focus their efforts on internationalization, working with countries outside the immediate region due to offers of preferential trade and investment. While internationalization brings investment and large markets with trusted partners, this strategy overlooks the enormous markets and opportunities within the region. The move to regionalize Asian economies will require building trust, breaking down barriers, and improved leadership from major states. Regionalization is while likely, by no means guaranteed.

Case Study

Lenovo: Global Expansion by Takeovers

Nat Pinnoi and Pongsak Hoontrakul

In 2003, China's Legend Computer was rebranded as Lenovo to prepare for overseas expansion. Its Chinese name, *Lianxiang*, means "connected thinking." Lenovo made use of such thinking as it eyed businesses that IBM and Google wanted to abandon.

IBM was among a triumvirate that dominated the global personal computer (PC) market in the late 1990s and early 2000s. But after losing nearly US$400 million in 2001, IBM pursued serious restructuring. At the same time, Lenovo saw in IBM's PC division what Lenovo lacked. Lenovo already enjoyed laser-thin manufacturing costs and dominated the domestic PC market, but IBM had a global brand and global business partners. In 2005, Lenovo bought the division for $1.25 billion.

To bring in experience in leading a global company, the head of IBM's PC operation was asked to serve as Lenovo's CEO and head an executive staff drawn in equal numbers from both companies. English was declared Lenovo's official language. Lenovo now has two headquarters—in Beijing and in Morrisville, North Carolina, in the United States. Main production facilities are in these two cities and in Singapore.

Lenovo has become the world's no. 1 PC maker. However, the global demand for PCs was forecast to fall from 321 million units in 2013 to 305 million units in 2014, a 5 percent decrease.[18]

In January 2014, Lenovo paid $2.91 billion for Google's Motorola mobile-phone business, a major brand that could help Lenovo compete with Apple and Samsung. That same month, Lenovo paid $2.3 billion for IBM's low-end server business, which provides services like hosting websites, tracking inventory, and managing banking transactions.[19] This move was designed to help in the server competition with Dell and Hewlett-Packard. Lenovo plans to lower prices in order to boost volume. Lenovo's current chairman and CEO, Yang Yuanqing, said the acquisition complemented his company's "PC Plus Strategy" for long-term profitability following the decline in the global PC market.

In China, Lenovo is the largest distributor in a market where PC sales are still growing and the server business is up-and-coming. The IBM and Motorola acquisitions also elevate the Lenovo brand globally and bring in production know-how and technology transfer. This is a case study in knowing and correcting your weaknesses in order to expand and compete globally.

Tata Motors and the Jaguar Land Rover Turnaround

Pongsak Hoontrakul

About 111.5 million people watched the telecast of American football's Super Bowl XLVIII game on February 2, 2014, when Jaguar made its first appearance in the iconic game commercials to tout its new F-Type coupe. But few of those viewers knew that Jaguar Land Rover Automotive Plc (JLR), Britain's largest car manufacturer, is a subsidiary of the Indian carmaker Tata Motors Ltd.

Tata Motors acquired JLR for $2.3 billion from Ford Motor Co. during the tough operating environment of 2008 just before the Great Recession began. Ratan Tata, chairman of the Tata Group—the family-owned, Mumbai-based conglomerate that is the parent company of Tata Motors—said JLR's luxury cars and sport utility vehicles (SUVs) added strategic value to Tata Motors, which specializes in the cheap small car the Nano.

Ratan Tata gave JLR's management a free hand and two years to improve the company's disappointing financials. When they did not, he replaced them with a new corps of executives from other European carmakers, including Ralf Speth as JLR's CEO in February 2010. Their mission was to turn the company around—and they did that in a spectacular fashion.[20] Tata also invested more than $200 million to set up an "IT ecosystem" in which the subsidiary Tata Technologies controlled and streamlined all the production processes at JLR. The program resulted in product rationalization, value engineering, and reduced costs for raw materials, employees, and warranties.[21]

JLR rebounded from a loss of 673 million pounds in 2009 to a profit of more than 1 billion pounds in just the first half of fiscal 2013. The importance of JLR to Tata Motors' revenue stream was evidenced by the results of the second fiscal quarter of 2013. Tata Motors lost about $130 million in the Indian market as sales of compact cars was disappointing. The luxury segment was another story; sales were buoyed by the right product mix, the global economic recovery, and strong demand in India and in China. JLR made a profit of $811 million, helping Tata Motors as a group make a profit of $577 million.[22]

"The key to success," Speth said, "is creating value and innovation to generate the right economic return to justify further investment in innovation—the perfect virtuous cycle."

Tata Motors' auto parts manufacturing business benefitted from JLR's global markets access, especially in the United States and the European Union. This coincided with the shift by all automakers to cut costs by using common spare parts in different car models.[23] Tata's auto parts business was forecasted to grow 25 percent, to 500,000 units, in 2014. With the domestic Indian market slowing in 2013–2014, JLR also opened the door for Tata exports to 169 countries. Furthermore, JLR has successfully moved into many high-growth and emerging markets.[24] In March 2012, JLR formed a 50/50 JV with a Chinese firm, Chery Automobile Co. Ltd., which makes SUVs, minivans, and passenger cars. JLR's aggressive expansion plan was to double its car-manufacturing capacity, from 400,000 units in 2013 to 800,000 units by 2017.[25]

Notes

1. J. Nederveen Pieterse, "Dynamics of Twenty-First Century Globalization: New Trends in Global Political Economy," *Prace Instytutu Profilaktyki Spo\ lecznej i Resocjalizacji*, 2011, 17, 107–132.

2. R. Feenstra, "New Product Varieties and the Measurement of International Prices," *The American Economic Review*, 1994, 84(1): 157–177; Timothy J. Kehoe and Kim J. Ruhl, "Why Have Economic Reforms in Mexico Not Generated Growth?," *Journal of Economic Literature*, American Economic Association, December 2010, 48(4): 1005–1027.

3. M. Ariff and H. Hill, *Export-Oriented Industrialisation*. Hoboken: Taylor & Francis, 2012, provide an in-depth review of the ASEAN experience.

4. L. Leviter, *The ASEAN Charter: ASEAN Failure or Member Failure?*, 2010 [e-book], accessed: April 1, 2014 (http://nyujilp.com/wp-content/uploads/2013/ 02/43.1- Leviter.pdf).

5. V. Rodriguez and A. Soeparwata, "ASEAN Benchmarking in Terms of Science, Technology, and Innovation from 1999 to 2009," *Scientometrics*, 2012, 92:3, 549–573, follow patterns in ASEAN nations.

6. B. Mercereau, *FDI flows to Asia* (Washington, DC: International Monetary Fund), Asia Pacific Dept, 2005, finds the economic fundamentals to be the main driver of FDI flows away from many Southeast and East Asian countries.

7. "The China Files: Chinese Economy through 2020," *Morgan Stanley*, November 8, 2010 (http://www.morganstanley.com/views/perspectives/China_Economy_2020.pdf)

8. Indonesia, being the most populous nation in Southeast Asia remains riddled with corruption, reducing the overall effectiveness of Malaysia and Thailand to thrive.

9. Belligerence in China—notwithstanding.

10. The East Asian Financial Crisis is a classic example of excessive hot money and insufficient government oversight.

11. Growth in Mercosur member nations in both real and nominal terms lags behind ASEAN nations.

12. Micronesia, while important, remains (with all respect) an insignificant percentage of demand.

13. Mercereau, *FDI flows to Asia*, finds China had impact on FDI flows to most of Southeast Asia.

14. Once removed from the major cities, the average level of English decreases considerably, discrediting the notion Indians throughout all of India are highly skilled English speakers.

15. India is ranked 117 in terms of ease of doing business.

16. The Indian government is in the midst of registering all Indians for identification cards.

17. The latest World Bank report describing India's growth gives credence to this fact

18. Thompson Wu,"Lenovo Group Ltd—FY3Q14 Preview: Raising FY 14/15E EPS Alongside Global Smartphone Increase," *Credit Suisse*, Asia Pacific/Hong Kong Equity Research, IT Hardware, January 8, 2014, pp. 1 and 3.

19. Stephen Shankland, "IBM Sells its x86 Server Business to Lenovo for USD2.3 Billion," *News.CNET.com*, Jan 23, 2014 (http://news.cnet.com/8301–1001_3–57617651–92/ibm-sells-its-x86-server-business-to-lenovo-for-$2.3-billion/).

20. Surajeet Das Gupta,"The Jaguar-Land Rover Turnaround," *Business Standard*, February 12, 2014 (http://www.business-standard.com/article/beyond-business/the-jaguar-land-rover-turnaround-113082001080_1.html)

21. Ibid.

22. Rupert Hargreaves, "Why Does Tata Motors Look Significantly Undervalued ?," *The Motley Fool*, January 16, 2014 (http://www.dailyfinance.com/2014/01/16/why-does-tata-motors-look-significantly-undervalue/).

23. Jatin Chawla and Akshay Sazena, "Tata Motors Ltd.: The Story Has More Legs Part 2," *Credit Suisse Equity Research*, January 9, 2014, 1, 4, and 11–12.

24. Hargreaves, "Why Does Tata Motors Look Significantly Undervalued?."

25. Chawla and Sazena, "Tata Motors Ltd.," 1, 3, and 4.

5

Harnessing the Power of Social Media and Mobile Technology in Asia

Pongsak Hoontrakul

Introduction

Social media transforms personal and group interaction into value creation with the speed, scale, and economics of the Internet. Up to two-thirds of value creation comes from improving communication and collaboration between people.[1] Social media nurtures a more open, non-hierarchical, and knowledge-sharing culture. It unlocks initiative, creativity, and passion for a more engaging society.

Asia's developed countries such as Japan and South Korea have much higher percentages of social network users than emerging countries such as India where information and communications technology (ICT) infrastructure constraints limit access to the Internet. But mobile devices are about to overcome this limitation and to transform Asia.[2] More than half of Asia's more than 3.8 billion people have no Internet access, most of them in rural areas.[3] However, 90 percent has mobile phones on average.[4] The emergence of cheap smartphones,[5] typically made in China, has expanded Internet access. More than 1.4 billion people, predominantly in rural areas of low- to middle-income countries such as China, India, Indonesia, and Vietnam, will access the Internet for the first time in their lives by 2020. This will enhance their quality of life and significantly impact telecommunications (telecom) industries, software application (app) providers, consumer retailers, and the banking sector.

SMAC (social, mobility, analytics, and cloud) is the next big business opportunity, worth more than $1 trillion by 2020, representing a 30 percent compound annual growth rate from now until then.[6] SMAC-savvy businesses will analyze the "big data" generated by social media in order to make profitable business decisions. And they will obtain inexpensive computing capacity through "cloud computing," or distributed computing over the Internet. A high-profile example of cloud computing success is WhatsApp, which was acquired by Facebook in February 2014 for $19 billion. WhatsApp, an "over-the-top" (OTT)[7] communication services firm, had 450 million monthly active users (MAU) who sent a total of more than 19 billion messages per day, including 200 million voice messages and 100 million videos.[8] Governments should leverage SMAC to create the high-quality educational systems that low-income countries need to advance to high-income, digital service economies.

In this chapter, we first discuss the economics of wireless data and its implications for telecoms. We then examine the social media economy followed by SMAC and the need to develop human capital.

The Economics of Wireless Data

Previously, people accessed the Internet only for email, information, entertainment, and shopping. Today, about two billion people around the world also log on to social media sites to communicate with other people.[9] These are the habits of "netizens," particularly in developed countries. But more than half of people in Asia do not even have access to the Internet. Generally, low- and middle-income countries have dual, urban–rural economies. Typically, the urban areas are more industrialized and have well-developed ICT infrastructure; the residents can afford Internet access. People in the rural or semi-urban areas with less-developed infrastructure have no shortage of desire to be online, but they are constrained by availability and budget. The emergence of affordable smartphones and low-cost bandwidth will provide life-changing benefits to these people.

In 2014, half of the world's total of 1.9 billion handsets were made and sold in Asia.[10] And they are getting cheaper by the day. Although the growth of handset shipments is forecast to plateau in the near future, Asia's proportion of half will remain unchanged. More than 70 percent of Asia's demand is forecasted to be in China (50%) and in India (22%) in 2014 and 2015.[11] Much of this demand is expected to replace old handsets with smartphones. China (42%), South Korea (35%), Japan (31%), and India (28%) had the highest replacement rates in 2014.[12] Even the poorest regions in Asia had a replacement rate of 27 percent.[13] Figure 5.1 summarizes these figures. Indeed, smartphones sales are forecast to account for

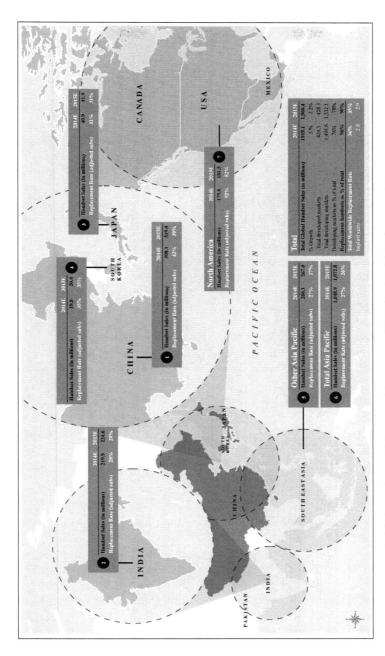

Figure 5.1 Map of Global Handset Model Regional Forecast and Handset Model Replacement Forecast

Source: Gelblum et al., 2014. Copyright © 2014, Pongksak Hoontrakul.

86 percent of volume and 98 percent of the value of all handsets by 2017.[14] The long-term growth of smartphone sales is projected to be at 16 percent compound annual growth rate worldwide, but it will be double but that if Long Term Evolution (LTE; G4) is successfully rolled out, especially in China and India.[15] Samsung, with a 32 percent market share in terms of units sold, and Apple, with 12 percent, dominate the global smartphone market.[16] But locally made handsets that for the first time are available for less than $50 per unit and "white box"[17] are gaining momentum rapidly.[18] In terms of units sold, the Indian brands Micromax and Karbonn are respectively second and third with a market share of 17.1 percent and 11.2 percent to Samsung (32.95%) in the domestic Indian market for the third quarter 2013.[19] In addition, Chinese brands Lenovo (12.9%), Huawei (8.2%), and Yulong (9.3%) are respectively second, third, and fourth in the Chinese market compared to the top brand—Samsung (18.6%) in January 2014.[20] These local brands are far ahead of Apple.

It is not difficult to see how mobile phones can enhance productivity by empowering users to have more connections, information, and choices in the marketplace. In southern India, Kerala fishermen used their mobile phones to connect with wholesalers and find the best market prices, according to one famous study in 2007.[21] Cheap mobile phones and cheap connections are paving the way for the "silent transformation" of India's grassroots.[22] (This will to be further discussed in the next chapter.)

To appreciate the potential of affordable wireless bandwidth—the other half of the equation reshaping the digital world—we need to understand the basic economics of wireless data. First, population density and spectrum[23] are important determinants of wireless data economics. At the early stage, 2G, the mobile phone business is driven mainly by voice services with a clear economy of scale. There is a high (82%) correlation between the length of use and the operating expense per minute.[24] Hence, the voice pricing structure is per minute, and to maximize revenue per user, telecom operators offer cheaper rates for higher volume. Population density is a clear positive for telecoms. For instance, India has one of the highest population densities in the world and telecom operators in its major cities like Mumbai and Delhi have the lowest capital expenditure per minute in the world.[25]

At the next level, or 3G, spectrum becomes more significant because data services are offered at variable levels of diseconomies of scale. 3G base transceiver stations in a cellular network operate quite differently from 2G because of the varying speed and diverse usage of data services. The faster the data transfer, the more drastic the shrinkage of cell site coverage areas. The more people use more data services, the more the coverage will shrink as well. The more spectrums the telecom operator has, the more "data throughput" capacity for speed and unit growth—hence greater efficiencies. Wireless data service pricing based on volume discounts like voice service will potentially lead to margin compression over time because of uneven data throughput during the day.[26] Telecom operators must manage the peak load and redistribute loads through marketing mix and bandwidth management. In a nutshell, the economics of 3G is a combination of spectrum, population density, and differential impact on base transceiver stations.[27]

China's case, however, is different. All its networks are state-owned and so require less return on capital, and spectrum resources are abundant. Telecom operators like China Mobile and China Unicom can aggressively monetize data revenues on their inexpensive rates based on volume discounts. As a result, China is well positioned for Internet economy expansion. China was projected to outgrow every other Asia-Pacific country in the "business-to-customer" space, or online retail, from 2013 onward.[28] Still, online retail in China represents only 11 percent of its total retail sales—a nascent stage compared to developed countries like the United States, South Korea, and Japan.[29] In addition to advertisements, commerce and games, China's netizens will increasingly go online for travel and financial services and digital apps as the prices of smartphones and usage drop. There is a "cannibalization" effect in this transition; as more people use mobile devices to access the Internet, they will have less use for personal computers (PCs). The search engine giant Baidu, the online game franchise Tencent, and the leading e-travel site CTrip are among the beneficiaries of this trend as they adapt quickly to mobile platforms.[30] China's subsidy of the infrastructure network has created a structural productivity driver and new jobs (e.g., apps developers, web designers, and big data analysts) and business opportunities (e.g., mobile payments, e-marketing, and digital services) for developing a high-wage, knowledge-based economy.

Southeast Asia, on the other hand, in general needs more spectrums for future growth in wireless data services. Thailand auctioned off nine slots of 5 megahertz (MHz) bandwidth of 2.1 (gigahertz) GHz or 3G spectrums for a total of $1.4 billion in October 2012.[31] Here, the actual economics of wireless data is driven by the revenue-sharing rate from the auction. The "holding spectrum" is comparable to a "land bank" in a property firm. Indeed, there is a significant correlation (85%) between a wireless operator's market capitalization and its estimated "spectrum bank" (or the supply side of data services) since spectrum drives the telecom operator's efficiency, margins, and earnings.[32] On the cost side (capital expenditure), there is very high correlation between base station density and subscribers per MHz.[33] In advanced economies such as South

Korea and Japan, wireless data demand growth can and will outstrip supply growth because of the rapid rise in both smartphone penetration and richer online content such as video. A proliferation of base stations is expected. Earlier, low population density in dispersed geographic coverage made it unfeasible to invest in base stations, similar to telephone posts in the fixed-line days. Thanks to new technologies, small cell (e.g., femtocell, WiFi, and WiMax) and satellite transmission can now be utilized together with 3G to create cheaper and wider coverage.[34] So instead of heavy investment in base stations, telecom operators should look into the unexploited territory in rural or semi-urban areas for voice as well as data services if the spectrum is available for the public. In brief, the 3G situation favors Internet access for rural areas in the near future.

At the latest level, G4 or LTE, the economics of wireless data is a function of technology choice as well as the spectrum and population density. G2 and G3 have different levels of scalability due to differential impacts of spectrum, population density, and base stations. LTE improves efficiency gains by consolidating larger noncontiguous spectrum bands. The race to roll out LTE is on. A pioneer in this field, Japan's NTT DoCoMo, says that from 2011 to 2015, the number of its subscriptions will increase by 400 percent, driving its data service to grow by to 1,200 percent, but revenue will grow only 150 percent during that period.[35] Thus, rapid data usage does not proportionally translate into revenue growth. China Mobile subsidized LTE-variant smartphone costs in order to achieve 100 million shipments in 2014; the US semiconductor firm Qualcomm and the Chinese network and mobile producer Huawei (white box suppliers) won the concession, driving the price to below 799 Chinese *renminbi* (RMB), or $128, per unit.[36] LTE upgrading costs vary greatly according to the industry structures and characteristics of telecom operators. The implied annual capital expenditure to upgrade for LTE deployment per subscriber is $24 for China and $10 for the ten countries of the Association of Southeast Asian Nations (ASEAN).[37] Moreover, to gain more efficiency in load balancing, wider spectrum ranges are needed. Hence, LTE favors operators with large spectrum holdings, and they tend to be the market leaders.[38] Because of the high investment costs, most emerging Asian countries are still in the process of preparing G4 auctions and rollout countrywide. India had its first 4G services in Kolkata in April 2012 and continued rollout in selected cities.[39] Thailand planned 1.8-GHz and 2.3-GHz spectrum auctions in the last quarter of 2015.[40] It is worth noting that in 2013, only advanced economies like Japan and Korea have 4G penetration rate of 27.6 percent and 79 percent for all mobile subscribers and the rest for 3G, respectively.[41] For less-developed nations like China, India, and Indonesia that have no 4G access have their 3G penetration rate of 31 percent, 16 percent, and 8 percent for all mobile subscribers and the rest for 2G, respectively.[42]

For more than a decade, Asia's telecom developments were largely in ICT infrastructure in highly populated cities. The easy moneymaking from spectrum licenses for the telecom operators to serve urban areas is over, especially in the high- and middle-income countries like Japan and China. The opportunity now lies in data services and in relatively untapped rural and semi-urban areas. New technology is available for cheaper and wider wireless coverage. The top ICT policy goal for governments and regulators should be to bring as many citizens as possible into the digital fold. Regulators may reserve some spectrum footprints and give incentives where the ICT market fails to provide reasonable services, such as in the rural areas, education sectors, and small operators.[43] Internet access is like water, power, and other utilities—it needs to be developed in order to improve productivity and competitiveness, so people can enjoy better living standards.

The Social Media Economy

Social media has revolutionized the way many millions of people live and communicate (see Figure 5.2). The wide range of apps in social technologies include networks, micro-blogs, forums, crowd-sourcing, games, media, and file sharing. Three basic features of social media are it: (1) enables information technology; (2) empowers users to create, add, and modify content and communication; and (3) enables distributed access to content and communications.[44] How do social media create value on a transformative scale?

Value Transfer

First, social media has transferred value in the communications business. The classical mode of conversation is one-to-one or one-to-many via phone call synchronously. These OTT service providers offer the classical mode in an asynchronous manner with rich content such as video. This not only makes it cheaper to communicate with others but also changes the way we communicate.[45] Consequently, the voice and SMS services offered by telecom operators are vulnerable in this value transfer to social media apps. It is comparable to the experience of brick-and-mortar book retailers versus Amazon in the early 2000s or radio versus TV during the 1930s to 1950s.[46] People will make less use of the telephone and more of social media platforms/OTT apps. This explains the recent pricey

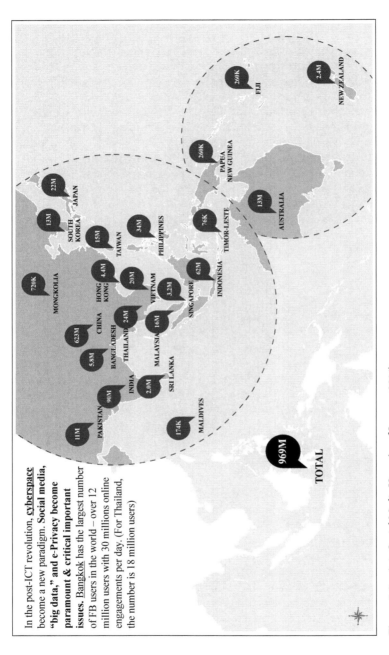

In the post-ICT revolution, <u>cyberspace</u> become a new paradigm. **Social media, "big data," and e-Privacy become paramount & critical important issues.** Bangkok has the largest number of FB users in the world – over 12 million users with 30 millions online engagements per day. (For Thailand, the number is 18 million users)

PAKISTAN 11M

INDIA 90M

SRI LANKA 2.0M

MALDIVES 174K

BANGLADESH 5.8M

CHINA 623M

MONGOLIA 720K

THAILAND 24M

MALAYSIA 16M

HONG KONG 4.4M

VIETNAM 20M

SINGAPORE 3.2M

INDONESIA 62M

TAIWAN 15M

SOUTH KOREA 13M

JAPAN 22M

PHILIPPINES 34M

TIMOR-LESTE 76K

AUSTRALIA 13M

PAPUA NEW GUINEA 260K

FIJI 260K

NEW ZEALAND 2.4M

TOTAL 969M

Figure 5.2 Asia Social Media Users (as of January 2014)

Source: Simon Kemp, 2014. Copyright © 2014, Pongsak Hoontrakul.

acquisitions of global communication apps by Facebook and others. In February 2014, Facebook, for example, acquired WhatsApp for $16 billion or at $36 per MAU for 450 million MAU.[47] In May 2013, for another instance, SINA acquired Weibo in China for $586 million or at $71 per MAU for 126 million MAU.[48]

Re-intermediary

Second, social media changes the nature of commerce. Traditionally, from a customer's viewpoint, there are at least four social interactions—information search, offers, purchase, and services—and the purchase transaction involves four parties—consumer/card holder, card issuer, card acquirer, and merchant. And before purchasing, people may seek advice from friends or others. Social technologies provide an integrated social platform for all of this.[49] With more than 300 million users, WeChat, a social network app from China's Tencent, links customers and merchants in an integrated platform.[50] In China, mobile payments amounted to 1.2 trillion RMB in 2013, an eightfold increase year-on-year. Total online and mobile payment was estimated to be $267 billion, a close second after the United States in 2012.[51] This mobile payment alone will boost productivity gains in managing transactions by at least 50 percent.[52] Like in India and Indonesia, in China about 60 percent of the population, mostly in rural areas, has no formal relationship with finance and banking institutions.[53] This represents a great opportunity for innovative mobile payment and mobile banking. Chinese Internet companies like WeChat are already challenging the banks, not just in mobile payment but also in all of financial services. These cheap, mobile links to financial services and credits may help fight poverty among Asia's rural poor.

Disruptive Force

Third, social media can unlock value and productivity of between $900 billion and $1.3 trillion in four industry sectors: retail finance, professional services, advanced manufacturing, and consumer packaged goods.[54] Sharing knowledge, collaborating in work, and improving communication create value within and across firms. Within firms, more engaged employees can fully realize their initiative, creativity, and passion. Social media interactions with customers shift the organizational culture from a focus on the supply side—the product and service provider—to the demand side—the consumer. Professional services, healthcare providers, education, banks, telecom, and software Internet sectors are examples of the high-value potential for social media in the United States.[55] Still, the potential is very difficult to evaluate since we are still in the early stage of the social media revolution (Web 2.0), especially in Asia.[56] Social media rips through traditional business models like the brick-and-mortar shops and the earlier Web version. It creates new value and enhances productivity while cannibalizing other businesses both online and offline.

There are five business layers in a telecom-related business.[57] The last three layers are network infrastructures such as base station, fiber, and LTE; commercial activity such as distribution, packaging, and pricing; and core operator applications such as Internet access, TV, and video distribution. The first two layers are OTT layers such as media, social media, commerce, banking, and terminal ecosystems such as Android, iOS, Windows, and smart TVs. The higher the layer is, the more value to customers. In only a short few years, social media has greatly impacted OTT layer businesses by re-intermediating, transferring value, and building new business opportunities, while destroying the old business model[58] (see "Sony: The Former Gadget King" case study).

Like WhatsApp, LINE in Japan provides, for example, OTT message and voice services; it had more than 347 million MAU around the world in January 2014. LINE was launched in Japan in June 2011 as a spinoff from Naver, the leading Internet search portal in South Korea. In January 2014, LINE had an implicit estimated value of at least $3 billion (or about $10 per user).[59] Other social media sites like Facebook have similar functionality to WhatsApp, WeChat, and LINE. These apps are getting better and more innovative. In 2014, LINE and WhatsApp launched "killer app"—OTT voice that costs "almost nothing" for users. This app shifts people's communication away from the traditional telecom operators' business of voice and SMS. Within three years, at least $20 billion in revenues from SMS will disappear from the global telecom sector.[60] Almost all of Asia's telecom operators now derive more than half of their revenues from voice services[61]; in the future, all this revenue also will disappear as people talk less on the telephone. Unlike most telecom operators in Asia, which are having a tough time adjusting to new reality, Singapore Telecom[62] and China Mobile[63] launched VoLTE (Voice over LTE) in the second quarter of 2014 to counter LINE and Skype. VoLTE offers higher-quality voice at low cost.

South Korea, Japan, Singapore, and Hong Kong have technologically savvy customers using advanced mobile payment systems. But more than half of Asia's population, especially in rural areas of China, India, and Indonesia, have no formal banking links. OTT digital banking service can bypass the traditional banking business.

China, which has the world's largest Internet user base, is developing its Internet finance system after years of subsidizing its ICT physical network. During the Communist Party's Third Plenum in November 2013, China adopted an Internet finance policy to make the financial industry more inclusive for its citizens. Two Internet giants, the games leader Tencent and the search engine giant Baidu, quickly went mobile and added financial services. Apart from competing in digital services in the classified advertisement, real estate, and automobile sectors, the two now are competing in finance as well (see Figures 5.3a and b). Tencent launched WeChat as an OTT communication service to build a social media network. Baidu focuses on mobile platform community services like Baidu Love, Baidu Games, and an app distribution channel. With more than 350 million MAU in 2013, WeChat dominates OTT communication services. It had more than 20 million mobile payment users with at least 200,000 new users per day.[64] In January 2014, Tencent launched a financial product platform and a taxi booking and payment platform on WeChat. By March 2014, about 7 percent of total taxi orders were being booked and paid for from mobile devices in major cities like Shanghai.[65] By 2014, WeChat had more than 600 million registered users. Baidu, which has a search engine market share of more than 70 percent, was transforming itself for more mobile business. Baidu's income is mainly from search advertisement. The nearly half a million advertisers who have a close relationship with Baidu can serve as a good customer base for its future financial products and services. Baidu successfully transformed its search engine to be on mobile platform. In 2014, Baidu planned to install its seven apps on 80 percent of China's smartphones in order to reach more than 400 million users, at the cost of 1.5–3 RMB for each app.[66]

Both Baidu and Tencent are trying to obtain one of new five bank licenses for private Internet firms announced by the China Banking Regulatory Commission in March 2014. The commission gives priority to new pilot banks with differentiated business models like small deposit and small loan or peer-to-peer lending schemes. Tencent's concept is micro-retail banking. Tencent has WeChat membership, social media apps, and monthly paid subscribed mobile game apps. Later, it may offer this young, affluent, and tech-savvy client base other financial products such as money market funds of up to 2 trillion RMB in 2014 and mobile payment with revenue opportunities of 22.8 billion RMB by 2015.[67]

China built an ICT infrastructure and a thriving Internet sector on its own domestic platforms and now is using the mobile revolution to give its rural poor access to financial services. India and Southeast Asian countries can learn from China's policies and experience.

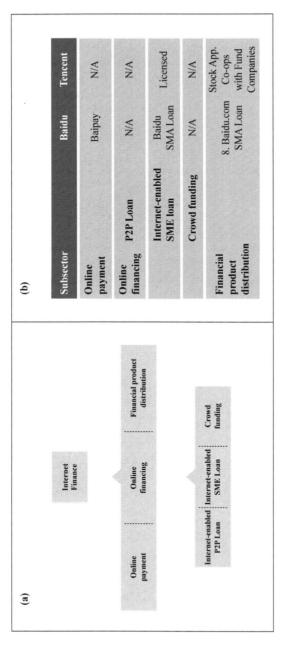

Figure 5.3 The Landscape of China Internet Finance (a) and Internet Finance exposure of Major Players (b)

Source: Chan, 2014, p. 2. Copyright © 2014, Vincent Chan, Credit Suisse.

SMAC and Its Implications

SMAC groups the core technologies that will drive innovation and competitiveness in companies. It will be a $1 trillion digital enterprise business opportunity by 2020. Each of its components is evolving in its own way, but firms are increasingly treating SMAC as an integrated system. Cloud computing and social media will represent nearly all SMAC opportunity size at $615 billion and $220 billion, respectively, with 32 percent and 40 percent compound annual growth rates, respectively. Mobile and analytics will represent opportunity sizes of $140 billion and $25 billion, respectively, with 15 percent and 45 percent compound annual growth rates, respectively.[68] Users' experience is the key to profitability in the convergence of SMAC trends. This means there needs to be more capital expenditure to upgrade both hardware and infrastructure and software. Affected by the SMAC trend will be ICT-related hardware businesses in Greater China, ICT export services in India, and software app development in South Korea and Japan. New ICT businesses will be developed, but old ICT businesses will be cannibalized.

SMAC involves first the social aspect of new wireless media. In 2012, Indians spent on average one-quarter of their online time on social networking sites like Facebook.[69] In June 2012 alone, 50.9 million Indians visited Facebook and engaged the site for nearly four hours.[70] From Chinese New Year's eve to New Year's Day (January 30, 2014), Chinese citizens sent more than 13.6 billion mobile New Year messages from all platforms of Tencent, surpassing the 11 billion SMS messages from all telecom operators in China in the same period.[71] At the peak, Tencent's Mobile QQ and WeChat handled 32.7 million and ten million messages per minute, respectively; during the Chinese New Year celebration period (January 30 to February 7, 2014), eight million WeChat members gave 40 million "red envelopes" through mobile payment with the average below RMB10 ($1.6) per transaction.[72] These massive mobile engagements reflect changing social behavior and a deepening and broadening relationship among people and between customer and service providers.

Mobile here means access to anywhere–anytime information and digital services. Modern mobile devices have more computing power and memory capacity than PCs a decade ago. "Bring your own device" to the workplace has become a new trend with improvement in data transfer between devices and in security protection. About 74 million homes are workplaces for netizens in India, whose online population was the third largest in the world after China and the United States in August 2013.[73] People also use wireless handsets for entertainment. In 2013, about 390 million Chinese watched online video on their handsets.[74] Mobile games growth is also very strong in China, South Korea, and Japan. In China, total mobile games revenue was estimated at 23 billion RMB in 2014, representing 21 percent of the total online games market.[75] All this requires easy- and fast-access broadband Internet, which requires more investment in advanced ICT infrastructure, which in turn means more ICT-related business opportunities.

Analytics is important because any successful online business must understand the crowds' trends, values, and preferences. Each day, Facebook generates 500 terabytes of data and Twitter generates 12 terabytes, according to a paper published in June 2013.[76] There are at least four dimensions to this "big data": volume, velocity, variety, and veracity. Businesses must know how to store this ever-growing data, how to quickly retrieve it, and how to make decisions based on it. Online marketers must analyze in real time big data from social media interaction that is rich in content and mostly unstructured. Social media analytics, including consulting, technology solutions, real-time engagement solutions, brand proficiency, and insights, is used to transform these data in business decisions. More than half of the global firms surveyed by India's Tata Consulting Services took initiatives in big data analytics in 2012, with expected return-on-investment of more than 25 percent.[77] The potential shortage of 150,000 database analysts and 1.5 million managers in this field by 2018 will create opportunities in outsourcing[78] for firms in India and elsewhere. Financial services and retail and telecom industries worldwide have been among the early adaptors of big data technologies.[79]

Cloud computing transforms a firm's information technology (IT) consumption to be like "utility computing" or "pay per use." Cloud computing is a hybrid between a telecom infrastructure provider (e.g., data warehouse and broad bandwidth) and an IT technology service (e.g., platform, software, and system integrator). Consequently, firms can enjoy low setup costs and cut capital expenditure on IT spending by 40 to 80 percent.[80] A client company uses cloud computing services from cloud vendors and cloud brokers. Vendors are infrastructure, platform, and software providers; brokers are system integrators, consultants, and aggregators. Each participant creates value by providing services to other participants. Telecoms can offer enterprise-grade infrastructure to cloud companies with different levels of service agreements. The core of the infrastructure is physical data centers but clouds are location-independent and cloud providers work across several data centers. Cloud may cannibalize software and platform service businesses first since customers pay for services instead of the old IT model where they "buy, own, and operate" themselves. Indian IT service firms are adapting to the

SMAC megatrend, especially cloud computing. (See case study on Tata Consulting Services (TCS), Wipro, and Infosys.)

Talent: Human Capital and the Middle-Income Trap

ASEAN has three tiers of economies. Singapore and Brunei are high-income economies where the gross national income (GNI) is about $40,000 per annum as indicated in Table 5.1. Thailand, Malaysia, Indonesia, and the Philippines are middle-income economies roughly from $3,000 for lower-middle to $12,000 for upper-middle income status. Cambodia, Laos, Vietnam, and Myanmar are low-income economies, below $3,000 (see Table 5.1).

Why have countries like Thailand been stuck in middle-income status for years, unable to climb to high-income status? A low-income country typically moves up the economic ladder with rapid growth rate that is resource driven (e.g., abundant and cheap land, labor, etc.). A country falls into middle-income trap with slowing down economy after depleting

Table 5.1   Human Development Index—HDI (Education) 2012 for ASEAN Nations

Country	HDI (Education)	Level of income		
	2012 Ranking*	GNI per capita level per annum (2005 PPP as of 2012)*	GNI per capita level per annum (Atlas Method, Current USD as of 2012)**	Status
Singapore	18	52,613.00	49,710.00	**High income**
Brunei	30	45,690.00	N.A.	**High income**
Malaysia	64	13,676.00	9,820.00	**Middle income**
Thailand	103	7,722.00	5,210.00	**Middle income**
Philippines	114	3,752.00	2,500.00	**Middle income**
Indonesia	121	4,154.00	3,420.00	**Middle income**
Vietnam	127	2,970.00	1,550.00	**Low income**
Laos	138	2,435.00	1,270.00	**Low income**
Cambodia	138	2,095.00	880.00	**Low income**
Myanmar	149	1,817.00	N.A.	**Low income**
China	101	7,945.00	5,720.00	**Middle income**
India	136	3,285.00	1,550.00	**Low Income**
Japan	10	32,545.00	47,870.00	**High income**
S. Korea	12	28,231.00	22,670.00	**High income**

Note: N.A. = Not Available; Copyright 2014 © Pongsak Hoontrakul. Last Update: June 30, 2014.

Source: * http://data.un.org/DocumentData.aspx?id=324
** http://data.worldbank.org/indicator/NY.GNP.PCAP.CD

its resource advantage and unable to achieve in productivity-driven stage to improve its competitiveness and finally innovation-driven stage for high-value, high-income level. There is a high correlation between a country's level of education as measured by the United Nations (UN)'s Human Development Index (HDI) and the country's level of income. Consequently, it seems that the lack of a good educational system holds back progress toward a knowledge-based economy (see case study on Thailand's educational system).

The Chinese government has spent heavily on ICT infrastructure and on lowering the costs of wireless devices and Internet access. The result is that more people have more information and more choices, especially in finance and education. A family in China on average spends about 60 percent of household income on children's education, after-school education, foreign-language classes, and extracurricular activities.[81] Along with the relaxation of the one-child policy, the government's rapid urbanization plan will result in 300 million more people in China's cities by 2020 and put more strain on the public education system. Private and online education has become a high-growth business worth an estimated 45 billion RMB.[82] Internet classes can only supplement regular classes because students still prefer offline classrooms with dynamic learning environments. One of the key factors for success in online learning is the maturity of the students. More than 40 percent of online students are more than 35 years old and have a college degree. Professional training programs are the most successful and popular. For online education, Thailand and other Southeast Asian countries should focus on vocational training and continuing education for adults in order to fill in the human development gap resulting from the chronically poor conventional educational system.

Case Study

India's Big Three IT Services Firms and the SMAC Race

Pongsak Hoontrakul

India's big three IT services companies—TCS, Infosys, and Wipro—are embracing the SMAC megatrend as their traditional businesses of enterprise resource planning, IT business process outsourcing, and Web 1.0 work are in structural decline.

Table 5.2 shows the range of services the three companies offered in 2013. TCS seemed to be ahead in mobility and Wipro had noteworthy schemes in cloud services.

Table 5.2   TCS, Infosys, and Wipro responding strategy to SMAC

Company	SMAC service offering	SMAC-related IP
TCS	Whole ranges from cloud services, mobility products and services, eMarketing solution, performance management, and business intelligence	CubbuZZ (Social, cloud), mKrishi (mobile), TCS mobile Point of Sale (PoS), Voice of customer (Social, analytics)
Infosys	Cloud services, enterprise mobility services	Cloud Ecosystem Hub, SocialEdge, Shopping Trip 360, mConnect (analytics)
Wipro	Cloud services, big data analysis, and information management system	Cloud Trust, Virtual Desk (cloud, mobility), NextGen Care Management (Cloud), Mobile Mining Dashboard

Sources: 1. Subramania Prasad M.K., "Are You Riding the Digital Wave with an Assurance Surfboard You Can Rely On?," Tata Consultancy Services (TCS), Accessed January 2014 (http://www.tcs.com/resources/white_papers/Pages/Digital-Wave-Assurance.aspx). 2. "Impact of SMAC on Enterprise Software Applications," Infosys, April 8, 2014 (http://www.infosysblogs.com/supply-chain/2014/04/impact_of_smac_on_enterprise_s.html). 3. "In Conversation with Bill Fearnley, Jr.," Wipro, Accessed January 2014 (http://www.wipro.com/Documents/resource-center/in-conversation-with-Bill-Fearnley.pdf).

With quite a few sets of proprietary SMAC service offerings, TCS has been the first to target the cloud computing space. It has built several datacenters overseas in order to create a private network of cloud services. For its mobility team, TCS built a Customer Collaboration Center in Santa Clara, California, in the heart of Silicon Valley. In India, TCS invests in a platform called mKrishi to deliver digital services to rural poor people and farmers via mobile technology.

In 2013, Wipro invested about $30 million for a minority stake in a US-based big data firm, Opera Solutions, and another $5 million in a US-based cloud computing firm, Axeda. The former specializes in cloud services in machine-to-machine (M2M) solutions; the latter provides cloud analytics services for selected industries. Wipro has a special arrangement for these two companies to work together and for them to give technical training and support to Wipro personnel.

Infosys has extensive experience with projects in North America. There, Infosys helped a railroad firm cut costs by 50 percent by migrating its legacy infrastructure and legacy apps into a private cloud. Infosys helped the city of Orlando, Florida, adopt Google Apps to streamline communication among city departments, saving more than $200,000 annually. In addition to offering cloud and enterprise mobility services, Infosys set a Social Customer Relationship Management for its social and analytics components.

It is too early to say which of India's big three will win the SMAC race.

Sony: The Former Gadget King

Pongsak Hoontrakul and Nisanart Thadabusapa

The yen's recent dramatic drop against all the major currencies has given hard-hit corporate Japan its biggest break in years, spurring a long-awaited earnings recovery. For Sony, the currency windfall buys time to launch the restructuring that the company needs if it wants to regain its once-iconic status.

The weaker yen makes Sony's made-in-Japan products more profitable when sold abroad and boosts overseas revenue when repatriated in the Japanese currency. According to Sony's annual report, every 1 yen/euro change results in a swing of about 6 billion yen in annual operating profit. This could boost Sony's weak competitiveness against South Korea's Samsung in TVs and smartphones. A weaker yen allows Sony to raise marketing spending, boost advertising, increase inventories, flesh out its product lineup, and take other steps to win back some market share.

Sony is still an enormous company with diversified businesses. Sony Pictures produced hit movies like "Spiderman" and Sony BMG Music Entertainment distributes the songs of Adele and Taylor Swift. The two units post profits. The company's biggest moneymaker is Sony Life, its insurance company. The problem is Sony's lackluster gadgets.

By the time its different divisions were corralled into cooperating, Sony had lost its foothold in two crucial product categories: televisions and portable music devices. As of fiscal year 2011, Sony had lost US$2.2 billion from its TV division alone.[83] The division had been in the red for eight years, hit by slowing demand for expensive TV products and growing competition from low-cost producers as well as the then-strong yen.

In fiscal year 2013, Sony's mobile products and communications unit, which sells the smartphones, reported that revenue grew in the quarter that ended September 30 by about 39 percent, to 418.6 billion yen. The average selling price of Sony's smartphones increased as it introduced new high-end models like the Xperia Z1. However, Sony still revised its overall annual revenue and net profit outlook downward. This was because the company's losses in the quarter widened to 19.3 billion yen ($196 million), from 15.5 billion yen in the same quarter of the previous year. In the last quarter, Sony made a modest profit of 3.5 billion yen, which it attributed to improved sales of smartphones and the favorable impact of foreign exchange rates.[84]

But the windfall profit from yen depreciation can only be temporary. For long-term competitiveness, Sony needs vigorous structural reform. The company needs to move away from a hardware-based business model to a high-value digital services model like Amazon and Apple.

Sony is plagued by stiff competition and lack of innovative products. It has been struggling in an environment where Apple and Samsung have grown to dominate consumer electronics with their vertically integrated businesses of hardware, software, and services. Sony has been stuck in its past success formula of creating the right hardware at a time when people are only paying premium for digitalized services. Sony used to lead the market with the Walkman and PlayStation 2. Now Sony is a follower chasing smartphone growth. It needs innovative products like Apple's software applications and Amazon's e-books. Samsung was among the first in the world to imitate Apple's success story in a different platform, Android. Samsung's smartphone offerings now span the entire market, from ultracheap to premium models.

Sony's smartphone sales in 2013 were encouraging but most of it came mainly from yen depreciation and its domestic consumers, Sony's captive market. Its 2014 guidance is a major shock to the market with a major downward earning revision.[85] On February 5, 2014, Sony also announced to exit PC business, a spin-off TV business as a standalone entity, and laid off other 5,000 employees. Streamlining its operation and restructuring its business units may not be enough. To be a top global player again, Sony must reinvent itself in the digital age.

Addressing the Binding Constraints: Reforming the Thai Education System

Nonarit Bisonyabut

In attempting to move from middle-income to high-income status, countries may face "binding constraints" in which market distortions prevent the best use of resources and thus economic progress. The education system is one of Thailand's most binding constraints.

Spending is not the problem. Measured as a percentage of gross domestic product (GDP), Thai public expenditure on education is a bit below that of the UK and the United States but is at the same level as Hong Kong, Japan, and Malaysia. Measured as a percentage of the total budget, Thai expenditure is notably higher than that of other countries except for Hong Kong.[86]

However, Thailand's education system is far behind those of the advanced economies in both quantitative and qualitative measures. For people 25 years and older, Thais have two to six years less total schooling than people in other countries. And Thai students score on average 60 to 120 points less on the Programme for International Student Assessment (PISA) test than students in the advanced economies.[87] These figures show that Thai education system will require much more than just increased investment.

There are at least three key binding constraints on the education system.

The first is that the education market in Thailand is operated mainly by the public sector and the possibilities for the private sector to improve the situation are limited. At the high school and university levels, about 85 percent of students attend public schools. In other countries, private schools pull good resources away from the public school system (funds, teachers, students, etc.) and create a high-quality niche market that eventually decreases the government's role in education. However, this is not the case for Thailand. Except for a few elite institutions, private schools do not have enough resources to compete with public schools.

The second binding constraint is the very weak link between education and the labor market in Thailand. There are simultaneously huge numbers of unemployed workers (excess demand) and unfilled jobs (excess supply), which indicates that schools are not teaching suitable work skills.

The last binding constraint is cultural. The current generation places a high social value on higher education. People expect that a university graduate will have a better life than a vocational school graduate. But the current university infrastructure (professors, equipment, etc.) cannot accommodate all the demand and universities will just end up producing worse and worse students. Second, the current stage of Thailand's economy requires vocational workers the most, not university graduates.

Three reforms would help relax these constraints.

First, we should require public schools to reveal data on their academic performance so that parents can choose the most suitable school for their children. Second, we should permit schools to manage themselves (in securing funds, choosing teachers, creating curricula, etc.); this would ensure that the blame for any bad performance will fall on the schools, not the government. The government's role would be to distribute financial support to schools based on market demand and each school's performance. These reforms would create incentives for schools to compete for government funds, resulting in higher-quality education. The first binding constraint would be alleviated.

Finally, a third reform is required to more closely link the schools with the current labor market (the second binding constraint), in order to reduce the labor mismatch problem. We must encourage the private sector to become an active partner of the education system. Private companies could grant financial subsidies to schools that teach students the skills these companies need. Alternatively, companies could organize workplace training programs for students as part of their degree requirements.

Although these three reforms do not tackle the cultural bottleneck directly, they would suppress the demand for higher education. They would signal to the schools that they must address the huge demand for vocational labor. And if the government provides more funds to schools that do that, the schools would have more incentive to produce vocational workers and less incentive to produce university graduates.

Notes

1. Michael Chui, James Manyika, Jacques Bughin, Richard Dobbs, Charles Roxburgh, Hugo Sarrazin, Geoffrey Sands, and Magdalena Westergren, "The Social Economy: Unlocking Value and Productivity through Social Technologies," *McKinsey Global Institute*, July 2012: 3 and 9 (http://www.mckinsey.com/insights/high_tech_telecoms_internet/the_social_economy).

2. Mitchel Winkels et al., "The Global Social Network Landscape: A Country-by-Country Guide to Social Network Usage," *eMarketer*, July 2013: 1–40 (http://www.optimediaintelligence.es/noticias_archivos/719_20130715123913.pdf).

3. Simon Kemp, "Social, Digital & Mobile in APAC in 2014," *We Are Social*, January 23, 2014 (http://wearesocial.net/blog/2014/01/social-digital-mobile-apac-2014/.)

4. Ehud Gelblum et al., "Comm Equipment and Data Networking: Recasting Citi's Global Smartphone Model and 2014 Update," *Global Communications Equipment Equities, Citi Research*, March 10, 2014: Fig. 13 on p. 10 (https://ir.citi.com/Zpghh/MHa2M89we 7g0YleGt2+If8m1Y96V8t5j973Mpx5qt9Zg2 qpg==).

5. These Internet-enabled mobile devices likely to use operating system (OS) to be an open standard, middleware Android on the Linux kernel. See (http://www.openhandsetalliance. com/ android_overview.html).

6. Anantha Naraya and Sagar Rastogl. "India IT Service Sector: The SMAC pack," *Credit Suisse*, July 2013 (https://doc.research-and-analytics.csfb.com/docView?language=ENG&source=ulg&format= PDF&document_id=1019813371&serialid=KDTcan6WWDtwPyROhjt1Ubh5pCqDjCoE198IXqKWkEc%3d).

7. Over-the-top (OTT) in telecommunication is defined as sending content (e.g., video, audio, and others) over the Internet without a multiple system operator's engagement in the control or distribution of the content.

8. "Getting the Messages," *The Economist*, February 22, 2014 (http://www. economist.com/ news/business/21596966-why-mark-zuckerbergs-social-network-paying-such-whopping-sum-messaging).

9. Kemp, "Social, Digital, & Mobile".

10. Gelblum et al., "Comm Equipment and Data Networking," 1–15.

11. Ibid.

12. Ibid.

13. Ibid.

14. See more details of the forecast at Kulbinder Garcha, Randy Abrams, and Achal Sultania, "The Wireless View 2014: Smartphones—A Slowing Disruptive Force," *Credit Suisse*, January 6, 2014: 5, 6, and 7 (https://doc. research-and-analytics.csfb.com/docView?language=ENG&source= emfro msendlink&format=PDF&document_id=805847640&extdocid=805847640 _1_eng_pdf&serialid=VKIqPfyGKvPXILC6%2bF%2bpFCXU1PjBAqhenh6 L1lN6AVE%3d).

15. LTE = Long Term Evolution, commonly known as 4G as a standard for high-speed mobile device with Internet connection. See more details of the forecast at ibid., pp. 3 and 5–6.

16. Gelblum et al., "Comm Equipment and Data Networking," Fig. 8 & 10 on pp. 6 & 7.

17. "White box" refers to "no brand," In this mobile "white box" space, Taiwanese Mediatek is the leading world supplier of application processors (AP).

18. Alvin Kwock, J. J. Park, Gokul Hariharn, and Chi-Chu Tschang, "EM Mobile Data Tipping Point: Brands, Whitebox, Carriers—Same Trend, Varying Fate", *J.P. Morgan*, March 12, 2013: p. 1, Fig. 2 and 3 on p. 4.

19. Alvin Kwock, Gokul Hariharn, William Chen, and Masashi Itaya, "Asian Technology: E-Commerce Hardware Winner & China Technology Landscape Changing Policies," *J.P. Morgan*, March, 2014: 1–32 (https://markets.jpmorgan. com/research/ArticleServlet? doc=GPS-1347867–0&referrerPortlet=EQCAS HASIA_accordion).

20. Ibid.

21. Robert Jensen, "The Digital Provide: Information (Technology), Market Performance and Welfare in the South India Fisheries Sector," *Quarterly Journal of Economics*, August 2007.

22. Neelkanth Mishra, Ravi Shangkar et al., "India Market Strategy: India: The Silent Transformation," *Asia Pacific/ India Equity Research, Credit Suisse*, March 13, 2013: 13–14.

23. Spectrum for wireless communication is defined as a range of radio frequencies. There are the upper and lower bound of the frequencies of this signal called bandwidth.

24. James R. Sullivan et al., "The Economics of Wireless Data—Part One: The Importance of Population Density and Spectrum," *J.P. Morgan*, May 4, 2011: 13–14.

25. Ibid., pp. 11–12.

26. Ibid., pp. 11–15.

27. Ibid.

28. Dick Wei and Evan Zhou, "China Internet Sector—Part One," The new thumb economy, *Credit Suisse*, May 26, 2013: on Fig. 4 on p. 2.
29. Ibid., p. 5.
30. Ibid. See mobile Internet growth by segments at Fig. 5 on p. 2 and takeaway theme on p. 3.
31. National Broadcasting and Telecommunications Commission (NBTC) (http://www.nbtc.go.th/wps/portal/NTC/!ut/p/c4/04_SB8K8xLLM9MSSzPy8xBz9CP0os3gTf3MX0wB3U08n8zAjA88wCzNXM09PA1MzE_2CbEdFALxking!/?WCM_GLOBAL_CONTEXT=/wps/wcm/connect/library+ntc/internetsite/eng/en_interesting_articles/en_interesting_articles_detail/ae185900400633288ac5ceabcb3fbcab).
32. "Spectrum bank" is estimated from MHz × KM2 MHz is the spectrum slot and KM2is the coverage area in square kilometers for BTS (Base Transceiver Stations) between users and network. This is a measure on the supply side of data service. See more details at James R. Sullivan et al., "The Economics of Wireless Data—Part Two: Valuing Air", *J.P. Morgan*, December 11, 2011: 1–5 and Fig. 13 on p. 9.
33. Ibid., pp. 1, 12–14.
34. Femtocell is a small cellular network that requires low power base station. WiFi is any wireless local area network that can be done in campus-wide or village-wide. WiMAX is designed for last mile wireless broadband that provides 30 to 40 megabit-per-second data rates. See more details at Sullivan et al., "The Economics of Wireless Data—Part Two," 52–64.
35. James R. Sullivan et al., "The Economics of Wireless Data – Part 3: What LTE Means for Asia," *J.P. Morgan*, March 26, 2012: 3–5.
36. Alvin Kwock et al., "China Technology EDGE: Five Landscape-Changing Policies to Watch," *J.P. Morgan*, March 18, 2014: 1–20.
37. Ibid., pp. 10–16.
38. Ibid., pp. 4–10.
39. Ibid.
40. Khettiya Jittapong and Viparat Jantraprap "NCPO delays 4G auction by a year," the *Bangkok post* and *Reuters*, July 18, 2014.
41. Kwock at al., "China Technology EDGE," table 4, p. 10.
42. Ibid.
43. Ibid., pp. 46 to 47 and 89 to 92.
44. Chui et al., "The Social Economy," Box 1 on p. 16.
45. Sasu-Petri Ristimaki, Glen Campbell, and Sean Johnstone, "Telecoms and Social Media—A Communications Value Transfer," *Global Telecom, Bank of American Merrill Lynch*, 2013: 1 and 3.
46. Ibid., pp. 1–8.
47. Stanley Yang and Sally Yoo, "Korea Internet: Focus on Overseas Business Momentum," *J.P. Morgan*, February 24, 2014: 1–27.
48. Ibid.
49. More discussion by Ashwin Shirvaikar et al., "UPWARDLY MOBILE II: A Long and Winding road for Mobile Payments—Eight Crucial Questions, Answered," *Citi GPS*, November, 2012: 1–60 (https://ir.citi.com/ %2fOx67R

G%2b6opqS844%2bjuDL13WNBhvedMsna%2b7HXAEvK7UCB4n9nSlgQ %3d%3d0).

50. Simon Ho, Muzhi Li, and Paddy Ran, "Chinese Banks: Digital Stormtroopers at the Gate," *Diversified Banks, Equities, Citi Research*, March 11, 2014: 1 and 24–29 (https://ir.citi.com/qFC87i81AZ3VMaJ7HQwZ8QA/tbL7tagU02S6Ez Bf+o3P6cjVx7HRMQ==).

51. Ibid., Fig. 25 and 26 on p. 21.

52. J. James Manyika et al., "Disruptive Technologies; Advances That Will Transform Life, Business and the Global Economy," *McKinsey Global Institute*, May 2013: Exhibtion 2 on p. 34, (http://www.mckinsey.com/ insights/business_technology/disruptive_technologies).

53. Ibid., Fig. 27 on p. 22.

54. Chui et al., "The Social Economy," 1–184.

55. Ibid., Exhibit E4 on p. 10.

56. Web 1.0 is the first conceptual evolution of the World Wide Web (www) in top-down approach where content creators are few at the top prior to 1990s. Web 2.0 is both platform and innovative technology as social media to enable many users to collectively create rich media (e.g., pictures, videos), exchange, share, edit, comment, vote, and other social engagements among their selected community members.

57. Ristimaki et al., "Telecoms and Social Media," 1–5.

58. Ibid.

59. Yang and Yoo, "Korea Internet," 11–12.

60. Ibid., pp. 6–7.

61. Colin McCallum and Jennifer Gao, "Asia Telecoms Sector: Killer App: OTT Voice," *Credit Suisse*, March 13, 2014: 1–45 (https://doc.research-and-analyt-ics.csfb.com/docView?language=ENG&source=ulg&format=PDF&docume nt_id=806056360&serialid=EYyrVAffwugU8gnE%2fn92ozsCAqUDqmjSio kQjxtUoPM%3d).

62. James R. Sullivan, "JPM Telcos: Tavel with Sully: In-Depth on VoLTE with SingTel," *J.P. Morgan*, March 17, 2014.

63. Kwock et al., "China Technology EDGE," 1.

64. Vincent Chan, Victor Wang, Dick Wei, Evan Zhou, and Frances Feng, "Sino Hotspot Series: Internet Finance," *Credit Suisse*, January 2, 2014: 1, 11 (https://doc.research-and-analytics.csfb.com/docView?language=ENG&sou rce=ulg&format=PDF&document_ id=1027329381&serialid=8eAbN9%2fP PyGY1TQzKiIyVlMXZT0RuanH0scnmqWnMMM%3d).

65. Alex Yao and Yong Wang, "Those Disrupted by Mobile Internet: Taxi-Hailing," *J.P. Morgan*, March 3, 2014: 1–7.

66. Alex Yao and Yong Wang, "Baidu.com: Reverse Engineer 2014 Margin Guidance: What Assumptions are Implied?," *J.P. Morgan*, March 18, 2014: 1–12.

67. Dick Wei, "Techcent Holdings: WeChat Payment—The Next Growth Frontier," *Credit Suisse*, January 17, 2014: 1 and 18.

68. Naraya and Rastogl, "India IT Service Sector," 1.

69. "In India, 1 in 4 Online Minutes Are Spent on Social Networking Sites," *ComScore*, August 19, 2012 (https://www.comscore.com/Insights/Press_ Releases/2012/8/   In_India_1_in_4_Online_Minutes_are_Spent_on_ Social_Networking_Sites).

70. Ibid.

71. Alex Yao and Yong Wang, "A Deepening and Broadening Consumer Relationship with Mobile," *J.P. Morgan*, March 17, 2014: 1–8.

72. Ibid.

73. "2013 India Digital Future in Focus," *ComScore,* press release, August 22, 2013 (https://www.comscore.com/Insights/Press_Releases/2013/8/comScore_ Releases_the_2013_India_Digital_Future_in_Focus_Report).

74. Alex Yao, "Youku Tudou Inc.: Increasing Uncertainties in Growth Outlook," *J.P. Morgan*, 2013: 1–13.

75. Alex Yao, "2014 China Internet Outlook: Investment Continues While Early Movers Approach Return Stage," *J.P. Morgan*, January 9, 2014: 6.

76. Note Bit is 0 or 1, Byte = 8 bits, Megabyte (MB) $=10^8$, Gibabyte (MB) $=10^9$ Terabyte (TB) $=10^{12}$. See more details in "Social, Mobile, Analytics & Cloud: The Game Changers for the Indian IT Industry," *DinodiaCapital*, June, 2013: 27 (http://www.saviance.com/whitepapers/SocialMobileAnalyticsCloud.pdf).

77. Ibid., p. 32.

78. Ibid., p. 35.

79. Ibid., p. 34.

80. Simon Weeden et al., "Cloud Computing: Every Silver Lining Has a Cloud," *Citi Research*, September 5, 2012: 3–6; Ross Barrows et al., "Cloud Computing Part 2: Market Sizing, Barriers, Value Network & Outlook," *Global Communications Equipment Equities, Citi Research*, December 5, 2012: 1–20 (https://ir.citi.com/P8MtBwhA6nIY2kp90iUuICj0HzOm1a1cZ7G   4B9KRg HbKw%2bEsHGf4Qz4zfpf9C9yDWiQ0LPbMZaM%3d; simon.weeden@citi. com Tel +44-20-7986-4204).

81. Muzhi Li, Ravi Sarathy, and Gregory Zhao, "China Education Service: Class Apart," *Citi Research*, February 7, 2014.

82. Ibid., p. 3.

83. J.J. Park, Jay Kwong, and Jesper J. Koll, "Sony: Still a Long Way to the End of Tunnel," *JP Morgan*, February 7, 2014: 1–20.

84. Ibid.

85. Ibid.

86. To assess whether a factor is a binding constraint in a country, we compare that country to other countries with lower, similar, and higher levels of economic development.

87. The test compares the quality of education systems worldwide by assessing the competencies of 15-year-olds in reading, mathematics, and sciences.

6

The Rise of China and India— Its Implications

Pongsak Hoontrakul, Christopher Balding, and Reena Marwah

Introduction

The rise of China and India could shift the political and economic center of the world to Asia in the next decade. China and India share many similarities: both have a huge population, high economic growth, and ancient civilizations (which provide them with strong national identities) without histories of colonizing others. Yet, both are distinct in terms of their political and economic structure and progress. Since opening up in 1978, China has developed into a nation with a larger and wealthier population than India, with the per capita income of an average Chinese citizen being three times that of an average Indian.[1] While China is considered "The Factory of the World" because of its reputation for exporting low-cost manufactured goods and merchandise, India is a global center for services, specifically, a hub for outsourcing business work processes and software. Thus, their actions impact the world in a big way.

The economic success in both China and India can be said to be the great triumph of a market-oriented economy and capitalism to some extent. Both nations began to prosper when they opened their markets and began to embrace technology along with foreign capital; however, the paths they took vary greatly. China has achieved immense success since its economy opened up. China is allowing foreigners and individuals to participate in both its financial and domestic markets as its economy transitions to a market, high-technology economy, which is gaining and giving know-how to firms in need of hard and human capital. India, on the other hand, has retarded its economic growth for much of the last century by inward-looking administrative policies and an overburdened bureaucratic system; private firms in the information technology (IT) and outsourcing industries have thrived partly from ingenuity and partly from the government's inability to regulate. With dissimilar starting points and distinctive paths in economic development, it remains to be seen how China and India would converge as they learn from each other.

Convergence will come from two distinct points. The Chinese government has overcome its early disappointments to effectively implement its ideology and state policy. The strict government control is tolerated largely due to the tremendous growth in gross domestic product (GDP) and improved quality of life; barring a real economic crisis, any change in the political setting will be small. In contrast, India as the world's largest democratic country is bogged down by excessive "red tape" and by special interest groups. Protests, debate, and lobbying are common for most of the issues. With diverse values, interests, and beliefs among the different ethnic and multireligious and linguistic groups, any thought of changing the Indian political and economic landscape seems formidable. While large Indian conglomerates are driving the formal economy, private microenterprises in the informal sector are vibrant. One wonders how the two nations would fare in a globalized world. As income disparity is widening, social and political tensions will continue to grow. In a world of unparalleled prosperity, sadly, the majority of Chinese and Indian people are still being deprived of clean water, energy, and dignity.

The next section will describe the different origins of Chinese and Indian revolutions in modern history. Section III will portray the rise of China and India in different directions. The economic policy implications are examined in Section IV. Selected issues are argued upon before the last section which provides the conclusion.

The Revolutions

China

After the Opium War, the end of the Qing Dynasty marked the conclusion of 2,000 years of brutally unified imperial rule. The Republic of China (1912–1949) was nominally unified and shaped by Sun Yat-Sen of the Kuomingtan (KMT) or The Nationalist Party, in the midst of civil unrest and foreign invasion. Despite their nation-building efforts to modernize the economy with its first constitution, internal conflicts among the KMT, the Communist Party of China (CPC), remnant warlords, and

Japan tore the country apart, and with the Communist win over the KMT, the People's Republic of China or PRC was established in 1949.

In 1949, Chairman Mao followed a Soviet-style centrally planned economy to radically transform China into a centralized, modern, and powerful socialist republic. Close to 70 percent of all modern industrial enterprises were state-owned and the rest were under public–private ownership. After land nationalization, collective farming was initiated under "communes." The initial success of the first plan brought more ambitious policies: first, the Great Leap Forward (industrialization), then the Agriculture First policy (agricultural reform). The combination of the two reforms led to the near collapse of political institutions and the economy. Without market competition and control, authority became concentrated at the center, at the expense of local government.

This protectionist policy resulted in poor management of resources and stagnation in the economy, and leaders such as Premier Zhou Enlai (1970–1974) tried to revive it without success. During the post–Mao era, in 1982, the de facto PRC leader Deng Xiaoping fundamentally altered China's basic policy to one of "reform and opening." To pursue market liberalization, the economic system was then oriented toward a more market-based mechanism. Trade and investment were opened to foreign investment and management. In agriculture, the contract farming responsibility system was to replace the collective commune structure. Farmers were once again allowed to sell their products in free market exchanges. Special economic zones (SEZs),[2] which were located in areas along the coastal provinces, were established to bolster the industrial sector by providing greater flexibility, autonomy, and market-friendly involvement. Enterprise managers gained control over their units, while incentive for profit sharing was now acceptable. In 1994, a new company law was promulgated, and in the following year, a policy of "grasping the large and letting go the small" was implemented which allowed private small and medium enterprises (SMEs) to flourish and privatized some state-owned enterprises (SOEs). Despite their weak performance and persistent government bailouts, SOEs accounted for about 40 percent of all industrial output in 2005. China's GDP grew, reflecting the various government policies during 1952–2005—from slow start till 1978, from disastrous policy (e.g., Great Leap Forward, Cultural Revolution, etc.) to double-digit growth till 2004 after opening up its economy (e.g., SEZ, World Trade Organization (WTO) entry, etc.).

Fast forward to the 18th Communist Party Congress in November 2012: President Mr Xi Jinping and Premier Li Kequiang along with their new members of the Politburo Standing Committee were officially elected to collectively rule China[3] and branded as the CPC's fifth generation to carry on a continuous revolution.[4] A year later at the CPC's Third Plenum, President Xi revealed the most ambitious and detailed roadmap to structurally reform China toward domestically oriented for sustainable growth.[5]

In 2013, China's total GDP stood at USD 9.0 trillion,[6] second only to the United States. China's foreign exchange reserve was over USD 3.82 trillion at the end of 2013, second to none.[7] It is estimated that in 2014, China's income per capita will be USD 7,277, which qualifies it to be termed as a middle-income country.[8]

India

Since the eighteenth century, the United Kingdom had colonized and unified maharaja-run kingdoms into one nation known today as India with its 29 diverse states[9] and 7 territories. Unlike China, India won its independence as a modern state from Great Britain in 1947 by widespread use of nonviolent resistance as a means of social protest. Mahatma Gandhi, Jawaharlal Nehru, and Sardar Vallabhbhai Patel, who led the civil disobedience against the colonial administration, declared India a Republic in 1950 as the parliament adopted its first constitution ever. Prime Minister Nehru introduced the Indian version of state planning and control over the economy and strict regulation over private enterprises, foreign trade, and foreign direct investment out of colonial paranoia.

Like China, the first Five-Year Plan in 1951 was introduced with a strong socialist and nationalist-inspired approach. The policy was a simultaneous mixture of capital- and technology-intensive industry along with subsiding manual, low-skill cottage and agriculture industries. Strategic industries such as mining, heavy industries, banking, and serving public interest utilities were invested in, owned by, and operated by SOEs. State-owned outputs were used to serve public interest and often served as checks to private firms' abnormal profits. In the agriculture sectors, land redistribution and resource endowment programs were envisaged. Projects, such as the construction of irrigation canals and dams, resulted in impressive growth; despite good intentions, some useful projects (such as the spread of fertilizers) during Nehru's tenure failed to alleviate India's widespread food shortage problem. Moreover, low productivity, low production quality, and dismal profitability exacerbated chronic unemployment and entrenched poverty. Nevertheless, Nehru's popularity and iconic image remained unaffected partly due to the large-scale infrastructure assisting the rural population and partly due to his passionate education and social reforms. Caste discrimination was, for example, considered a criminal offense. Continuing education centers, vocational training colleges, and technical schools were created for adults.

By the turn of the twentieth century, India had changed its policy toward a free-market economy with substantial reduction in state control through the economic liberalization of 1991 under Prime Minister Narasimha Rao and, the then, Finance Minister Manmohan Singh.[10] SOEs were slowly privatized bit by bit in the midst of political debate, especially on foreign interest. Deposit rate unregulation in 1997, bringing import duties, on average, down to 7 percent in 2012 from 78 percent in 1992, and reserving over 900 manufacturing items for locals are among the fine examples of these economic liberalization initiatives.[11] License Raj (i.e., investment, industrial, and import licensing) was also coming to an end. Prior to 1990, for example, almost every imported item required governmental license, but now little or no license is needed for all importation. At the same time, India's large population of young, fluent English-speaking workers (a legacy of British colonialism) and trained professionals had become an important target of the world's outsourcing and service industry. Today, business processing outsourcing (BPO), information technology-enabled services, software development, financial research, and medical tourism are among the fine services exported from India. Over 23 percent of the workforce is employed in the business services sector with an average growth of more than 7.5 percent per year. Foreign exchange reserves have risen from a mere USD 5.8 billion in March 1991 to USD 292.33 billion as of February 15, 2014.[12] With GDP growth close to 10 percent for more than a decade (as shown in Figure 6.1), Indian GDP is equivalent to USD 1.848 trillion in 2011. So far, with a nominal USD 1,145 per capita income in 2012, according to an International Monetary Fund (IMF) report, World Bank has classified India as a nation of *lower middle-income* economy.[13] As a direct result of its huge illiterate population, poverty remains a serious issue: One estimate finds that roughly 27 percent of the Indian population lives below the international poverty line of USD 1.25 per day.

The general consensus GDP forecast for 2014 points to a growth of about 6 percent. The economy is expected to see some market volatility due in part to the country's elections to be held on nine separate dates from April 7 to May 12 for 814 million eligible voters—the world's largest electorate.[14] After Bharatiya Janata Party (BJP) won a landslide victory commanding an absolute majority in the parliament by his highly personalized campaign and inclusive outreach approach, Mr. Narendra Modi became the fifteenth Indian prime minister (PM) on May 26, 2014. Despite his tall mandate, PM Modi may fulfill high expectations in terms of the country's economic direction. Indian history points that PM Modi

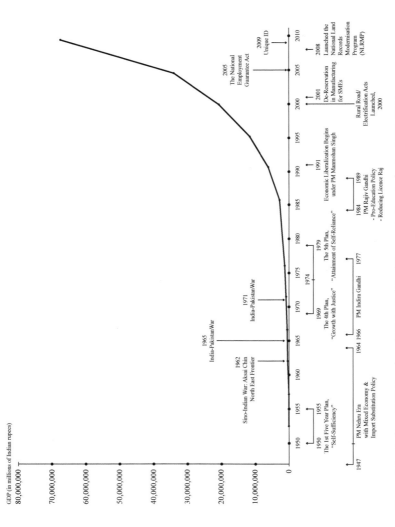

Figure 6.1 Indian GDP Graph and Major Political Economic Events during 1950–2010

Source: "Handbook of Statistics on Indian Economy," *Reserve Bank of India (RBI),* (http://www.rbi.org.in/scripts/AnnualPublications. aspx?head=Handbook+of+Statistics+on+Indian+Economy). Copyright © 2014, Pongsak Hoontrakul.

may be eventually forced to compromise on policy decision making with states and bureaucratic system.[15] Moreover, it is interesting to note that coalition government formation or the fragmentation of the central government is not an impediment to economic growth (and hence the stock exchange performance) in India because of three primary reasons.[16] First, under India's loose federation, the central government sets the policy and the state governments drive the execution, typically in infrastructure and social welfare-related policies. (See Table 6.1 for the division of responsibilities between the center and the states.) Thus, any state that implements well both the central and its own state policies would generally enjoy prosperity. In short, the central government may initiate its policy but there are lag effects in implementation for a nation-wide scale with divergence among the state-wise adjustment and growth rates. Second, there is really no major difference in the economic ideologies of the leading parties. The contest is all about local issues (e.g., caste, religion, corruption, etc.). Third, an election does not really matter much in economic terms as central policies can take between six and eight years for any meaningful impact to be felt. Figure 6.2 shows for a selected case of central government policy reforms and time lag in economic impact. National Highway Development Program, Telecoms Reform, and Electricity Act, for example, initiated in 1998, 1997, and 2003 took about six years in average to have impacts nationwide.[17] A corollary to this pattern is the remarkable predictability and continuity of the impact in the reform process with

Table 6.1   Division of responsibilities between the center and the states in India

Central	State	Concurrent (state and center)
Defense, atomic energy, foreign affairs	Law and order (police, prisons, adm. of justice)	Education
Currency, foreign trade	Local government	Drugs and poisons
Financial services (banking and insurance)	Transportation (state and local highways, ports)	Labor welfare
Control of industries, mines, etc	Land revenue, taxes on vehicles, luxuries, etc.	Newspapers, books, etc.
Telecommunication	Agriculture, forests, fisheries, irrigation, etc.	Electricity
Transportation (rail, air, national highways, major ports)	Public health and sanitation	Economic and social planning
Income tax, customs and excise duties, etc.		Ports

Source: Constitution of India, Mishra and Shangkar, 2013, Fig. 14 on p. 5. Copyright © 2013, Neelkanth Mishra and Ravi Shankar, Credit Suisse.

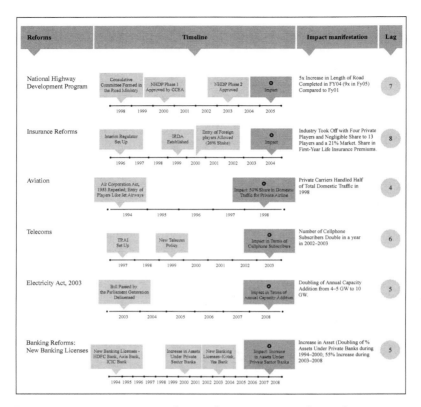

Figure 6.2   Time to Impact on the Broader Economy in Indian Reforms

Source: RBI News, Mishra and Shankar, 2013, Fig. 17, p. 7. Copyright © 2013, RBI News, Credit Suisse.

different time lags in different states.[18] In sum, the fruits or positive economic impact will typically lag 6–8 years after the passage of the reform in the central parliament.

China and India Stumbling in Different Directions

Chindia

First coined by Mr Jairam Ramesh, *Chindia* is an economic reference to the combination of the names China and India, which will contribute the most to world growth over the next 50 years. In addition, the economic strength between these two countries is widely considered complementary, since China is a strong, industrial powerhouse, while India is a leader in services. This relationship is deeply rooted in history since the Silk Road era. In 2015, *Chindia*'s GDP will be 1.25 times that of the US GDP, estimated in purchasing power parity (PPP) adjusted term,[19] while Chindia's world trade is forecast at 1.5 times of US trade.[20] By 2030, *Chindia*'s trade, equivalent to 2.5 times of US trade, will account for about quarter of world trade.[21] China is currently challenging the top economic power spot from the United States in terms of total GDP and trade. India is rising fast as well to be second to China by 2030. In the last two decades of rapid growth after opening up, China has now become a big consumer of base metal (43% world demand), of major agriculture crops (24%), and of nonrenewable energy resources (20%).[22] Many are looking at India to repeat the same phenomenon. Simply put, consumption in services, commodities, and consumer goods will be prominent. The rise of *Chindia* will be a game changer in global economy.[23] So does it seem probable?

Growth Story

The "growth story" of China and India has occurred in parallel to the rise of the Association of Southeast Asian Nations (ASEAN) and Asia. The main factors responsible for this growth are demographic trend, cross-border trade, direct investment, infrastructure, and urbanization. In fact, one could even say that while the story is really about China today (ASEAN for tomorrow), it is India for the future. Yet, China and India have the unpleasant history of political mistrust on the disputes along the borders from Arunachal Pradesh in the east to Kashmir in the west. Their dissimilarity in political economic development does not help either. This leads the two giants to be stumbling in different directions.

First, demographically speaking—after enjoying over two decades of stellar economic growth—by adding a more productive workforce, China is heading for a workforce deficit and an aging population by 2030 while India (and Indonesia) will have more population of working age representing one-third of the world. India will enjoy a demographic dividend of an additional 241 million absolute productive labors or 30 percent growth rate during 2010–2030.[24] Owing to its one-child policy[25] in 1979, China will face −1.8 percent and −8.2 percent growth in working-age population for the 2020s and 2030s, respectively.[26] Even after announcing a relaxation of the one-child policy during the CPC's plenum in November 2013, additional annual births in China will be 1.8 million, not sufficient to offset the persistent declining fertility rate in the next two decades.[27] This divergent workforce has a strategic importance in shaping future economic activity. Commercially speaking, one can antici-pate new increasing demands in baby products (e.g., diaper, baby food, etc.) in China[28] (and India). Conversely, there already are strong demand trends for health-related products and elderly care services in China like in other developing nations (e.g., Japan, Korea, etc.). Strategically, China has to focus more on capital-intensive production (e.g., chemical, rail-ways, etc), high value-added industry and services (e.g., digital services, semiconductor, etc.), and to relocate their labor-intensive industries (e.g., footwear, textiles, etc.) to lower wage and younger population nations like India (and ASEAN). This is in line with China's policy to rebalance its economy to be more domestic driven, whereas India's policy tends to be outward looking, particularly to the East and more open to foreign direct investment (FDI). As India eases FDI restrictions and adopts China's SEZ model, billions of dollars in FDI in the industrial sector will be required: energy, telecom, real estate, and other infrastructure development will be among the top priority for Indian development. In the next two decades, redeploying their labor from agriculture to the industrial sector and accommodating the fast-growing service sector are among India's goals.

Second, China is India's largest trading partner while India is China's tenth trading partner in the world, but the largest in South Asia. Their combined trade is set to increase to USD 100 billion by 2015. However, the balance of trade is in China's favor with a surplus of USD 30 billion 2013.[29] The common man in India is happy to purchase the cheap Chinese products (e.g., mobile phones, household appliance, etc.) but many Indian businesses complain about Chinese import restrictions. Indian pharma-ceutical firms that are known for their world-class products and generic drugs have, for example, complained that China tactically denies India access to their market.[30] (See Dr Reddy's case study.) Furthermore, ser-vices exports (e.g., software development, back office outsourcing, etc.) have traditionally been the Indian GDP driver. The composition of ser-vices has changed and continues to change to more communication and business services along with financial services and more high-value soft-ware development. As a result, India would also like to penetrate these highly protected and regulated industries in China. Trade imbalance, antidumping concerns, and nontariff barriers would be among the con-troversial issues between these two giants in the coming decades.

Third, despite a few political hiccups, infrastructure buildup and urbanization are one of the most promising growth stories, due to a low base effect, especially for India. The two interrelated supply-side factors are set to enhance productivity and to nurture the middle-income class for both China and India (along with ASEAN). The urbanization rate in Asia, which on average is 61 percent, is below that of the developed nations (80%), Group of 7 (G7).[31] India has the lowest rate, 32 percent in Asia, while China's rate is 53 percent, which is still below the Asian average.[32] Strong infrastructure investment needs in Asia of over USD 7 trillion are estimated, of which China and India account for USD 5.8 trillion and USD 1 trillion, respectively.[33] Transportation and power sectors worth USD 2.18 trillion each for China and worth over USD 340 billion each for India are top of the list.[34] Regional connectivity is another key theme that can create a virtuous cycle of trade, consumption, and income distribution for many decades to come. While China pushes for linkages by road and train to the west, south and inland, and for access to sea-lanes via ports in South Asia, India is gravely concerned over its impact on the subcontinent. For example, when state-owned Chinese Oversea Port Holding won the contract to manage Gwadar port (about 600 km from Karachi), Pakistan, in February 2013, Indian Defense Minister A. K. Antony sounded the alarm since China had already funded and was operating ports in Hambantota, Sri Lanka, and Chittagong in Bangladesh.[35] All these ports are in India's neighborhood and provide access to the Strait of Hormuz, a key oil shipping route, and access to the Indian Ocean, where they could end competing with Indian naval forces, as long warned by the Indian PM Manmohan Singh in his rare public criticism against China.[36] Furthermore, when China is aggressively pursuing a North–South Economic Corridor linking southern China to the rest of ASEAN through Thailand via road and high-speed train, India is offering USD 500 million soft loans to Myanmar to build a part of a 3,200-km highway to be completed in 2016 to link up the East–West Economic Corridor between India and Thailand to the rest of ASEAN.[37] Though China wishes to invest in Indian infrastructure and manufacture, the newly manifested Chinese assertiveness in the region makes India uncomfortable.

China's Rebalancing Formula

The economic policy implication to move China into the next level is intriguing. In August 2013, the State Council had approved the establishment of the Shanghai Free-Trade Zone (SFTZ) as part of a new round of economic reform and opening-up in China. This is similar to the setting up of an SEZ in Shenzhen in the 1980s to prepare China for the entry into the WTO in 2001. This time the SFTZ is a pilot project to facilitate China's bid to join Trans-Pacific Partnership (TTP). SFTZ will enjoy the suspension of various laws to ease the burden in doing business. Critical financial liberalization in SFTZ will include securitization, enabling private entities to invest overseas, *renminbi* (RMB) convertibility, and interest rate as well as capital account liberalization. If the SFTZ is successful and provides answers to China's future policy challenges for the next five to ten years, RMB will likely be internalized. Shanghai will challenge Hong Kong as the financial center, not only for China but also for Asia. Backing SFTZ as testing ground announced on September 29, 2013, Premier Li asserted the next round of radical economic reform measures. RMB convertibility, unrestricted foreign currency exchange, a tax holiday for ten years, and uncensored Internet access would be among the liberal measures. The rationale is to emulate the success of Shenzhen's SEZ in 1980, which paved the way for China's entry into WTO by trying out SFTZ to facilitate its bid to join TPP. If this so-called opening-up 3.0 or new round of economic reform initiative from trade to investment liberalization is successful, then China could expedite its nationwide reforms and reclaim Shanghai as the international financial center and economic growth engine.[38] Premier Li understands well that China needs an upgrade in its economic institutions before moving up to become a high-income level nation.

In November 2013, during the Third Plenum, President Xi announced the most comprehensive reform in Chinese history, which addressed 16 areas with 60 major initiatives across nearly all sectors. Over 20,000 words of blueprint cover briefly four basic agenda of reforms: ideology, political, economic, and social.[39] First, Xi stresses that internationally China has to safeguard its sovereignty as well its interests and that domestically, the emphasis is on CPC's leadership and its long-term path in socialism. Second, judicial reform with centralized and efficient law enforcement is one of the keys to ensure people's livelihood, such as food and drugs, environmental protection, labor and social security, and anticorruption measures. Third, economic reform is impressive both in scope and in scale. Shaping a new role between government and private sector to deepening the market-based economy in various sectors (e.g., utilities, banking, real estate, etc), protecting property rights of private citizen,s and fiscal and tax reforms are among the fine examples of the most relevant measures to its economy. While Xi emphasized more on market-based economy, the SOE's economy model has not been abandoned. Land reform and urbanization are stressed to ensure the dual urban–rural structure. Last is social reform. Easing the one-child policy to counter the aging population trend, reforming "*hukou*" or "household registration system" to help migrant workers and farmers, and protecting the natural resources and environmental protection are emphasized by Xi during his deliberation. Summary of key reforms are shown in Table 6.2.

In sum, following a top-down approach, Chinese collective leadership has committed to continuously deepen structural reform and open up its

Table 6.2   Summary of key reforms of the Third Plenum (Plenary Session) in Nov. 2013

Key reforms	Some details and our comments
Trade and investment	Greater openness to foreign investment. Acceleration of setting up free trade zones like SFTZ
Financial	Interest rate and capital account liberalization to be speeded up. A system of deposit insurance will be set up. The bankruptcy system will be upgraded. Private banks will be allowed. Government control over company IPOs to be relaxed. The tax regime will be reformed to bring in more revenues, rate liberalization, encouraging two-way capital flows, introducing deposit insurance scheme. However, there were no details on sequencing and timetable of these reforms
Market based	Market forces will play a "decisive function in resource allocation." Prices of natural resources should be determined by market demand. The private sector is to be encouraged, but the principal position of the state sector is reaffirmed
One-child policy	Couples living in cities are now allowed to have two children, if at least one of the spouses is an only child
Residency or "hukou"	The household registration system, *hukou*, will be relaxed. This will allow more rural people who migrate to work in the cities to qualify for basic social welfare and housing
Rural land	Farmers will be granted more rights on what they do with the land they lease from the state
Fiscal	Some local governments will allow to issue their own bonds for their own financing for trials. VAT, resource tax levied on natural resources, particularly on coal, tax cut for small business, and registration for property tax and environment protection-related tax are fine examples of tax reform deepening
State-owned enterprises	More mixed ownership is encouraged at a different speed for different corporate levels. On March 26, 2014, CITIC groups taking over CITIC Pacific as the backdoor listing, for example, became the second major initiative after Sinopec announcing its divestment of its division in marketing
Service sector	Health-care service, medical institutions, and medical insurance system will be participated more by private sectors

Source: 1. Salidjanova and Koch-Weser, 2013.

2. Song, 2013.

3. "Road to the Chinese Dream? Xi Jinping's Third Plenum Reform Plan," *Knowledge@Wharton, University of Pennsylvania*, December 10, 2013. Accessed May 8, 2013 (https://knowledge.wharton.upenn.edu/article/road-chinese-dream-xi-jinpings-third-plenum-reform-plan/).

4. and 5. Authors.

economy in the coming decade. The scope and scale of these reforms aim to rebalance every political and economic aspect of the challenges facing China, from its economic system to its political agenda, from environmental protection to social issues. In the coming years, it remains to be seen how China will push forward for bold changes in the countryside where the majority of the people live and for the restoration of their individual basic property rights that has been long denied after the end of Mao's disastrous scheme of "people's communes."

Indian Silent Transformation

The Indian economy faces many challenges, from a slowdown in the economy, the plunging rupee, to corruption scandals and protests dominating the news headlines in 2014, an election year. In fact, the Indian economy is driven largely by global business cycle and consumption patterns of the robust low-income group rather than politics.[40] Many would like to see India follow the Chinese success formula of having a strong central government with command and control over economic planning. Others feel that India is an underachiever when compared to the immense success achieved by the Chinese. The truth is India can never emulate Chinese economic development because of its diversity. The nation has at least 15 major languages, over 100 dialects, several major religions with more than 10,000 gods, and thousands of tribes. A strong central government and high-speed growth regardless of social and environment costs may not be a viable option in India because these could easily lead to labor chaos, farmer protests, religious pogroms, and class wars.[41] In a nutshell, India is like at least 28 separate nations that have been loosely united in confederation by technologies—railways and arms—since its colonial days.[42] What most people miss to observe is the ongoing silent transformation, which hopefully will extend into the future too.

India is now in the middle of a once-in-a-life-time transformation from the grassroots level up. Many of the past social economic reforms are already improving the productivity of rural people. This structural and sustainable productivity growth at the grassroots level is happening in an unparalleled scale. Because the rural people and farmers are nearly all in the informal sector, the improvement in their quality of life and their active economic engagements are often overlooked and not officially recorded.[43] But it shows in their robust consumption from the bottom of the pyramid.[44] (See Figure 6.3 for a pictorial presentation.) Fundamentally, the four drivers for this structural productivity growth are as below.[45]

Rural Roads: Almost 360,000 km of rural roads was built under the prime minister's Rural Plans (*Pradhan Mantri Gram Sadak Yojana*—PMGSY) launched in 2000 and an additional 250,000 km of roads will be done in the next five years. First, PMGSY road connection substantially improves labor mobility, wage, and employment opportunities and reduces the loss

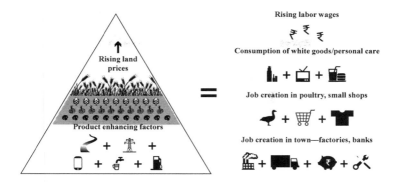

Figure 6.3   Indian Silent Transformation: Self-Sustaining, Productivity-Driven Job Creation Transforming India

Source: Mishra and Shankar et al., 2013, p. 1. Copyright © 2013, Neelkanth Mishra, Credit Suisse.

incurred by farmers due to the perishing of produce (e.g., fruits, vegetable, poultry, etc.). This rural road equates to more job access and income diversification. Second, these road links boost land prices. The wealth effect cannot be underestimated since 94 percent of land is rural and about 400 million rural people own more than one acre of land.[46] For example, after newly paved roads built in 2009, in Mogra Ram village of Madhya Pradesh state, the road frontage land price has increased at compounding annual growth rate of 31 percent between 2007 and 2013.[47] Huge price changes may seem "bubble like," but it could be justified from lower base, the norm of using land as saving means in rural and more economic use of the land (e.g., retail shop, clinic, food stalls, etc.).[48] Thus, rural land price increases alleviate the well-being of the Indian majority.

Rural Electrification: In modern society, electricity is life, but in India more than a third of the population has no power at all. The number of households in India that have been electrified has risen from 44 percent to 55 percent in the last decade as the direct result of the Rural Electrification Programme (*Rajiv Gandhi Grameen Vidyutikaran Yojana*—RGGVY) initiated in 2000.[49] The percentage will continue to rise until 2017 as the RGGVY program has the funding. The per capita output of each state is highly correlated to the percentage of power usage from rural households, and this usage of electricity implies its use in lighting, automation, cost saving, and comfort.

Mobile Phone: Mobile phones connect people and connect subsistence economy to the markets in India, of course with other supporting infrastructure like road links.[50] Intuitively, fishermen and farmers, for example, can improve their productivity and profitability with more efficient price discovery of their fishes and agriculture products.[51] Micro and small enterprises, for another instance, may serve their clientele better with personal touch and save their traveling time. Indeed, rural represents 40 percent of mobile subscribers in India with a rapid growth.[52]

Other drivers: TV, water, and cooking gas are among the "new discretionary consumption" goods that new vibrant rural pay for and this helps to create new jobs with higher wage in the areas. So far one factor that stands out in driving rural prosperity is computerized land titles, which was implemented in August 2008 under the National Land Records Modernization Programme (NLRMP) with the aim to be made available nationwide in 2017. This is really a big issue because in 2001 about 90 percent of land titles in India were found to be unclear.[53] With NLPRMP's title guarantee, landowners now monetize their land asset for their consumption and investment with asset-backed commercial bank loans and credit card issuers. Currently, about 82 percent of land in India across 20 states are completely recorded through the use of technology.

Wealth creation from the silent transformation is widespread from the bottom of the pyramid that currently derives from multiple dimensions—from rising agricultural output to new job creations, from market connection to credit access. It is intriguing as to how the next move forward should be for the Indian economy when half of its GDP and 90 percent of employments are informal.[54] Perhaps the future transformation may lie in "distributed capitalism" growth from bottom-up. Instead of the Chinese classical industrialization style with cheap labor, mass production, and coal and electrical power, India may opt for the third industrial revolution type.[55] India can break its gigantic problems—in ever-growing megacities like Mumbai, complicated government regulations, and enormous physical infrastructure constraints—into manageable size.[56] Basically, given its strength in information and communications technology (ICT) services, Indian can use Internet technology to transform power grid to be a "smart grid" that connects all renewable energy sources from potentially millions of existing and new smart homes and "green" buildings. Power can optimally be rationed and its allocation may induce the informal sector to participate toward which unique ID cards have been issued for every citizen from the 2009 initiative. In this process, millions of "green" jobs will be created, power shortage will be minimized and ICT serviced works will be provided. The new era of micro-enterprises and SMEs for renewable business and home-based industry will flourish if right incentives and strong supports are provided by the central government. By letting each state compete for these incentives and funding schemes, they can be assured of improving their economic health. This may sound like fantasy, but the technology is already here. At least one Indian conglomerate is building a city outside Chennai as the prototype called, "Mahindra World City."[57] This self-sustainable and wealth-creation approach will create a virtuous cycle of productivity improvement and inclusive investment with high-wage jobs, and may propel India into the forefront as a world economic leader.

Selected Issues for Discussion

Barriers to Riches

The United Kingdom first industrialized, followed by the United States and West Europe. Nearly 40 years after World War II (WWII), Japan transformed to be one of richest countries. Thailand, China, and India have followed the leading industrialized nations and have reached middle-income status in the 1980s, 1990s, and 2000s, respectively (see Figure 6.4). Growth in Asia is fascinating in that catch-up occurs after market liberation, the acceptance of foreign investment, and adoption of technological advancement.

The different income levels of different countries based on productivity improvement can be theoretically explained.[58] The countries' relative efficiencies as the direct result of effective technology adoption are exposited to relate to the evolution of international income levels over the last millennium. The level of production efficiency at different settings, not only the different stock of knowledge, differs in the amount of society-imposed constraints on the choices of the technology that their citizenry may opt to adopt. As a country loses their institutional constraints and embraces technological advancement in different points in time, the country will "catch up."[59] There are two critical constraints that reduce productivity:

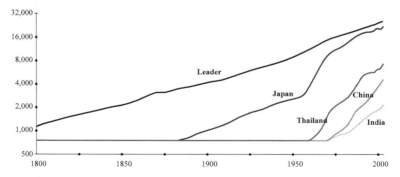

Figure 6.4   Different Nations with Different Endowment Start at Different Times with Different Development—Per Capita GDP Trends (1990 US $)

Source: Prescott, 2005. Copyright © 2013, Edward C. Prescott.

use[60] and integration[61] of technology. Regulation, laws, capital market, and bribes are among the constraints of technology and innovation.

What China has done right is to reinvent market-based mechanism and to open up trade and investment for foreign businessmen. The coastal SEZs (e.g., Dailian, Tianjin, Shanghai, Guangzhou, Shenzhen, etc.) have been established with independence, special tax incentives, and well-defined laws and regulations since 1980. These have quickly transformed into commercial and industrial centers where foreign investment receives special treatment. China first began the reform process by clearly defining the right to property: by 1984, almost 98 percent of all farm households were granted long-term land leases under their own responsibility, allowing income from farming to grow rapidly. Entrepreneurs—both local and foreign alike—had incentives to work hard with modern technology and management skills. Competition flourished because the free flow and exchange of goods and services beyond their communes were allowed. Corrupt officials who abused their power were trailed and severely disciplined—often by capital punishment.

India, on the contrary, always had a legal infrastructure for free market activity as the direct result of its colonial legacy. The fear of foreign dominance, however, has been paramount in its postindependence history, which led India to adhere to a quasi-socialist approach by partially controlling the private sector, particularly foreign trade and FDI. It was after the financial economic crisis in 1991 that India gradually liberated its markets through economic reforms and reduced the overpowering role of the state. Nevertheless, the bureaucratic system has prevented people from realizing their full economic potential; only large corporations with political connections are able to perform well in the formal sector. Millions of small entrepreneurs are vibrant and fare better in micro-enterprises (e.g., street vendors and self-employment initiatives), which are based in the informal sector. What is intriguing is how the Indian business service sector has evolved and prospered from small groups of self-employed knowledge workers to becoming the global outsourcing center because of the lack of regulation in this sector. Hence, the main lesson here is that a well-designed market at the household level allowed free decision making to shape and support the process of business transactions. Trade increases social welfare, the more open it is.

Power Rivalry

After being newly elected as the Chinese premier, Li chose India to be his first official foreign visit in May 2013, to signify the importance of

Sino–Indian relationship. But his maiden state visit was overshadowed by the news of Chinese troop intrusion nearly 19 km deep into Indian terrain earlier in the month. This incident highlights the inherent power rivalry between the two giants in terms of territory, population, and civilization.[62] The two behemoths are billion-plus population nations that are geographically separated by the Himalayan terrain. Both share a long common border and compete for natural resources. The "line of control" of troubles and tensions in Arunachal Pradesh that, for example, was fought in the Sino–India war in 1962 has spillovers into the unfriendly neighbor—Pakistan—that has filled modern history with wars and conflicts. Apart from issues of religious and ethnic differences, river water and freshwater reserves, even from the Tibetan plateau, are contentious issues as both nations already have water-stressed economies, which may even trigger a war.[63] One dangerous idea China may have is to divert the Brahmaputra (or Yarlung Tsangpo) River that flows through Arunachal Pradesh, India. In fact, China began construction of a 700-MW hydro dam on the river in 2012 and plans to construct 20 more dams.[64]

At sea, India sees the great potential threat from China to actively engage in developing and managing seaports—so-called string of pearls in all surrounding neighbors—Pakistan, Sri Lanka, Bangladesh, and Myanmar for strategic accesses in India Ocean. China fears India is developing a naval relationship with Vietnam, South Korea, Japan, and, most importantly, United States to counterbalance its influence. In short, China is desperately seeking to secure its sea-lanes for their energy supply and international trade to the world. India is uncomfortable to have the Chinese naval force challenge them in its own ocean.

With great economic capacity and strong central government, China is intimidating India in many ways. India has no choice but to open up and move closer to United States, Japan, South Korea, and ASEAN nations. Its military also has to adopt a minimum deterrent capacity to defend itself. At the end, it is the bipolar geopolitical world which is shaping the relationship between China and the United States and the US alliance including India as the counterbalance.[65] To a large extent, the Asian century hinges on how well the Sino–India relationship develops.

Upgrader Consumers

Much hype has been raised on the rising middle-class consumers in recent years. Many retailers are disappointed to find that the reality is far less exciting than the statistics indicate. This has a lot to do with the law of averages. When the annual income of all citizens of China and

India are summed up on a macro level, the average shows impressive rising middle-class consumers. However, the fact is both China and India have a dual economy—rich urbanites and poor rural. The rising trends of the two segments on a micro level have different implications in terms of consumer market opportunities. Few analyze in depth and discuss the new market niche opportunities and trends in both countries. The rural poor typically have higher income elasticity than the urban rich. In other words, the poor would spend more in percentage wise than the rich if they have more discrete income. Naturally, the poor would spend more on basic needs and small ticket items for a better future. In the context of this chapter, the rising rural income in India and the potential market from the relaxation of the one-child policy in China present good examples of identifying the new market niche—"Upgrader Consumer" for business opportunities from structural changing trends.

The silent Indian transformation has made the robust rural spending divergent from urban spending in almost all categories despite the slow-down in 2013. For example, though nearly (97%) everyone owns mobile phones in India, the rural population has a greater desire to upgrade to a smartphone. Interestingly, nearly 60 percent of Indians would buy smart-phones in order to use software applications, especially for social media even though only 30 percent Indians have access to Internet.[66] The Indian urban, for instance, experiences stagnant automobile vehicle penetrations in the last three years, but the rural consumers have doubled their vehicle penetrations during the same period.[67] Naturally, rural people would prefer a two-wheeled vehicle first and then upgrade to a compact car later. The rising rural would enjoy their mobility freedom by traveling mostly to domestic destinations rather than flying internationally as evidenced by India's very low air-travel penetration rate.[68] Perhaps in the near future after aviation liberalization, more low-cost airlines would operate, then this travel spending pattern may change drastically.

On the other hand, for China as a centralized planned economy, the impact of relaxing the one-child policy provides a fine study example for marketers. The group of young parents and parents-to-be between the ages of 18 and 29 and 20 and 45 have the potential for huge purchasing power as the result of this new policy to boost fertility. About 66 percent of the first group and 72 percent of the second group who have high confidence in their future believe it is either good or excellent to spend now to prepare for a bigger nest.[69] This translates to about RMB 2.3 trillion spending from the prime-age group of parents for themselves and their children from now through 2020.[70] Dairy product is one of the biggest beneficiaries. The big gap in dairy purchase penetration between the two parental groups in China (75%) and India (90%) will be progressively narrowed since approximately an additional 8.3 million births are expected by 2020.[71] Interestingly, the "feeling good" factor drives the young and confident parents to spend more on soft-line discretionary goods (e.g., fashion apparel, sportswear, etc.) but less in hard-line discretionary goods (e.g., watch, jewellery, etc.) as not a priority. It is intriguing to note that a new record high 70 percent of both parental groups in China intends to do shopping online in sharp contrast to about 20 percent in counterparts in India.[72]

Conclusion

The rise of China and the emergence of India are indeed a triumph of market-based economy. India and China both have their own strong points and weaknesses. While India is the world center of business and high-tech outsourcing to competitively deflate business process and services cost, China is the factory of the world to export cheap goods to every corner around the globe. The speed of both nations to "catch up" with the advanced economy will depend upon a lot of factors, but their way of approach and who will succeed and who will sustain the growth and so on will be an interesting phenomenon for all scholars and policymakers.

With different values, endowments, and starting points, China and India have their own way of charting their political and economic progress. The Chinese one-party system offers effective executive branch strives for a strong nation and central planned economy. There is no denial of Chinese stellar growth in the last two decades after "opening up." But one should also remember that when Chinese top-down approach failed like during the CPC's earlier years, it failed miserably. Next, the world is watching how effectively China would implement its most ambitious reform roadmap announced during the Third Plenum in November 2013 to rebalance its political economy. Though the blueprint is wide in scope and scale across 16 areas with 60 major initiatives across nearly all sectors, many will watch how China pushes forward for bold change in the countryside where the majority of the people live and whose individual basic property rights have been long denied after the end of Mao's disastrous scheme of "people's communes."

On the other hand, India's political system in federal republic parliament style is rooted in colonial legacy and nonviolent belief in respect of the different views of its multiethnic, -linguistic, and -religious communities. India can never emulate the Chinese style of success. Still, India is now in the middle of a once-in-a-lifetime transformation from the grassroots level. Many of past social economic reforms are already improving the productivity of rural people materially. Going forward, India may adopt the third industrial revolution type for inclusive growth rather than the "distributed capitalism" approach. This may induce another half of its GDP—informal sector to join the mainstream. Niche markets driven by Indian silent transformation in comparison to China's relaxation of its one-child policy are discussed.

Potentially, a more balanced economic development in India and a more balanced political evolution in China may be desirable for world peace and prosperity as *Chindia* thrusts forward to proclaim its position as rightful world leaders. An overemphasis on growth in China has caused several issues, including rising income inequality as well as a lack of social security. Water scarcity and security apprehension are highlighted among the potential global issues with suggested solutions. This is an immense challenge with global implications. Asian century hinges, to a large extent, on how well the Sino–India relationship develops.

Case Study

From Local to International: Dr. Reddy's of India

Pongsak Hoontrakul

Dr. Reddy's Laboratories Ltd is a publicly listed Indian pharmaceutical company based in Hyderabad that manufactures and markets a wide range of medications and active pharmaceutical ingredients across the world. It has eight active pharmaceutical ingredient plants (six in India, one each in Mexico and in the UK) and nine formulation manufacturing facilities (seven in India and two in the United States).

Founded by Dr. Kallan Anji Reddy in 1984, Dr. Reddy's began by producing branded formulation drugs for the local market. The following year, the company produced its first well-known brand, Norilet (norfloxacin antibiotic), which sold for 25 percent of the competitors' price.[73] After Dr. Reddy's became the first Indian firm to export active pharmaceutical ingredients to Europe, it exported its brands to other, less-regulated markets. Today, Dr. Reddy's has a presence in major emerging countries including China, Russia, and Brazil. The company's drug research and development (R&D) is focused on joint R&D with many laboratories in developed countries including the United States and the UK. One of Dr. Reddy's key strategies is to produce first-to-market, tough-to-make products.[74] Dr. Reddy's has numerous US Food and Drug Administration (FDA)-approved brands, although more than half of its global business is in generics. Memantine with Namenda brand for Alzheimer therapy,

Ixaberpilone with Ixempra brand for breast cancer treatment, Eszopiclone with Lunesta brand for insomnia therapy, and Desvenlafaxine succinate with Pristiq for depression treatment are among fine examples of Dr. Reddy's key products in 2014.[75]

Dr. Reddy's total sales and net profit for 2015 would reach 164 billion rupees ($2.57 billion) and 25.4 billion rupees ($420 million), respectively, a year-on-year growth of 13.5 percent and a 14.7 percent, respectively.[76] Geographically, the revenue for 2011 derived mainly from North America (31%), Europe (21%), India (19%), and Russia (19%).[77] Despite a direct presence in China, Dr. Reddy's has done very little there due to the country's heavy regulation.

Developing the Offshore RMB

Pongsak Hoontrakul and Jonathan A. Batten

For the first time in the history of mankind, one nation plans to have its currency to be a world currency. China is strategically planning to internationalize its currency, the RMB. The RMB was used to settle trade with China's immediate neighbors, including Vietnam and Mongolia, as far back as the 1980s, and there were also a number of Bilateral Currency Trade Settlement Agreements signed in more recent times (such as with Russia and Belarus in 2010 and 2011). However, the personal use of RMB is a more recent phenomenon that began in 2004[78] with the creation of offshore renminbi (CNH) for settlement in Hong Kong. Unlike the RMB that is used inside China (termed "onshore renminbi" or CNY), offshore renminbi is not subject to the tight band within which China's central bank, the People's Bank of China (PBoC), controls domestic exchange rates. In fact, the Hong Kong Monetary Authority (HKMA) will also not directly intervene in the offshore RMB market even though Hong Kong remains one of the main trading centers for the CNH.

The separation of the onshore and offshore RMB markets is intended to manage volatility in the domestic economy, while allowing offshore RMB to be used for trade and financial transactions without fully opening up China's capital account. A detailed comparison of these two markets is undertaken that while spot foreign exchange trading in the offshore RMB market is smaller (CNH turnover is about US$5.1 billion per day in 2013 compared with US$17.6 billion per day in the case of the CNY), transaction costs are also significantly higher with average bid-ask spreads of 33 basis points compared with 17 basis points in the onshore market.[79] One important distinction is the price formation mechanism between CNY and CNH. The former is a managed float system by PBoC—Chinese central bank; the latter is a free float and market-based system regulated by the HKMA. Consequently, the market intervention in CNY market may be anticipated whenever PBoC deems appropriated.[80]

Since the global financial crisis began in 2008, China has intensified efforts to promote offshore RMB, initially for cross-border settlements in spot and forward markets, then as a currency for more bonds and other debt securities and now more complex financial products such as swaps, options, and other derivatives. The growth in the RMB has been explosive. Offshore RMB in cross-border trade settlement grew from virtually nothing in 2010 to over RMB one trillion in 2013.[81] About one-third of global trade is anticipated to be settled in RMB by 2020.[82] In addition, the outstandings of bonds and Certificates of Deposit (CDs) issued in RMB leaped from a negligible amount in 2010 to over RMB 400 billion in 2013.[83] It is interesting to note that the first foreign nonfinancial company to issue offshore RMB-denominated bonds (or "dim sum" bonds) was McDonald's.

Because China is now the second largest economy in the world, a number of policy makers and economists have predicted that offshore RMB will become one of the top three currencies for world trade by the end of this decade.[84] This should occur more recently within the Asia-Pacific region given China's extensive trade with Asian emerging markets. Currently, within the Asia-Pacific region, Hong Kong, Singapore, and Taiwan should remain leading offshore RMB centers, with London taking a leading role for trading outside of this group's time zone. Note that China's 12th Five-Year Plan (2011–2015) states that it will "Support Hong Kong to develop as an offshore RMB business center and international asset management center."[85]

The SFTZ, which opened in 2013, is a pilot project that allows companies in the zone to borrow and trade in offshore RMB in order to facilitate currency risk management, e-commerce settlement, and currency exchanges for cross-border direct investment. This experiment in currency convertibility will pave the way for the RMB to become a global currency in the near future.

Notes

1. Minggao Shen et al., "China & India Equity Strategy: Two Plays, One Portfolio," *Citi*, October 8, 2010: Fig. 2, p. 3.
2. During the 1980s, China separated the country into Eastern, Central, and Western regions and developing each of these regions in stages. The Eastern contains SEZs and open coastal cities (e.g., Shanghai, Canton, etc.) and the main drive for Chinese high economic growth rate. The Western region (e.g.,

Tibet, Sichuan, etc.) has many minorities and is rich in natural resources. The economic development has been impaired and social problem is increasing as the disparity between other regions is growing. Chinese government is prioritizing this area and allocates more assistance and support.

3. Andrew Naylor, "China's Leadership Change 2012," *Cicero-Group*, November 15, 2012: 1–10.

4. "China Next Generation of Leaders, Looking to 2012," *Stratfor*, September 17, 2012 (http://www.marketoracle.co.uk/Article22759.html).

5. Helen Zhu et al., "Third Plenary: Ambitious Blueprint to Boost Sentiment," *Goldman Sachs*, November 18, 2013: 1–13.

6. IMF (http://www.imf.org/external/pubs/ft/weo/2013/01/weodata/weorept. aspx? sy=2012&ey=2018&scsm=1&ssd=1&sort=country&ds=.&br=1&c=9 24&s=NGDPD%2CNGDPDPC%2CPPPGDP%2CPPPPC%2CGGXWDG_ NGDP&grp=0&a=&pr.x=41&pr.y =17).

7. The People's Bank of China (http://www.pbc.gov.cn/publish/html/kuangjia. htm?id=2013s09.htm), [In Chinese]. Also China was already reported to have the foreign exchange reserves of USD3.663 trillion, highest in the world as of the end of November 13. (See Joseph Lupton and David Hensley, "Global FX Reserves Near $12 Trillion in 2013", *JP Morgan*, February 28, 2014: 1–5.)

8. IMF.

9. It should be noted that a formation of Telengana as the new 29th state of India, separating from the rest of Andra Pradesh state, was declared to be effective on June 2, 2014. It is interesting to note that the city of Hyderabad is now the joint capital of both Telangana state and the rest of Andhra Pradesh state.

10. As a member of the Indian National Congress headed by Sonia Gandhi, Prof. Dr. Manmohan Singh was the 14th Prime Minister of India. PM Singh was the first Sikh ever to become PM on May 22, 2004.

11. Neelkanth Mishra and Ravi Shankar, "India Market Strategy: Reforms: The Past and the Future," *Asia Pacific/India Equity Research, Credit Suisse*, November 8, 2012: 3.

12. "RBI Weekly Statistical Supplement," RBI. Retrieved 2012–08–24 (http:// www.rbi.org.in/scripts/wssviewdetail.aspx?type=section&param1=2).

13. World Bank, "Country and Lending Groups" (http://data.worldbank.org/ about/country-classifications/country-and-lending-groups).

14. Rohini Malkani and Anurag Jha, "India Macroscope: Looking Beyond Elections," *Citi*, March 7, 2014: p 1, Fig. 54 on p. 8, Fig. 66 on p. 24, and pp 8–9.

15. See for more discussion, Rohini Malkani and Anrag Jha, "India Macroscope: Modiscope: Mandate, Mantra and More," *Citi*, June 6, 2014: 1–28 and Neelkanth Mishra and Ravi Shankar, "India Market Strategy: 2014 Outlook," *Asia Pacific/India Equity Research, Credit Suise,* December 2, 2013: 1–21.

16. Mishra and Shankar, "India Market Strategy: India 2014 Outlook," Fig. 2 on p. 2 and Fig. 12 and 13 on p. 5.

17. Ibid., Fig. 17 on p. 7.

18. Mishra and Shankar, "India Market Strategy: India 2014 Outlook," 1, 17–18.
19. IMF, *World Economic Outlook: Slowing Growth, Rising Risk*, Washington, DC: Imfbookstore, 2011 (http://www.imf.org/external/pubs/ft/weo/2011/02/pdf/text.pdf and also available at http://en.wikipedia.org/wiki/List_of_countries_by_future_GDP_(PPP)_ estimates).
20. Willem Buiter and Ebrahim Rahbari, "Trade Transformed: The Emerging New Corridors of Trade Power," *Citi GPS: Global Perspectives & Solutions*, October 18, 2011: Fig. 39 on p. 22 (https://www.citivelocity.com/citigps/ReportSeries.action?recordId=1).
21. Ibid.
22. David Lubin et al., "China & Emerging Markets: China is About to Rebalance. How Will EM be Affected?" *Citi GPS: Global Perspectives & Solutions*, July 16, 2012: 1–56.
23. See for more discussion, Sajjad Ashraf, "Rise of China and India: Global Game Changer?" *RSIS Commentaries no 024/2013*, the S. Rajaratnam School of International Study, Nanyan Technology University (NTU), Singapore, 2013.
24. Adele Hayutin, "Population Age Shifts will Reshape Global Work Force," *Standford Center of Longevity*, April 2010 (http://longevity3.stanford.edu/wp-content/uploads/2012/10/Pop-Age-Shifts_Work-Force_April-2010_v2_FINALWEB_0.pdf).
25. The impact of one-child policy is enormous. China's fertility rate is 1.63 children born per women as opposed to 3.01 in 1975–1980 and 6.11 in 1950–1955. More discussion by Ebru Sener Kurumlu, Shen Li, Henry Tan, and Celine Pannuti, "Baby Boosts and Consumption," *Asia Pacific Equity Research, J.P. Morgan*, No. 17, 2013: 1.
26. Adrian Mowat et al., "China 2020: 130 Million Swing: How Demographics Change the Economy," *Emerging Market Equity Research, J.P. Morgan*, May 31, 2011: Table 3 on p. 6.
27. Kurumlu et al., "Baby Boosts and Consumption," 1, 5–11.
28. Tina Long et al., "Global Beneficiaries if China Retires Its One-Child Policy," *Consumer Product—Hongkong/China Equity Reseach, Bank of America Merrill Lynch*, May 22, 2013: 1–44.
29. Ananth Krishnan, "India's Trade Deficit with China Nears Record USD30bn," *The Hindu*, December 14, 2013.
30. See for more discussion, Rupakiyoti Borah, "Rise of China and India: Global Game Changer?" *RSIS Commentaries no 118/2013*, the S. Rajaratnam School of International Study, Nanyan Technology University (NTU), Singapore, June 27, 2013.
31. T. Moe et al., "Asia Pacific 2014 Outlook: Back on Track," *Goldman Sachs*, November 21, 2013.
32. Ibid. It is also interesting to note that advanced economies like South Korea, Malaysia, and Taiwan have the urbanization rate of 83 percent, 74 percent, and 71 percent, respectively. In contrast, not-so-advanced economies like Thailand, Philippines, and Indonesia have their urbanization rate of 34 percent, 49 percent, and 52 percent, respectively.
33. Ibid.

34. Ibid.
35. Alistair Scrutton, "Indian PM Warns of Rising China," *REUTERS*, reprinted by Bangkok Post, September 8, 2010.
36. Ibid., More discussion see Anurag Kotoky and A. Ananthalakshmi, "India 'Concerned' by China's Role in Port," Reuters, reprinted by *Bangkok Post*, February 8, 2013.
37. Nophahun Limsamarnphun, "India Funds Three-Nation Road," *The Nation Daily Newspaper*, August 12, 2012.
38. Minggao Shen, Shuang Ding, and Enjiang Cheng, "China Macro View: SFTZ: Testing the Waters of Reform," *Citi Research*, August 27, 2013: 1–15.
39. Michael Yu, Joanne Cheung, and Adrian Mowat, "The "Decision"—The Details: More on China's Reforms," *Asia Pacific Equity Research, J.P. Morgan*, November 17, 2013: 1–14.
40. Hak Bin Chua et al., "Asia Macro Weekly: India: Do Politics Matter for Economics?" *GEM Fixed Income Strategy & Economic for Asia, Bank of America Merrill Lynch*, May 16, 2013: 1–21.
41. Anand Mahindra, "Toward a Uniquely Indian Growth Model," *McKinsey & Company*, November, 2013 (http://www.mckinsey.com/insights/asia-pacific/toward_a_uniquely_indian_growth_model).
42. Fareed Zakaria, "The Rediscovery of India," *McKinsey & Company*, November 2013.
43. Neelkanth Mishra and Ravi Shankar, "India Market Strategy: India's Better Half: The Informal Economy," *Asia Pacific/India Equity Research, Credit Suisse*, July 9, 2013: 1–44.
44. Neelkanth Mishra and Ravi Shankar et al., "India Market Strategy: India: The Silent Transformation," *Asia Pacific/India Equity Research, Credit Suisse*, March 13, 2013: 1–44.
45. Ibid., pp. 8–16.
46. Ibid., p. 17.
47. Ibid., Fig. 23 on p. 9.
48. Ibid., pp. 17–20.
49. Ibid., pp. 11–13.
50. Ibid., pp. 13–15.
51. Robert Jensen, "The Digital Provide: Information (Technology), Market Performance and Welfare in the South Indian Fisheries Sector," *Quarterly Journal of Economics*, August 2007.
52. Mishra, Shangkar et al., "India Market Strategy: India: The Silent Transformation," 13–15.
53 Ibid., pp. 21–23.
54. Mishra and Shangkar, India Market Strategy: India's Better Half: The Informal Economy.
55. Jeremy Rifkin, *The Third Industrial Revolution: How Lateral Power is Transforming Energy, The Economy and the World* (New York: Palgrave Macmillan), 2011.
56. Mahindra, "Toward a Uniquely Indian Growth Model."
57. Ibid.

58. Stephen L. Parente and Edward C. Prescott, "A Unified Theory of the Evolution of International Income Levels," *Research Department Staff Report 333, Federal Reserve Bank of Minneapolis*, March 2004 (http://apps.eui.eu/Personal/rmarimon/courses/ parenteprescott333.pdf).

59. Edward C. Prescott, "Overcoming Barriers to Riches," presentation at the seminar organized by Sasin of Chulalongkorn University, Bangkok, Thailand, 2005.

60. Work rules, inspection and bribes, and general technological know-how.

61. Obstacles that prevent free flow of technology.

62. Roert D. Kaplan, "The India–China Rivalry," *Stratfor*, August 25, 2012.

63. Brahma Chellaney, "Coming Water Wars," *International Economic*, Fall, 2009 (http://www.international-economy.com/TIE_F09_Chellaney.pdf).

64. Prem Shankar Jha, "Why India and China should leave the Yarlung Tsangpo alone," *Chinadialogue*, March 5, 2014 (https://www.chinadialogue.net/article/show/single/en/6753-Why-India-and-China-should-leave-the-Yarlung-Tsangpo-alone).

65. Kaplan, "The India–China Rivalry."

66. See Survey of 2,596 Indian respondents across ten cities in both urban and rural cities by Arnab Mitra and Akshay Saxena, "India Consumer Survey 2014: Rural Continues to be the Bright Spot," *Credit Suisse*, 2014: Fig. 63 and 64 on p. 19 and Fig. 71 on p. 22.

67. Ibid., pp. 6–8, 14–16.

68. Ibid., pp. 22–23.

69. See Survey of over 2,000 Chinese consumers who are potential prime-age parent age between 1829 and 30–45 years old by Kevin Yin and Vivian Zhao, "China Consumer Survey 2014: Unlock the Power of 'Shopaholic'," *Credit Suisse*, February 14, 2014: 1–25.

70. Ibid., pp. 7–8.

71. Ibid., Fig. 19 on p. 11.

72. Ibid., Fig. 27–28 on p. 16.

73. Dr. Reddy's Company site (http://www.drreddys.com/25yearsofhealth/1990.html).

74. Dr. Reddy's, "Investor Presentation," February 2014, slide no. 15 (http://www.drreddys.com/investors/pdf/drreddys-investor-presentation.pdf).

75. Neha Manpuria, Pinakin Parekh, and Sean Wu, "Dr. Reddy's Laboratories Limited," *Asia Pacific Equity research, J.P. Morgan*, March 6, 2014: 1–11.

76. Ibid.

77. Anjan Ghosh et al., "Indian Pharmaceutical Sector", ICRA Rating Feature, March 2012: 23–24 (http://icra.in/Files/ticker/Indian%20Pharmaceutical%20Sector.pdf).

78. The announcement was made in November 2003 and Bank of China Hong Kong branch was designated as the RMB clearing bank in Hong Kong. See more discussion at Zhongxia Jin, "The Use of RMB in International Transactions: Background, Development and Prospect," Peoples Bank of China, 2011 (http://china.ucsd.edu/_files/renminbi/pdf-rmb-JinZhongxia.pdf).

79. Chang Shu, Dong He, and Xiaoqiang Cheng, "One Currency, Two Markets: The Renminbi's Growing Influence in Asia-Pacific," *BIS Working Paper Number 446*, Monetary and Economic Department, Bank for International Settlements, Basel, Switzerland, April 2014: 5 (http://www.bis.org/publ/ work446.pdf).

80. Ibid.

81. Sean Craig, Changchun Hua, Philip Ng, and Raymond Yuen, "Development of the Renminbi market in Hong Kong SAR: Assessing Onshore–Offshore Market Integration," *IMF Working Paper*, May 2013: 1–23.

82. Petchanet Pratruangkrai, "Yuan to Become Major Currency in World Trade: HSBC," *The Nation*, April 25, 2014 (http://www.nationmultimedia. com/business/Yuan-to-become-major-currency-in-world-tradeHSBC- 30232162.html). More discussion see Beck Liu, "Offshore Renminbi Bonds—Outlook for 2014," *Global Research*, Standard Chartered Bank, February 5, 2014: 4 (https://research.standardchartered.com/ configuration/ ROW%20Documents/Offshore_Renminbi_bonds_%E2%80%93_Outlook_ for_2014__05_02_14_02_42.pdf).

83. Sean Craig et al., "Development of the Renminbi Market in Hong Kong SAR: Assessing Onshore–Offshore Market Integration," *IMF Working Paper*, May 2013: 1–23.

84. Pratruangkrai, "Yuan."

85. In July 2010, the PBoC signed the modified RMB Clearing Agreement with the Bank of China HK branch. See more discussion at Jin 2011.

7

The Rise of ASEAN 2.0—AEC and Regional Connectivity

Pongsak Hoontrakul

Introduction

The Association of Southeast Asian Nations (ASEAN) comprises ten countries south of China and east of India. Together, by 2011 estimates, ASEAN has more than 600 million people and a gross domestic product (GDP) of more than $2.2 trillion, the sixth largest GDP in the world.[1] The ASEAN Economic Community (AEC) to be formed in 2015 is the natural next step in ASEAN's economic transformation. The ASEAN Free Trade Area (AFTA) was established in 2010 to increase intra-regional trade by reducing all tariff barriers. The AEC's main objective is to promote the free flow in the region of five essential economic drivers—goods, services, investments, capital, and skilled labor—to strengthen ASEAN's competitiveness as a single production base.

Despite ASEAN's motto—"One Vision, One Identity, and One Community"—its members are at considerably different stages of economic development. Singapore and Brunei are the rich city-states with small, aging populations. The "ASEAN-4"—Indonesia, the Philippines, Thailand, and Malaysia—are middle-income countries that have long had market-based economies. Cambodia, Laos, Myanmar, and Vietnam—the CLMV countries—are low-income countries that previously had centrally planned economies. In 2012, the ASEAN-4 represented ASEAN'S critical mass; it had more than 70 percent of its population and more than 65 percent of total GDP, as shown in Figure 7.1. To narrow the gap and to spur equitable economic growth, the Master Plan on ASEAN Connectivity was adopted in October 2010.[2] The plan mapped physical infrastructure linkages in three areas: transportation, information and communications technology (ICT), and energy. It envisioned more intra-regional-oriented economies, urbanization, and infrastructure buildup. More than half a trillion dollars are needed to build these linkages and ASEAN-4's infrastructure needs, mainly for road, rail, and power, by 2020[3] (see Figure 7.1).

Because of its diversity in GDP, populations, and demographic patterns, ASEAN's integration offers great economic opportunities. The CLMV countries present the last investment frontiers in Asia. The ASEAN-4 are newly industrialized and emerging consumer countries following Japan's early development pattern. ASEAN's aggregate economy is sizable owing to its large working-age population rather than a high per capita income. Situated between China and India, ASEAN is emerging as the core of Asian regionalism and at the crossroads of the world's most vibrant economies.

Unlike the European Union (EU), ASEAN has no monetary union, common currency, or central ruling body. It has operated through consensus and informality since its establishment on August 8, 1967. ASEAN's institutional weakness is also its strength; it has served as a neutral platform for China, the EU, and the United States to partner comfortably. In fact, ASEAN has become "ASEAN + 6" after the bloc concluded separate bilateral free trade agreements (FTAs) with the other big Asia-Pacific countries—China, India, Japan, South Korea, Australia, and New Zealand. The United States has been pursuing a "pivot to Asia" policy and is trying to conclude the Trans-Pacific Partnership Agreement (TPP) with Asian countries,[4] while the EU has been pursuing FTAs with individual Southeast Asian countries.[5]

In subsequent sections, we will discuss the potential of ASEAN as a trading bloc and single community; efforts at regional connectivity for economic gain; and the plans and opportunities in infrastructure development and urbanization.

ASEAN'S Economic Potential

ASEAN is one of the world's four major trade blocs.[6] With more than 600 million people, collectively ASEAN's GDP was bigger than India's and about 30 percent of China's in 2012.[7] With among the fastest growth rates in emerging markets, ASEAN's GDP is projected to reach more than $3 trillion (or 21% larger than India's) by 2017. ASEAN's average GDP per capita will rise more than 50 percent to $5,800 by 2017, from $3,600 in 2012.[8] Its most populous member, Indonesia, is predicted to overtake

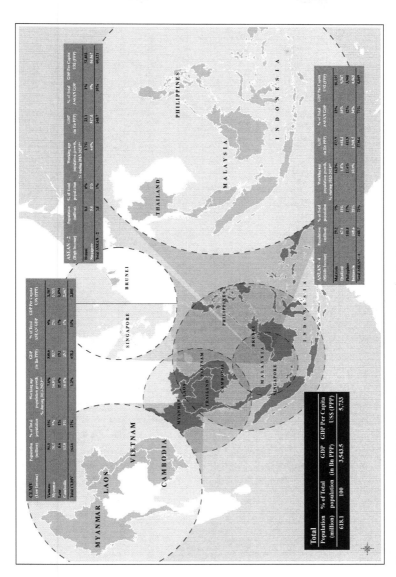

Figure 7.1 Map of ASEAN 2012: Population, GDP, GDP Per Capita

Note: PPP is Purchasing Power Parity. *The total GDP is 5,459 in weighted average.

Sources: 1. CIA World Factbook, 2011.

2. ** Chua et al., 2013, Table 2, p. 4. Copyright © 2014, Pongksak Hoontrakul.

France and the UK as the eighth-largest economy in the world by 2025[9] (see Figure 7.1).

The main growth drivers for ASEAN are favorable demographics, urbanization trends, and structural reform.

First, ASEAN will benefit from a "demographic dividend" of young societies for at least the next 15 years while other Asian countries like China, Japan, and South Korea face the problem of aging populations. In the CLMV countries and in Indonesia, the Philippines, and Malaysia, the working-age populations are growing as a percentage of the total populations. Indonesia, Philippines, and Vietnam—the top three populous nations representing over 70 percent in ASEAN—had population of 249 million, 104 million, and 91 million, respectively in 2012[10] with population growth of 17.6 percent, 10.9 percent, and 7.8 percent for the next 10 years.[11] The three nations' productive workers are more than 65 percent of their population and young with an average age of around 32 years.[12] On the other hand, China and South Korea have about 4 percent population growth during 2013–2023 with their median age over 42 years by 2030.[13] Worse is Japan where the population will shrink further by 2.3 percent during the same period with its median age well over 50 years by 2030.[14] In short, ASEAN has the strongest workforce in Asia second to India.

Second, the percentage of people living in cities in Southeast Asia is expected to grow to 55 percent (351 million) by 2025, from 47 percent (264 million) in 2010.[15] With the growth of middle classes in the cities, business opportunities are huge in the consumer market and are even better for infrastructure buildup in property development, power supply, public transport, water supply.

Finally, trade and economic structural reforms have been brought about by AFTA and the AEC. Under AFTA, the average tariff rate on imports fell to zero percent for the ASEAN-4, Singapore, and Brunei in 2010 and to 1.69 percent for the CLMV countries in 2012.[16] The AEC will bring about a second economic transformation. Its main theme is connectivity for competitiveness. The business implications for ASEAN may be viewed in three perspectives: as producers, consumers, and facilitators.

As Producers

For centuries, Southeast Asia was viewed only on the supply side, as a source of commodities and producer of basic goods for Western consumption. Japan became a leading industrialized nation from the 1970s. As Japanese wages became expensive, labor-intensive and low-value-added industries like textile and assembly works left Japan for other

Asian countries. In the 1980s, South Korea and Taiwan followed Japan's model of export-led industrialization. So did Thailand, Malaysia, and Singapore. Newly industrialized countries are trading up into the international merchandise supply chains like the "flying geese patterns" (see Figure 7.2) according to an international division of labor, specialization, and technological development.[17] In other words, industrialization continuously spreads from the more-advanced to the less-advanced countries in order to take comparative advantages of the gaps in wages, land prices, and resources. However, after the 1997 Asian financial crisis the ASEAN-4 selected political/economic stability policy as their top priority over rapid economic advancement at all costs.[18]

In the World Economic Forum's Global Competitiveness Report 2012–2013, Singapore ranked second in the world; the ASEAN-4's rankings varied from 25th (Malaysia) to 65th (the Philippines); and the CLMV countries all fell below the 74th rank, as shown in Figure 7.3. Although macroeconomic stability is better in most ASEAN countries than in Europe, their performance in the report's 12 "pillars" of competitiveness is inconsistent across dimensions, as shown in Figure 7.3[19]. The CLMV countries are not on the world business map. The ASEAN-4 has lost its competitiveness to China in some low-value and labor-intensive industries including clothing, footwear, office machines, and electronic

Figure 7.2   Flying Geese Patterns
Source: Done by Author. Copyright © 2014, Pongsak Hoontrakul.

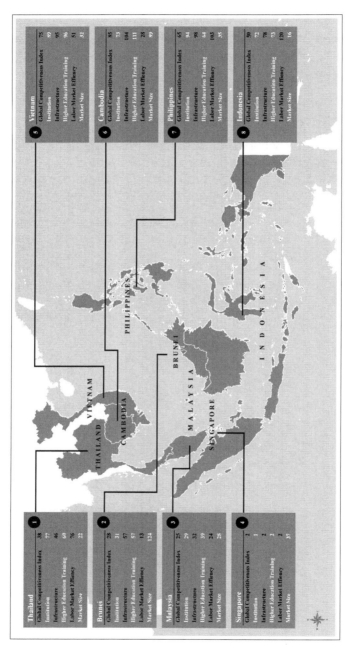

Figure 7.3 Map of ASEAN's Competitiveness Landscape

Source: Geiger, 2013. Copyright © 2014, Pongsak Hoontrakul.

assembly. The ASEAN-4 retains its core basic strength in commodities and some industrial sectors. Internationally, Thailand is still competitive in some sectors like automobile and road vehicle parts, primary plastic, chemicals, and food processing.[20] Malaysia relies more on soft commodity exports like palm oil and crude rubber. Indonesia's exports are more of hard commodities like coal, metals, and minerals. The ASEAN-4 also has realized more significant potential in service industries during the past decade.[21] Thailand and Malaysia enjoy a travel and tourism boom, while the Philippines has become the world's largest voice business processing outsource.[22]

ASEAN established AFTA and then the AEC to shore up competitive weaknesses among its members according to its Master Plan on ASEAN Connectivity in 2011. Essentially, the plan calls for three types of connectivity: people-to-people (e.g., for tourism, education, and culture), physical connectivity (e.g., via air, land, and sea along with ICT and power networks), and institutional connectivity (e.g., trade liberalization and law and regulations harmonization, especially on trade and investment).[23] AFTA and the AEC are catalysts for "creative destruction"[24] to drive out weak firms or industries and to consolidate or to create new innovative, strong, and competitive ones. The Master Plan aims to facilitate this process by improving logistics networks and institutional supports. ASEAN'S competitiveness as a whole has risen in recent years owing much to the progress made by the bottom-tier countries. On average, ASEAN as a whole increase, for example, its competitive ranking in the world from 45th in 2010 to 38th in 2013 after effective AFTA.[25] One hope AEC will be another round of catalyst would further boost ASEAN's competitiveness and hence social welfare.

Wages and land prices began to rise in China because of unfavorable demographics and rapid urbanization. Monthly industrial estate rental in Shenzhen, China, in 2012 was, for example, about USD 4.75 per square meter that was over ten times than in Ho Chi Minh, Vietnam, and twice over in Manila, Philippines.[26] Minimum wages in Shenzhen, China, was about USD 240 per month in 2012, for instance, is about five times than in Ho Chi Minh, Vietnam, and 50 percent more in Jakarta, Indonesia.[27] The wage gap between ASEAN and China should remain wide as ASEAN enjoys demographic dividend in decades to come.[28] More foreign direct investment (FDI) from China, Japan, and newly industrialized countries have been pouring into ASEAN. In 2012, FDI to China peaked at $121 billion (2.5 % year-on-year growth); ASEAN-bound FDI continued to close the gap with China at $111.3 billion (2.5 % year-on-year growth).[29] Despite the US quantitative easing (QE) tapering and initial capital outflow shock, Japanese industries decided to relocate more high-value-added plants into ASEAN, particularly Thailand.[30] These industries had plentiful liquidity as the Bank of Japan aggressively expanded its own QE while the Japanese government's "Abenomics" policy directed private firms to invest overseas with a target of 35 trillion yen ($350 billion) by 2020.[31] Indeed, ASEAN is on the verge of a fixed asset investment (FAI) upswing, especially to Singapore, the ASEAN-4, and Vietnam.

As Consumers

In the wake of the 2008 global financial crisis, like China, ASEAN has been rebalancing its economies to be more oriented toward domestic consumption and trade with its neighbors rather than with the West. The opening up of the CLMV countries and urbanization trends are adding large numbers of new consumers to ASEAN every day. On the demand side, as people achieve higher incomes, their consumption shifts from beyond basic needs toward discretionary and value-added consumer services. The estimated consumer market for the more than three billion people in Asia ex-Japan should reach $25 trillion by 2020; at least a fifth of that market, or $5 trillion, will be in ASEAN.[32] In ASEAN, Indonesia, the Philippines, and Malaysia will benefit from the demographic dividend—increasing middle-class and working-age populations with more propensity to consume.[33] Among emerging consumers in Indonesia and China, the young (18- to 29-year-olds), who typically have higher education and incomes than older people (46- to 55-year-olds), spend more on discretionary items such as brand products and property.[34] As in India, rural consumption in the ASEAN-4 is growing faster than urban consumption as the result of spillover effect from migrant workforces and "trickle-down" prosperity.[35] These rural consumers are more willing to spend on small-ticket items like watches, sportswear, and cheap smartphones to improve their quality of life, while basic necessities like food, education, and health care are still the largest components of spending.[36] This presents a great opportunity for businesses.

Retail trade is being reshaped by the rising affluence and infrastructure levels. In the first stage, traditional mom-and-pop stores are prevalent in lower-income (less than $5,000 per capita per year) and poor-infrastructure environments, leading to low trade by modern retailers (such as convenience stores and hypermarkets) as a percentage of total retail trade.[37] Modern retail stores such as in Thailand and Malaysia emerge when the GDP per capita reaches middle-income level ($5,000 to $20,000) and moderate infrastructure has been built up. Of total retail trade in Thailand and Malaysia, 35 percent and 10.3 percent, respectively, is accounted for by convenience stores, and 37 percent and 66 percent, respectively, by hypermarkets.[38] E-commerce in Thailand, Indonesia, and the Philippines is still limited by infrastructure and logistic bottlenecks.[39]

The automobile sector provides an insight into durable goods or big-ticket spending patterns in the ASEAN-4—and the huge potential. ASEAN car penetration in four-wheel-drive vehicles per 1,000 people (VPTP) has been drastically increased in recent years. Sales have increased more rapidly in Thailand than in the other ASEAN-4 countries. In 2012, Thailand's car penetration rate was close to 190 VPTP. Indonesia's demand increased steeply from 1996 to 2012, while the Philippines is just beginning to have sizable car sales. Specifically, in 2012, Indonesia had around 70 VPTP compared to Philippines' rate of less than 30 VPTP. There are plenty of more rooms to grow as they are getting richer from FAI-driven industrialization and, in turn, more urbanization. Also, Thailand is projected to produce three million autos by 2017.[40] Thailand is pushing ahead with an eco-car program while Malaysia is offering strong incentives and subsidies in order to become an energy-efficient vehicle hub for the region.[41] Because of the domestic critical mass sales growth in Indonesia and Thailand, Japanese automakers have relocated their plants to these two countries and use them as hubs for regional distribution.

Economic Gains from Greater Connectivity

A facilitator or middleman is very important to the challenge of tapping fast-growing business opportunities in frontier markets like the CLMV countries. Singapore, Thailand, and Malaysia have high potential as facilitators to link these countries with the rest of the business world. They can provide benefits in:

Financial Services

The more developed the financial system, the more efficiently it allocates resources to needed sectors. In late 2013, the total of the equity capitalization markets in the ASEAN-4 exceeded $1.5 trillion, second to China's market within the emerging markets universe.[42] The ASEAN-4 had a $3 billion daily trading volume; Thailand, with a $392 billion market size, accounted for $2 billion daily trade, the highest turnover in ASEAN. Thailand and Malaysia have greater financial depth than the rest of ASEAN except for Singapore.[43] In contrast, CLMV stock (and bond) markets are extremely small with very few listed firms. While Vietnam's economy was about half of Thailand's in late 2013, its equity market was less than 10 percent of Thailand's—though it is much bigger than the sum of the rest of the CLMV countries.[44] This is likely due to the lack of institutional supports (e.g., legal and tax structures and pension funds) in the CLMV countries and the lack of economies of scale and of scope. Occasionally, CLMV firms that have their primary assets and income in the CLMV region have to raise funds overseas. For example, Yoma Strategic Holdings Ltd did a reverse takeover in a Singapore Exchange-listed shell company in 2006 to raise funds to build its real estate conglomerate in Myanmar.[45]

The CLMV banking industry is minimal in both scale and scope since the economies are predominantly cash-based.[46] Checks, automatic teller machines (ATMs), and internally accepted letters of credit from local banks are rare. Because none of the CLMV currencies is internationally convertible, Thai baht and dollars are extensively accepted at shops. Since these countries frequently experience high inflation and financial instability, their currencies often fluctuate, generally with a high depreciation bias. Foreign investors in the CLMV countries should find financing outside of the CLMV group, perhaps in Thailand, Singapore, and possibly Malaysia. The Bangkok-based construction firm Ch Karnchang Plc, for instance, raised $1,581 million to finance construction of the Nam Theun 2 hydropower dam near Vientiane, Laos, for electricity export to Thailand. The loans were syndicated among Thailand's top six commercial banks—a good model for sustainable banking in ASEAN.[47]

Although the AEC encourages all ASEAN central bankers to work toward financial and banking integration, full banking liberalization in the CLMV region is still a long way off. But all the big commercial banks from the ASEAN-4 and Singapore maintain presence in the CLMV region to serve the basic needs of companies.

Land Bridge Connectivity

Thailand is located in the heart of ASEAN, and at the crossroads of China and India. Particularly for the Greater Mekong Subregion, all physical infrastructures that connect countries—whether highways, railways, power grids, or telecommunications lines—have to go through Thailand (see Figure 7.4). When China's outgoing Premier Wen Jiabao and incoming Premier Li Keqiang separately visited Thailand in a span of less than one year (in November 2012 and October 2013, respectively), they had one aim in common: to pursue two multibillion-dollar high-speed train linkages between the two countries as part of the Greater Mekong Subregion's North South Economic Corridor. The first line, of about 600 kilometers,

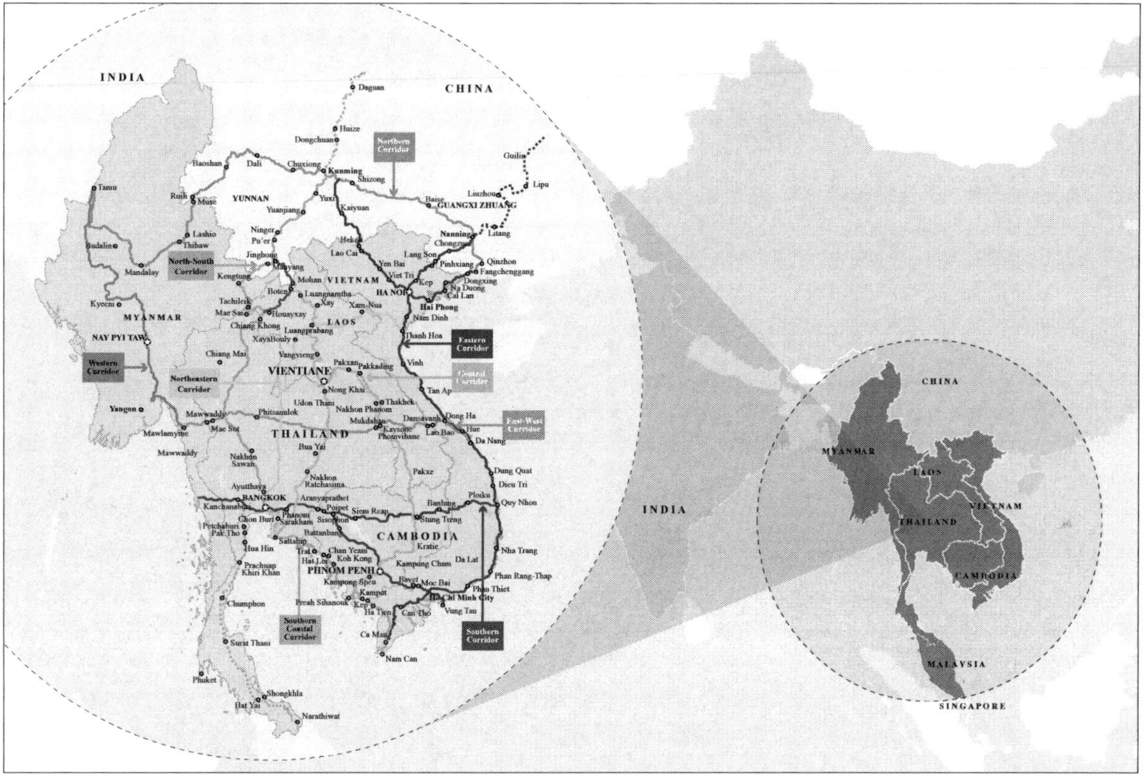

Figure 7.4 Greater Mekong Subregion—GMS Economic Corridors

Source: Asian Development Bank, 2012. Copyright © 2014, Pongksak Hoontrakul.

is to connect Kunming in southwestern China with Chiang Mai in north-ern Thailand and the second line, of about 450 kilometers, is to connect Kunming with Nong Khai in northeast Thailand via Laos.[48]

Indeed, China is now ASEAN's biggest trade partner with 600 percent growth over the last decade; the China–AFTA agreement is the world's third largest FTA between a country and an economic bloc; they are aim-ing for bilateral trade of $1 trillion by 2020.[49]Although China accounted for only $4.4 billion in investment in ASEAN in 2012, this represented a 52 percent increase year-on-year.[50] The trend is expected to continue as Chinese wages and land prices rise sharply.

When Indian Prime Minister Manmohan Singh visited Myanmar in June 2012 as part of a new "Look East" policy to counter Chinese influence, India offered Myanmar a $500-million grant to participate in a 3,200-kilometer trilateral highway running from Moreh, in India's northeast, to Bagan, Myanmar, and on to Mae Sot in western Thailand.[51] A 1,600-kilometer road will be built to accommodate container trucks in Myanmar and about 71 bridges on the Tamu-Kalewa Friendship Road in Myanmar will be repaired by Indian account.[52] The project reportedly can be completed within four years. This signifies the importance of the East–West Economic Corridor and recognizes Thailand as the gateway to the CLMV countries and ASEAN. India seeks to increase trade with ASEAN from $80 billion in 2013 to $200 billion by 2022, and has offered to build a $120 million port in Sittwe on the Myanmar coast to shorten the maritime logistics between Myanmar/ASEAN and India.[53]

After it ended nearly 50 years of isolation in 2011, Myanmar and its rich natural resources have attracted the attention of neighboring coun-tries eager to achieve energy security. Myanmar, which took over the chair of ASEAN in 2014, awarded 20 offshore oil and gas exploration licenses that year. The biggest awards went to its two largest foreign investors, China with $14 billion worth of deals and Thailand with $10 billion.[54] ASEAN would like to build a regional power grid using the existing net-work in Thailand to tap Myanmar's energy sources. China is completing a $1.5-billion oil pipeline and a $1-billion gas pipeline from Kyauk Phyu seaport across Myanmar to Kunming, southern China.[55] India is propos-ing together with the United States to build a super power grid stretching from India to Southeast Asia.[56]

Outside the CLMV region, another intriguing development is the Iskandar Development Region (IDR) in Nusajaya, Johor, on Malaysia's southern border with Singapore, as illustrated in Figure 7.5. The IDR's land size is three times that of land-starved Singapore. The idea is for Singapore's low-to-medium-value-added industries to relocate to the IDR, so Singapore can concentrate on upgrading to a knowledge- and

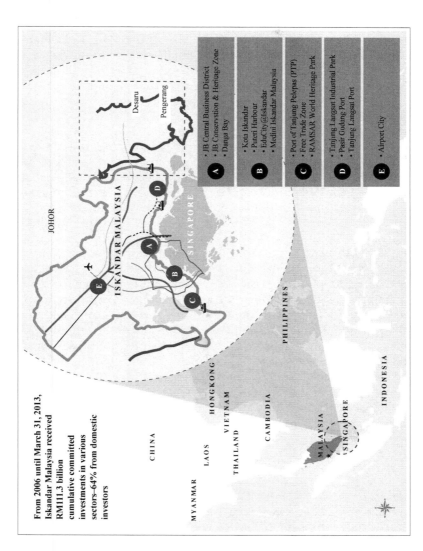

Figure 7.5 Iskandar Project by UEM Land Holdings Bhd. Malaysia

Source: Presentation from UEM Land KL, and done by Author. Copyright © 2014, Pongksak Hoontrakul.

services-based economy. For Malaysia, the IDR attracts foreign investors, expedites infrastructure buildup, and creates high-wage jobs, in following the government's Economic Transformation Program. Also, Singapore and Malaysia announced in February 2013 a plan to build a 40-billion Malaysian ringgit ($12.3 billion) high-speed rail line connecting Kuala Lumpur with Singapore in 90 minutes. Expected to open in 2020, it is potentially a "game changer." The enhanced flow of people and businesses will impact sectors including real estate, aviation, hospitality, the gaming business, and manufacturing in the medium to long term.[57]

A total of more than 111 billion ringgit ($34 billion) in investments was committed for the IDR project from 2006 until March 31, 2013. Forty percent of this has been spent in development, mainly in the property development and manufacturing sectors. Specifically, total investment in the top three sectors—manufacturing, property and government—was realized exceedingly by USD 6 billion, USD 3 billion, and USD 2 billion, respectively by June 2012.[58] The IDR's key economic indicators and projections indicate the population in the area will reach three million by 2025 representing 5.8 percent growth target with 9 percent growth job creation during 2010–2025.[59] The project is similar to the development of Shenzhen bordering Hong Kong under China's Special Economic Zone policy. (See case study of The Iskanda Project and Lessons from Shenzhen.) A 10-billion ringgit ($3 billion) rail system between Johor and Singapore and a 60-billion ringgit ($18.5 billion) rail system in Klan Valley will be constructed soon. These are needed to accommodate the IDR's projected population increase from 1.6 million in 2010 to 3 million in 2025.[60] Also noteworthy is that UEM Land, Malaysia's largest property developer, owns 5,833 acres of land bank in Iskanda for development.[61] The Iskandar Investment Board, which is majority-owned by Khazanah Nasional Bhd., Malaysia's sovereign wealth fund, owns about 2,008 acres.[62] This is a joint public–private partnership with UEM Land as the main project manager and master developer.[63]

The "Sweet Spot" in Urbanization

Urbanization is a natural result of the economies of agglomeration (e.g., economies of scale and greater specialization) in an industrialized country. Massive infrastructure buildup, especially in the ASEAN-4 and Vietnam, would create multiple decades of virtuous cycles of productivity growth by reducing logistics costs, power consumption, and travel times.

ASEAN's urbanization level is currently in "sweet spot." Urbanization's benefits follow a bell curve trend line. As a country progresses through the 40 percent urbanization line, it generally will achieve peak real per capita GDP growth of close to 8 percent. In 2012, the urbanization rates for Vietnam (33%), Thailand (36%), Indonesia (45%), and Philippines (50%) were in the sweet spots ranging from 30 percent to 50 percent.[64] The growth of ASEAN's consumer markets is linked to urbanization and its corresponding rising incomes and middle classes. Internet penetration, mobile device subscriptions, ownership of electrical appliances, and water usage are examples of potential market size and growth as a function of urban density.[65] More importantly, urban agglomeration improves efficiencies in delivering better education to create a pool of workers for higher-value industries. In short, urbanization improves productivity and creates wealth.

If ASEAN's income is to double in the next 10 years as projected, the demand for infrastructure will drastically increase by well over half a trillion dollars in the ASEAN-4 alone.[66] The breaks down of the infrastructure needs in the ASEAN-4 are similar to the heavy need in building up most in power and next in land transportation—road and railways capacity. About 40 percent of the demand for infrastructure investment is for ASEAN's most populous and largest economy, Indonesia, particularly for power (USD 99 billion), roads (USD 52 billion), and highways (USD 50 billion).[67] About $100 billion each is necessary for Thailand and Malaysia to boost infrastructure investment—about USD 40 billion each for power and USD 65 billion each for road and railways to enhance manufacturing capacity and productivity.[68] The Philippines requires the highest percentage of GDP in infrastructure investment with similar investment requirement with Thailand.[69]

With high private saving rates and room to broaden tax revenue bases, it is not too difficult to finance infrastructure in the ASEAN-4. The need for government funding is feasible due to low public debt.[70] Government burdens could be eased considerably by public–private partnership schemes. Under the Indonesian government's new promotion program for private–public partnerships, Japan's J-Power Consortium in 2013 won the bidding to build a 2,000-MW coal power plant in Central Java that will provide electricity for eight million people in three years.[71] In December 2013, Indonesia issued a list of 27 public–private partnership projects in infrastructure worth more than $47.3 billion—including rail, power generation, roads, and port construction—for public tender in the following year. In 2014, China Railway Construction Corp. was to sign an estimated 225-trillion-rupiah ($19.6 billion) public–private partnership deal for the Sunda Strait Bridge connecting Indonesia's islands of Sumatra and Java.[72] Furthermore, in 2014, the Indian–Philippine consortium Megawide-GMR Group won a 17.5-billion peso ($390 million) concession under a new public–private partnership program to build and operate the Philippines' second busiest airport, Mactan Cebu International Airport.[73] These are encouraging signs.

Welcoming Passengers and Textile Plants

"ASEAN Open Skies" Policy

Tourism creates high-wage jobs in the tertiary sector and has a large multiplier effect in the economy. In 2007, ASEAN agreed to the ASEAN Single Aviation Market, commonly known as the "ASEAN Open Skies" policy,[74] to be established in 2015 in time for the AEC. Under the policy, an ASEAN airline has the right to fly from its home country to other countries with unlimited passengers (or cargo) and to fly into and out of an airport of another ASEAN country without intergovernmental approval as long as the flight ends in the originating country.[75] The policy allows ASEAN-based shareholders to own up to 70 percent of an ASEAN airline, up from the previous 49 percent limit. Airlines professionals like pilots are allowed to freely work in other ASEAN countries with proper accreditation (but the domestic routes remain regulated).

Along with the region's few visa requirements, the "Open Skies" policy and the growth of low-cost carriers have opened a dynamic era for travel and tourism in Asia.[76] About 94 million travelers were projected to visit ASEAN countries in 2014, and a 5.8 percent compound annual growth rate was projected for the next five years.[77] The seat capacity of ASEAN low-cost carriers is forecast to grow 20 percent per year until 2016, making their 3.5-hour flight parameter one of the most competitive and busiest routes in the region, if not the world.[78] Air Asia of Malaysia and Lion Air of Indonesia will be among the biggest beneficiaries. Jakarta Soekarmo-Hatta International Airport is set to be the busiest airport in Southeast Asia, followed closely by Singapore's Changi Airport, Bangkok's Suvarnabhumi International Airport, and Kuala Lumpur International Airport.

Here, however, ASEAN may become a victim of its own success. There is wariness about possible overdevelopment in tourism in some areas. A more immediate issue is on-ground capacity to accommodate this surge in air travel. Safety procedures and regulations and the availability of hotel rooms and tourism professionals are among the serious shortcomings that need to be addressed. (See exclusive interview with Myanmar's minister of hotels and tourism.) The disappearance of Malaysian Airlines Flight 370 from Kuala Lumpur bound for Beijing on March 8, 2014 highlighted concerns about airport security. The huge disparity among ASEAN countries in airline sizes, airport security standards, and services capacity on the ground will limit the realization of the open skies potential. Cross-border joint ventures along with mergers and acquisitions in the aviation, airport, and related service sectors may strengthen the industry.

Textile Tax Privileges

Development of labor-intensive industries such as textiles is crucial to the CLMV countries to provide jobs and exports and to start up industrialization. The United States has offered duty-free access to its market for textile imports as part of the TPP trade agreement being negotiated among 12 Pacific Rim countries; Vietnam is one of these countries.

Vietnam's textile and garment industry reached a new pinnacle of $20 billion in exports in 2013.[79] This represented an 18.6 percent year-on-year growth.[80] Total exports to the United States grew 15,000 percent from 2000 to 2012 and reached $7.1 billion in 2012 alone.[81]

The US textile industry has filed complaints because most of Vietnam's textile inputs like yarn are forwarded from outside ASEAN, mainly China.[82] Indeed, China has rushed to relocate its plants in Vietnam. Pacific Textiles Group, a fabric producer publicly listed in Hong Kong with market capitalization of HK$15 billion ($1.93 billion) in 2013, planned to have one-third of its operation in Vietnam within 2014. This is a part of the company's strategy to reduce geographical risk and rising labor costs in China and to take advantage of the special exemptions from tariff duties and quotas that exports from Vietnam enjoy or will enjoy from the United States and Japan. As one of the main apparel sources for brands like Victoria Secret, GAP, and WalMart, Pacific Textiles is projected to have sales of more of than HK$10 billion ($1.29 billion) in 2016, a 13 percent year-on-year growth compared with 2015, and a net profit of HK$1.5 billion ($0.2 billion), a 14.27 percent year-on-year growth.[83] Another example is Shenzhou International Group Holdings, one of China's largest textile exporters; it is listed in Hong Kong with a market capitalization of HK$34.6 billion ($4.5 billion) in March 2014.[84] Shenzhou is major fabric and garment producer for brands like Nike, Puma, Adidas, and UNIQLO. It had production bases in China—Ningbo (70% of the production line) and Anhui (15%)—and in Cambodia (15%) at the end of 2013.[85] The company's second-phase expansion in Cambodia started in late 2012. A new plant in Vietnam will open in 2015. Shenzhou International's strategy is to secure at least 80 percent yarn in China and forward it to its local and overseas plants in order to diversify its risks in *renminbi* (RMB) revaluation, and rising wage and land prices.[86] Shenzhou forecast its total sales in 2016 to be 14.3 billion RMB ($2.3 billion), a 12.5 percent year-on-year growth compared with 2015, and net profit to be 2.7 billion RMB ($0.43 billion), a 13.5 percent year-on-year growth.[87]

The ASEAN Way

Unlike the EU, ASEAN does not have a top-down policymaking and implementation body. After nearly a half century of existence, ASEAN still decides by consensus because it places top priority on regional stability and solidarity. ASEAN's diplomacy is based on the principles of noninterference, informality, minimal institutionalization, consultation, and avoidance of confrontation. It can be described as multilateralism for Southeast Asia. Each member is allowed to restructure its economy at its own pace. The ASEAN-4 and the two rich city-states initiate the agendas and time frame, as they did for AFTA and the AEC. The CLMV countries are given time to try to catch up to the rest. The thought is that some may be slower than others, but that with steady progression, everyone would get there. Some say the common objectives are realized too slowly in a fast-changing world. But the ASEAN way is a realistic approach to multilateral relations in a region of diverse economic and political development and cultures. ASEAN's supporters say that if member countries were forced to compromise on the needs of their individual domestic constituencies, the organization would break up.

ASEAN has served well to preserve peace and stability in the region. Slowly but surely, ASEAN now is emerging as an economic pillar and engine for growth for the world.

Case Study

Interview with H. E. U Htay Aung, Minister of Hotels and Tourism, Myanmar

Pongsak Hoontrakul

Q: The country had about half a million visitors in 2011 while its neighbor, Thailand, has over 18 million tourists arriving annually. How will Myanmar promote itself as a tourist destination?

A: When you look at Myanmar's tourism, you will find that it grew 50 percent compared to the previous year. Though the growth is high, the number of arrivals is very few, approximately 400,000 by air in 2011. As international visitors are more curious about Myanmar, naturally the arrivals have been increasing.

As a destination, we can see glimmers of hope, but there are many things to be done in harmony with the growth of tourism. The Ministry of Hotels and Tourism has laid down the tourism policy to focus on systematic development of infrastructure, tourism-related services, human resource development, product development, and so on. Tourism cannot be in a development stage while infrastructure and other services are poor.

At present, FDI hotels (operators) are requested to build four- or five-star hotels. In Bagan and Inlay, leisure or recreation-oriented hotels and resorts are being developed. In Yangon, a commercial city, you can find various types of hotels. Under the Myanmar Investment Law, foreigners can enjoy tax exemption, tax holidays, and other incentives when doing business in Myanmar.

Q: There are many unregulated casino businesses along both the Thai and Chinese borders. What is the official policy going forward? Would you like to legalize gaming and/or to establish integrated resorts like in Vietnam, Cambodia, or Singapore?

A: Casinos are a question mark for us. The hotel investors, especially in the remote areas, are demanding official licenses for this activity. The Gambling Act is still in practice and it is very restricted. However, in the long run, this kind of attraction can entice foreign visitors at hotels in the Special Zones.

Q: Will Myanmar's newly introduced managed float of its currency hinder or foster foreign direct investment and trade in this sector? Will you allow foreign banks to engage in lending and exchanging of local and foreign currency?

A: As Myanmar is not familiar with international monetary systems, it is very difficult to change everything in a short while. The constraints are technology, resource people, skilled staff, and equipment. In the beginning, with the support of the IMF, we have introduced the floating of the currency, which can enhance the interests of FDIs to make investments in the country as there is no exchange control between foreign and local currencies.

For the time being, foreign banks are allowed to open offices in Myanmar and local banks are permitted to accept designated foreign currencies from entrepreneurs. In the future, I think that foreign banks can also engage in the money-changing business. Mitigating these exchange risks needs time. Though the official exchange rate of Myanmar has not been realistic for a long time, FDI hotels have invested here since 1990 and we will ensure that the current changes are very encouraging for the new investors to come.

Q: Are Myanmar's reforms irreversible?

A: We all are very delighted to drive forward. The main reason is that the government, the system, and the direction have been changed since the new administration was established.

The Iskandar Project and Property Development: Lessons from Shenzhen[88]

Pongsak Hoontrakul

To project commercial property development trends in Malaysia's Iskandar project, one can look back at the development since 1979 of China's special economic zone in Shenzhen, bordering Hong Kong's northern New Territories.

Aided by convenient cross-border rail transportation, Hong Kong businesses relocated their low- and medium-value-added production to Shenzen's much cheaper land prices and operating costs. That allowed Hong Kong to transform itself into a high-value-added, services-based economy. This has been a "win–win" formula for both cities for more than three decades.

Shenzhen's population had increased over 3,000 percent in three decades from a mere 330 thousand people in 1980 to 10.5 million people in 2010. Its GDP per capita also leaped 13-fold in the same period from 835 RMB in 1980 to 110,421 RMB in 2010. Consequently, Shenzhen's GDP grew from 27 million RMB (US$43.52 million) in 1980 to 1.3 trillion RMB (US$210 billion) in 2012, a remarkable 30 percent compounded annual growth rate. Below are GDP and population indicators for Shenzhen from 1980 to 2010.

A key measurement of the real estate value trend is the increased passenger traffic at the Lok Ma Chau Spur Line Control Point (immigration) between the two cities. Generally, the higher the traffic is, the higher the real estate prices. Shenzhen residential property demand did not take off materially until the 2000s. Then the Shenzhen secondary residential property price index had more than double its price from June 2007 to March 2013 as traffic flow has also doubled by road at Shenzhen Bay and 2.5 times by rail at Lok Ma Chau Spur Line during the same period. Residential property prices in Shenzhen and the northern New Territories remain robust as one-third of the demand is from Hong Kong and Macau residents. In 2012, housing prices in the northern New Territories were similar to those in downtown Shenzhen, around 40,000 RMB (US$6,446) per square meter. Close to 20 million people crossed the border in 2012, up from 2.1 million in 2002.

The Shenzhen experience indicates that two keys to whether the Iskandar project succeeds may be how efficiently people can travel across the border and whether Malaysia can find enough laborers and professionals to grow Iskanda's GDP.

Notes

1. Edward Teather, "ASEAN Linkages and Why They Matter," *UBS Investment Research*, June 24, 2011: 4.

2. ASEAN, *Master Plan on ASEAN Connectivity* (Jakarta: The ASEAN Secretariat), reprint in January, 2011: 1–91 (http://www.asean.org/resources/publications/asean-publications/item/master-plan-on-asean-connectivity-2).

3. In fact, just ASEAN 4 (e.g., Indonesia, Philippines, Thailand, and Malaysia) already require more than half trillion dollars for infrastructure buildup. See more discussion at Tilton, Andrew et al., "Asia Economics Analyst: ASEAN's Half a Trillion Dollar Infrastructure Opportunity," *Goldman Sachs*, May 30, 2013, Issue no: 13/18, 1–18.

4. Pasha L. Hsieh. "The Roadmap for a Prospective US-ASEAN FTA: Legal and Geopolitical Considerations," *Journal of World Trade*, January 2012: 1–35 (http://works.bepress.com/cgi/viewcontent.cgi?article=1013&context=pasha_hsieh).

5. Alexander Mohr, "A Boost for Thai-EU Relations," *Nation Daily Newspaper*, February 28, 2013 (http://www.nationmultimedia.com/opinion/A-boost-for-Thai-EU-relations-30200854.html).

6. The first three main trade blocs/pillars are 1) EU—European Union, 2) NAFTA—North American Free Trade Agreement and 3) MERCOSUR—the Common Market of the South America.

7. Zheng Kit Wei and Brian Tan, "ASEAN Economic Long View: Singapore Swing-Refocusing on ASEAN Regionalization," *Asia Pacific, Economics, Citi Research*, December 4, 2012: 20 (https://ir.citi.com/Zm%2ffnwe7sD0v9l1rVs xjf00tcmEH6OVl PyAzX9tPdLJ4PVq1eGpHWD%2bxleGmla0xY1FdHpNb Z4A%3d).

8. Ibid.

9. Ibid.

10. Teather, "ASEAN Linkages."

11. Hak Bin Chua et al., "Asia: Demographic Divide & Peaks," *Bank of America Merrill Lynch*, August 23, 2013: Tables 2 and 3, p. 5.

12. Ibid.

13. Ibid.

14. Ibid.

15. Helmi Arman, "ASEAN Economics Long View: Indonesia: En Route to a Top-10 World Economy by 2025," *Asia Pacific, Economics, Citi Research*,

March 20, 2013: 21–22 (https://ir.citi.com/qkmmp1WC%2fe3%2bW5lRWDa qFNK7YrFGd1Psy403a%2fEmpAt2tmrIZinuaCx3Bj%2b7bbTV9k6HYSRM AmU%3d).

16. ASEAN, *ASEAN Economic Community in Chartbook 2012* (Jakarta: ASEAN Secretariat), January 2013: slide no. 15 (http://www.miti.gov.my/cms/documentstorage/com. tms.cms.document. Document_a6d0d796-c0a81573-26-b77801cda8bcf8/AEC%20 Chartbook%202012.pdf).

17. Kaname Akamatsu, "A Historical Pattern of Economic Growth in Developing Countries," *Journal of Developing Economies*, March–August 1962, 1:1, 3–25; and S. Kasahara, "The Flying Geese Paradigm: A Critical Study of Its Application to East Asian Regional Development," *United Nations Conference on Trade and Development, Discussion paper #169*, April 2004.

18. Viktor Shvets and Chetan Seth, "ASEAN 4- Risks & Returns," *Macquarie*, August 16, 2013: 1–63 (https://www.macquarieresearch.com/rp/d/r/publication.do?f=E&pub_ id=7210925&file_name=ASEAN4_160813e157384. pdf&uid=NzQ2MjQ4).

19. Thierry Geiger, "Charting ASEAN's Competitiveness Landscape," *World Economic Forum Blog*, June 6, 2013 (http://forumblog.org/2013/06/charting-aseans-competitiveness-landscape/).

20. Shvets and Seth, "ASEAN 4- Risks & Returns."

21. Ibid.

22. Viktor Shvets and Chetan Seth, "APAC—Competitive Edge: Separating Winners from Losers," *Macquarie*, March 21, 2013: 51–53.

23. More details at ASEAN, *Master Plan*.

24. Creative destruction in the Schumpeter (1942) sense is the capitalism evolution process that gradually and continuously drives out the uncompetitive firm or industry and simultaneously creates a new and innovative firm or industry. See more discussion at Joseph A. Schumpeter, *Capitalism, Socialism and Democracy* (New York: Harper), 1975 [original publication 1942].

25. ASEAN, *ASEAN Economic Community in Chartbook 2012* (Jakarta: ASEAN Secretariat), January 2013: 1–64 (http://www.miti.gov.my/cms/documentstorage/com. tms.cms.document. Document_a6d0d796-c0a81573-26-b77801-cda8bcf8/AEC%20 Chartbook%202012.pdf).

26. Source: Japan External Trade Organization (JETRO) Survey 2012, *Citi Research*; and Wei and Tan, "ASEAN Economic Long View," Fig. 57, p. 37.

27. It should be noted that after 2013, Jakarta had increased its minimum wage toe at USD229/month. And more discussion by Zheng Kit Wei, Jun Trinidad, Helmi Arman, and Brian Tan. "ASEAN Macro Flash: Should We Worry about Wage Inflation in ASEAN?" *Citi Research*, December 3, 2012: Fig. 11, p. 8.

28. Ibid.

29. Zheng Kit Wei, Helmi Arman, and Jun Trinidad, "ASEAN Macro Flash: ASEAN-bound FDI Continued to catch up with China in 2012," *Citi Research*, June 28, 2013: Fig 1, p. 2 (https://ir.citi.com/xmORZempYjFDQL0DcYH-pylJj8CT5yQgOh24Eg7QTOm XUNRr5UAWKfQ%3D%).

30. Raymond Maguire, "Thai Equity Strategy: Will Foreign Manufacturing Shift from Thailand," *Global Research UBS*, March 19, 2014: 1–11.

31. Athaporn Arayasantiparb, "Strategy—Thailand: The Japan Effect And More," *UOBKayHian*, 2014: 1–2 (http://research.uobkayhian.com/content_download.jsp?id= 19512&h=7487db4b18866f75529483d51e31fd49).

32. Ebru Sener Kurumlu et al., "Asia Consumer 2014 Outlook and Strategy," *J.P. Morgan*, January 22, 2014: 1—146 (https://markets.jpmorgan.com/research/ArticleServlet?doc=GPS-1353431 -0&referrerPortlet=EQCASHASIA_accordion).

33. Karim P. Salamatian, "Consume 2013 Outlook: Momentum Change," *Credit Suisse*, January 2, 2013.

34. Ella Nusantoro, Priscilla Tjitra, and Jahanzeb Naseer, "Indonesia Consumer Survey 2014: Small Tickets to a Better Future," *Credit Suisse*, February 18, 2014: 5–6 (https://doc.research-and-analytics.csfb.com/docView?language=ENG&source= ulg&format=PDF&document_id=10296 07411&serialid=96t%2fiJvRXsfm%2baxcYSaB2Z0BlMWKJSUB%2fDzaQgo WCvE%3d).

35. Kurumlu et al., "Asia Consumer 2014," 38–39.

36. Nusantoro et al., "Indonesia Consumer Survey 2014," 6 and Fig. 22 on p. 20.

37. Kurumlu et al., "Asia Consumer 2014," 19.

38. Ibid.

39. Ibid., p. 21.

40. "Thailand close to achieve 3mn auto production milestone," *The Nation*, April 2, 2014 (http://www.nationmultimedia.com/business/Thailand-close-to-achieve-3mn-auto-production-mile-30230641.html).

41. Nalin Viboonchart and Jen Rita, "Malaysia's Eco-Car Ambitions: New National Automotive Policy Envisions the Country as an Energy-Efficient Vehicle Hub, but Even Generous Incentives Might Not be Enough to Woo Big Players to a Small Market," *Bangkok Post*, February 3, 2014.

42. Shvets and Seth, "ASEAN 4- Risks & Returns."

43. Financial depth is defined as total debt and equity of a country as percent of GDP. See more discussion at ibid., pp. 47–48.

44. Ian Gisbourne, "Strategy—Thailand: New frontiers CLMV," *Phatra Securities*, January 17, 2013: 72–75.

45. From company website—http://www.yomastrategic.com/html/about_milestones.php, and more reading on LVMC markets at Gisbourne, "Strategy—Thailand."

46. "Banking in CLMV: Things to know before making an investment," *Bangkok Post*, September 3, 2012 (http://m.bangkokpost.com/business/310561 and http://scbeic.com/ THA/document/topic_bkkpost_banking_clmv/ref:topic_all).

47. Carl Middleton, "Thailand's Commercial Banks' Role in Financing Dams in Laos and the Case of Sustainable Banking," *International Rivers*, 2009: 1–39 (http://www.banktrack.org/manage/ems_files/download/thailand_s_commercial_banks_role_in_financing_dams_in_laos_and_the_case_for_sustainable_banking/110707_sustainablethaibanks_ir_dec09.pdf).

48. Thanida Tansubhapol, "Beijing Eyes Train Deal: Premier Wen Calls for Fair, Open Competition," *Bangkok post*, 2012 (http://www.bangkokpost.com/news/local/322448/beijing -eyes-train-deal).

49. Bao Chang, "China Playing a rising role in ASEAN business," *ChinaDailyAsia*, October 11, 2013 (http://www.chinadailyasia.com/business/2013–10/11/content_15092349.html).
50. Ibid.
51. Tony Arora, "Indian PM Visit Put India Back in Step with Reform Momentum," *Bangkok post*, June 4, 2012 (http://www.bangkokpost.com/business/economics/296453/pm-visit-puts-india-back-in-step-with-reform-momentum).
52. Ibid.
53. Ted Osius et al., "Enhancing India–ASEAN Connectivity," A report of the (Center for Strategic & International Studies) CSIS Sumitro Chair for SE Asia Studies and the Wadhwani Chair for US-India Policy Studies (NY: Rowman & Littlefield), June 2013: 14 (http://csis.org/files/publication/130621_Osius_EnhancingIndiaASEAN_WEB.pdf).
54. Sophie Gong, "Myanmar Awards 20 Offshore Oil And Gas Exploration Tenders," *ibtimes*, March 26, 2014 (http://www.ibtimes.com/myanmar-awards-20-offshore-oil-gas-exploration-tenders-1563719).
55. Carl Berrisford, "Asia Pacific Equities: Myanmar in Transition," *UBS*, 2012: 1–11.
56. Osius et al., "Enhancing India-ASEAN Connectivity," 17.
57. Joy Wang, Simone Yeoh, Sumedh Samant, and Hoy Kit Mak, "ASEAN Property: Crouching Lion, Hidden Dragon," *J.P. Morgan*, April 28, 2013: 8.
58. Ibid., p. 9.
59. Ibid.
60. Ibid.
61. Ibid., pp. 30–31.
62. Ibid.
63. Ibid., pp. 27–39.
64. Alexander Redmand and Fan Cheuk Wan, "Opportunities in an Urbanizing World," *Emerging Market Research Institute, Credit Suisse*, 2012: 1–52 (https://publications.credit-suisse.com/tasks/render/file/index.cfm?fileid=88E9D3D8 -83E8-EB92 -9D5DAF8ECA39029A).
65. Ibid.
66. Tilton et al., "Asia Economics Analyst: ASEAN's Half a Trillion Dollar Infrastructure Opportunity."
67. Ibid.
68. Ibid.
69. Ibid.
70. Ibid.
71. "Indonesia's Infrastructure Investments: Finally Taking Off," IFC (http://www.ifc.org/wps/wcm/connect/region__ext_content/regions/east+asia+and+the+pacific/news/indonesia+infrastructure+investments) and more details at Shamin Razavi and Bintang Hidayanto, "Power Projects in Indonesia You Should Know," *Asian-Power*, October 21, 2013 (http://asian-power.com/project/commentary/power-projects-in-indonesia-you-should-know-about).

72. IFC, "Indonesia's Infrastructure Investments."
73. Miguel R. Camus, "Megawide-GMR may bag P17.5bn PPP deal," *Philippine Daily Inquirer,* December 13, 2013, (http://business.inquirer.net/156125/megawide-gmr-may-bag-p17–5b-ppp-deal).
74. See more discussion for all nine types of aviation freedom at Mohshin Aziz and Jaroonpan Wattanawong, "ASEAN Open Skies: What is it, What it Means to US?," *Maybank Kim Eng,* June 21, 2013: 1–7.
75. Alan Khee-Jin Tan, "Toward a Single Aviation Market in ASEAN: Regulatory Reform and Industry Challenges," *ERIA Discussion Paper Series,* October, 2013: 1–42, (http://www.eria.org/ERIA-DP-2013–22.pdf).
76. Michael Beer and Vivan Tao, "Southeast Asia Transportation," *Citi Research,* 2014: Fig. 48, p. 34.
77. Ibid., Figs 79 and 80, p. 44.
78. Ibid.
79. "Vietnam's Textile Exports Set for Strong Growth in 2014," *Viet Nam News and AsiaNewsNet,* January 7, 2014 (http://asianewsnet.net/Vietnams-textile-exports-set-for-strong-growth-in – 55833.html).
80. Ibid.
81. Michaela D. Platzer. "US Textile Manufacturing and the Trans-Pacific Partnership Negotiations," *Congressional Research Services,* November 20, 2013: 16–17 (https://www.fas.org/sgp/crs/row/R42772.pdf).
82. Ibid.
83. Eva Wang and Kenny Lau, "Pacific Textile Group," *Credit Suisse,* November 25, 2013.
84. Becky Han. "Shenzhou International Group Holdings: Solid 2013 Results: Vietnam Expansion on Track", *Standard Chartered,* March 25, 2014.
85. Leon Chik, Andrew Hsu, and Ebru Sener Kurumlu, "Shenzhou International: Headwinds to Growth Dissipating," *J.P. Morgan,* September 23, 2013: 1–22.
86. Ibid., p. 6.
87. Han, "Shenzhou International Group Holdings."
88. This is an excerpt from Wang, "ASEAN Property," pp. 40–44.

8

Asia's Energy Innovation after Shale Gas Revolution

Chanathip Pharino and Pongsak Hoontrakul

Introduction

Conventional fossil fuels form the backbone of today's energy supply. Reserves are diminishing and these fuels damage the environment and cause climate change. Thailand and its fellow Association of Southeast Asian Nations (ASEAN) members are facing challenges on developing alternative, renewable sources of energy and find additional reliable sources of energy in order to achieve long-term sustainable growth and energy security.

Like many ASEAN countries, Thailand still heavily relies on conventional energy sources. In 2010, when its economy grew 7.8 percent, for example, the ratio of the nominal value of Thailand's energy consumption to gross domestic product (GDP) was 17.8 percent.[1] Expenditures on energy imports accounted for 9 percent of the GDP. The value of total energy imports increased 19.8 percent over 2009. In 2010, the country's electricity generation used the following fuels: natural gas, 72 percent; coal/lignite, 18 percent; hydropower, 3 percent; electricity import and exchange, 4 percent; oil, 0.4 percent; and others, 2 percent.[2] Renewable energy development in Thailand, despite its strong growth in recent years, accounted for less than 10 percent of the total electricity generation annually.

As of 2013, ASEAN and Asia's economy appear to be in an upward trajectory, which in turn implies growth of energy demand. To supplement conventional fossil fuels, many countries start investing in renewable energy through green economy initiatives. Importing of energy in various forms and means also becomes crucial. One of the most favored choices of energy imports is in the form of liquefied natural gas (LNG) imported via LNG carriers through regasification terminals. Importing gas from producers located in remote areas is often more economical through LNG chain unless onshore pipeline can be constructed with high confidence in pipeline operational security.

This chapter will start with a discussion of shale gas and its future and potential impacts on ASEAN and Asia's economy. A brief discussion of green economy in ASEAN and Asia is then followed by an overview of key renewable energy sources and summary of their potential to support sustainable growth of the region. Cooperation among ASEAN and Asia countries is of vital importance to the success of sustainable economic development of the region. This topic is also discussed in this chapter.

Over the last few decades, there has been significant development in drilling and hydraulic fracturing technology. These developments make it economically feasible today to produce natural gas (mostly methane) from shale layer located deep underground. Shale Gas has significant potential to become a major energy contributor.

The Energy Information Administration (EIA) published a study outlining shale gas reserves in 33 countries worldwide (see Figure 8.1). It estimated global technically recoverable reserves (TRR) at 6,600 trillion cubic feet (tcf).[3] This is an extremely promising level of TRR for natural gas, equivalent to approximately 60 times the current global consumption at 113 tcf.[4] However, several studies since then have estimated lower TRRs. China, for example, estimated the TRR of its shale gas at 886 tcf, approximately 30 percent lower than the EIA estimate.[5] However, this reduced estimate still pointed to significant reserve of shale gas with strong potential to sustain economic growth while renewable energy industry is being developed.

Recent successes in the United States show that shale gas can be produced economically. There remain some concerns over potential environmental impacts of hydraulic fracturing and chemical involved in the process. However, with sufficient safeguards and regulations, risks to environmental damage can be quantified and mitigated. Shale gas, either produced locally or imported via LNG carriers, offers an exciting potential solution to today's increasing energy demands of ASEAN and Asian countries.

The Future of Shale Gas in Asia

The emergence of shale gas as a viable energy source in the United States has opened up the possibility of low-cost natural gas supply. US shale gas production increased drastically from a negligible level in 2001 to

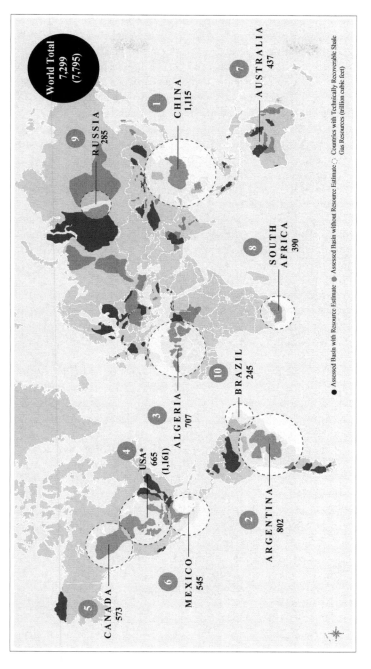

Figure 8.1 Top Ten Countries with Technically Recoverable Shale Gas Resources

Note: *EIA estimates used for ranking order. ARI estimates in parentheses.

Source: "Technically Recoverable Shale Oil and Shale Gas Resources: An Assessment of 137 Shale Formations in 41 Countries Outside the United States," Independent Statistics & Analysis, US Energy Information Administration (EIA), US Department of Energy, June 2013 (http://www.eia.gov/analysis/studies/worldshalegas/pdf/over-view.pdf). Copyright © 2014, Pongksak Hoontrakul.

approximately 7.5 tcf in 2011. This produces two major impacts: (1) A significant decrease in the Henry Hub natural gas benchmark and decoupling of the historical linkage with crude oil prices as US's energy production has boomed since 2007,[6] and (2) the United States, a country with a vast reserve of shale gas and a net natural gas importer, is transforming into a net exporter. Net imports of natural gas dropped from a peak of approximately 17 percent of total consumption in 2001 to approximately 6 percent in 2011.[7]

The rise of shale gas production has been most prominent in the United States due to its significant lead in the exploration and production of shale gas reserves and advances in technology. While shale gas offers promising potential, it is important to understand several key aspects of shale gas development and potential impacts:

1. Commercially feasible production of shale gas requires commercially acceptable shale gas reserves, favorable geological conditions, reasonable transportation costs, available market, and/or export facilities and end customers.
2. There are limited available exploration data in many areas.
3. Reserves are not spread around the world but rather concentrated in a few countries, including the United States, China, Argentina, Mexico, Australia, Canada, Algeria, South Africa, Libya, Brazil, and France.
4. We have limited experience in developing shale gas fields. While the United States has been successful, other countries have trailed behind significantly on development of skilled technical personnel and technology. Development of skilled technical personnel, in particular, will take time.
5. The environmental impact of "fracking" can also be significant. "Fracking," or "hydraulic fracturing," involves pumping a large quantity of fracking fluid at high pressure into the well. The main purpose is to create fractures in shale formations and stimulate the natural gas flow. Fracking fluid generally comprises water, sand, and range of chemicals. Fracking can cause contamination of aquifers through direct entry into aquifers via well bore; incorrect disposal of waste fluid on the surface; and migration upward through soil/rock layers. There are means to limit potential damage to the environment such as by using thick concrete casing to enclose the well to prevent fracking fluid entering the aquifer directly or utilizing best-practice storage and disposal of waste fluid.
6. It is no longer in dispute, according to the EIA, that fracking induces seismic activities, although the levels so far have been relatively low.

However, care should be given in cases of shale formations located near fault lines.

7. The release of methane during production of shale gas can be substantial and very harmful to the environment. The key question is the level of released methane. Several studies disagree on this key issue. The EIA estimates the rate of escaped methane per volume of natural gas produced at 2.4 percent. A recent study by the University of Colorado put the estimate at up to 4 percent.[8] This difference is sufficient to turn shale gas from a "clean" to a "dirty" energy source. *The Proceedings of the National Academy of Sciences of the United States of America*[9] reported that a 3.2 percent rate of escaped methane neutralizes the benefit of gas-fired power over coal-fired power. Thus, further research is needed to ensure that shale gas extraction offers real benefit over other energy sources before we move ahead with full-scale production worldwide.

Shale gas can play a vital role supporting the development of renewable energy. It will take some time before renewable energy can compete with conventional energy sources without government subsidies or policy support. Large-scale development of renewable energy infrastructure also takes significant time to build up. In the meantime, low natural gas prices supported by large supplies from shale gas can help supporting growth in energy demands and allow for a gradual, smooth transition to green energy economy.

Another important key characteristic of shale gas (or conventional gas) is the ability to provide baseload supply. Key renewable energy sources, such as solar and wind, are intermittent in nature and so cannot be used as baseload supply. Natural gas can act as the baseload with renewable sources like solar and wind helping to provide peak-load supply. With increasing use of renewable energy in various suitable mixes, the use of conventional energy sources can remain at the same level or even decrease as a proportion of the total consumption.

Current Situation of Shale Gas in ASEAN and Asia

Current data indicate that ASEAN countries do not possess significant reserves of shale gas, although this may change with increasing exploration. In the Asian region, China appears to have the vast majority of shale gas reserve and thus stands to benefit greatly from shale gas exploration and production. Currently, the future of shale gas in ASEAN rests on importing of shale gas via LNG technology from exporting countries or via pipeline from China under an assumption that China may become a net exporter of shale gas in the future.

Shale gas in the form of LNG can be imported in the same way as importing LNG from conventional gas sources. Receiving countries require a regasification terminal that allows off-loading capability, storage, and regasification of the LNG back to the gaseous state. The gas then can be transmitted through pipeline network to end customers. Exporting countries need to construct liquefaction plants (generally referred to as LNG plants) to process natural gas into a liquid form ready for transport. Transportation is done on specially designed LNG tankers (see Figure 8.2). A complete LNG chain typically is a very large investment, often $10 billion or more as of 2013, and requires significant negotiation and contract administration on the sales of LNG.

Although the cost of LNG chain construction and operation is very high, the recent sharp decrease in natural gas prices makes it a viable solution to export and import natural gas. Another way to transport gas over a long distance is a pipeline system. In Asia, as mentioned previously, China has large estimated shale gas reserves and can potentially become a net exporter of natural gas. A pipeline connecting China to ASEAN countries could be built for exportation. Or the existing pipeline (or one under development such as the gas pipeline connecting Myanmar to Kunming) for importing gas into China could be used for exporting in the future.

Among the ASEAN countries, Thailand has a strong lead in reaping the benefits of shale gas. It has been expanding regasification terminals (see Figure 8.2) and has a good network of electrical grids[10] (see Figure 8.3). Thailand could benefit from cheaper natural gas prices (from increase in global gas supply) or direct importation of shale gas LNG. The national oil company PTT is exploring the possibility of investing in shale gas in the United States for importing into Thailand.

Other leading ASEAN and Asia economies are developing LNG regasification terminals. Indonesia began construction of a floating storage and regasification terminal in West Java in 2013. Commercial startup of Malaysia's first LNG regasification terminal in Sungai Udang was expected in April–June 2013. Two other LNG regasification terminals were under construction in Pengarang Johor and LahadDatu. Singapore commissioned its first LNG regasification terminal. Vietnam is developing the ThiVai and Son My LNG regasification terminals, with operations expected to start in 2014 and 2018, respectively. The Philippines Shell Petroleum Corp is exploring the potential of developing an LNG regasification terminal next to its refinery facility in Tabangao, Batangas province.

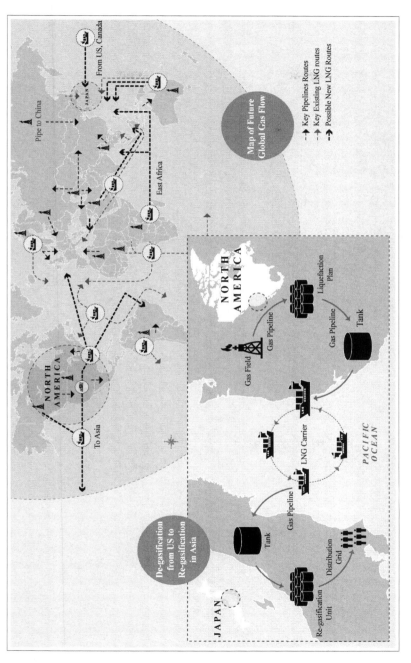

Figure 8.2 Map of Future Global Gas Flow and De-gasification from United States to Re-gasification in Asia

Note: Schematic only; size of arrows not reflective of actual flow; arrow directions indicative only.

Source: 1. Yuen et al. 2. adria-lng.hr, "LNG CHAIN – FROM EXPLORATION TO FINAL CONSUMERS." Copyright © 2014, Pongksak Hoontrakul.

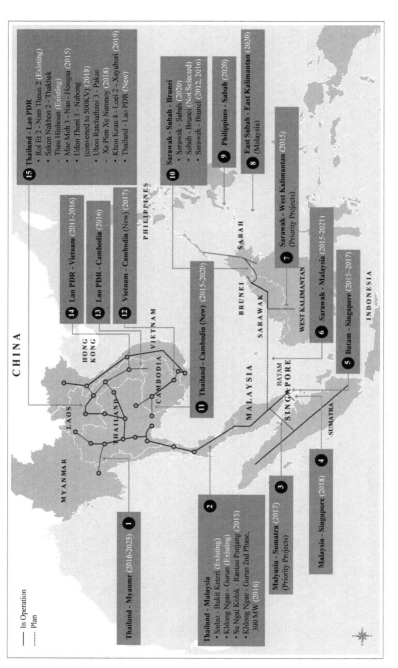

Figure 8.3 Power Grid Connecting ASEAN

Source: 1. Suthep Chimklai, 2013. 2. Electricity Generating Authority of Thailand, "ASEAN POWER GRID." Copyright © 2014, Pongsak Hoontrakul.

Other countries in the region have different priorities and abilities to develop the required infrastructures. Myanmar is focusing on producing oil and natural gas for export and domestic consumption. Cambodia lacks the venues and/or infrastructures to support large-scale LNG importation. They can, however, benefit indirectly from low gas prices and increased supplies from shale gas.

The Green Energy Economy in ASEAN and Asia

A green energy economy aims to reduce reliance on fossil fuels while sustaining economic growth and energy security. Sustainability is a key principle. It means enhancing and maintaining the economy, quality of life, and environment over the long term by integration of these three systems. But it is difficult to achieve sustainability with short- or medium-term investments and plans. Renewable energy investment appears expensive today compared to fossil fuels if we focus on short-term profitability. But if we measure risks and opportunity costs while facing the fact that fossil fuels are limited resources, we may find that renewable energy is a very promising solution.

Conventional hydrocarbons are generally cheaper sources of energy now because over the past century or more, society has made large investments in developing supporting technology, equipment, infrastructures, and logistical network. We have developed great expertise on how to explore, produce, refine, transport, and utilize these products. They are mature industries. Advancements in technologies and infrastructure have dramatically reduced the costs for consumers. The renewable energy industry, on the other hand, is an infant industry. The challenge is to make renewable energy price-competitive with the conventional fuel market by formulating the right strategic plans and supporting policies. We need to identify the most promising renewable sources and make long-term investment in research and development, new technology, infrastructure, and networks.

This investment is most effectively made through government funding of research and development in conjunction with initiatives from private enterprises and educational institutes. The Internet evolved in a similar way: The US government made the initial investment, and subsequent advancements by private enterprises brought the technology to maturity.

Key Renewable Energy Sources

Key alternative or renewable energy sources include wind energy, solar energy, hydroelectric power, nuclear power, and biofuels. Switching to these sources requires strategic investment of capital and time. For ASEAN and Asian countries, the key challenge is: "What types of renewable sources of energy or energy mix can provide energy security for the sustainable future?" In this section, we will explore potentials of key renewable energy sources and how they might be applied or developed for ASEAN and Asian countries. The potentials and limitations of renewable energy in the region are briefly discussed in the section "Green energy economy: In Summary."

Solar Energy: Costs and Consistent Policy Support
Solar energy can be harnessed by using solar modules to convert solar energy directly into electricity (photovoltaic) or by converting solar energy into heat, which is, in turn, used to produce electricity. Electricity generation from solar energy emits, for example, only 30 grams per kilowatt-hour (g/kwh) in greenhouse gas (GHG) compared to 512 g/kwh for natural gas-based generators and 960 g/kwh for coal-based generators.[11] Energy power from diesel source is, for another instance, a heavy polluter—650 g/kwh emission compared to other near-zero emissions like biomass (46), wind power (10), and nuclear power (170), respectively.[12]

ASEAN countries have large areas that are exposed to the sun throughout the year. The energy intensity varies over different areas in Thailand.[13] Thailand has 4 to 6 hours of peak sun per day. Germany, the world leader in solar energy development, has only 2.5 hours. Thus, Thailand has a strong advantage in solar energy development, especially when solar insolation and system price have drastically fallen in recent years.[14] The key issues remain the investment costs and the need for consistent policy support from governments.

In Thailand, developing solar farms with solar panels requires an initial investment of 100 to 200 baht per watt. SPCG, a leading solar energy developer in Thailand, reported that it could build a 6-megawatt (MW) solar farm with an all-in capital expenditure of 600 to 630 million baht. It is worth noting that the costs of solar panels and the land combined account for 90 percent of the expense.

At this cost level, presently it is very difficult to achieve an acceptable rate of return without government support. The cost of solar modules is high partly because of low demand. And demand is low partly because of inconsistent policy support for solar farm developments.

In December 2011, the Lopburi solar power plant in central Thailand, one of the world's largest solar farms using solar panels, started operations with a 73-MW installed capacity, more than twice the installed capacity of the Sirindhorn hydroelectric dam (36 MW). Companies that already hold licenses for solar development are in a strong position because the government has been subsidizing electricity produced by solar energy at very high rates (6.5 baht/kwh since 2010 and 8 baht/kwh before that, compared to 3.5 baht/kwh for wind-produced electricity). However, the industry is still growing quite slowly because of the private sector's lack of confidence in long-term government policy. In 2010, all requests for solar energy contract licenses were suspended and the additional "adders" (subsidies) to all existing applicants that were still waiting for approval were reduced and new requirements for licenses were added. A main reason for this move appeared to be that there were many groups applying for licenses with no actual intention to build solar farms.

For long-term development of the industry, it is essential to establish a permanent independent institution (e.g., a royal-sponsored institution or an independent foundation) that would guide or participate in policy-making, implementation, and monitoring. It should focus on funding for research and development and providing consistent policy in supporting the growth of solar energy. A good model of solar energy-promoting policy is Germany, which allows households to sell back excess electricity generated from rooftop solar installations. Recently in late 2013, Thai Government initiated the program to buy energy generating from solar rooftop. This is a positive and major progress toward future of solar energy adoption.

ASEAN and Asian countries are in good position to take the lead in this field. The countries have the strong engineering bases and workforce skills needed for the production of solar modules and for research and development in solar energy equipment and components.

Wind Energy: Reliability and Scalability

Wind power emits no CO_2 during its operational life and the basic technologies are mature. However, harnessing power from wind commercially can be difficult because of the generally low and variable energy intensity of wind and the need for connection to an existing electrical grid.

For large-scale wind farms, site selection and government policy support are critical. Accessibility and grid connectivity are also main concerns. The west-central and east-central regions of Thailand have sites with good wind speeds (Tanem Range, Lomsak, and Chaiyaphum). These sites are difficult to develop because of their high elevation, difficult terrain, and logistical factors. However, development of wind farms in less-developed areas would create jobs and improve the local economies.

In most parts of Thailand, monsoon patterns make wind speeds either too low or unreliable for wind farm development. Remote rural areas with low wind power (class 4 or lower, see Table 8.1) and poor connection to the national electricity grid should focus on small-scale community

Table 8.1   Wind power classes

	Elevation			
	10 m		50 m*	
Power class	Wind speed m/s	Power density W/m²	Wind speed m/s	Power density W/m²
1	0	0	0	0
2	4.4	100	5.6	200
3	5.1	150	6.4	300
4	5.6	200	7.0	400
5	6.0	250	7.5	500
6	6.4	300	8.0	600
7	7.0	400	8.8	800
	9.4	1000	11.9	2000

Note: *Showing elevation effect based on 1/7 power law.

Source: US DOE Wind Energy Resource Potential, 2006. Copyright © Ministry of Energy.

wind power developments in which small wind turbines are used to support water pumping.

A study conducted in six developing countries including Thailand indicated that wind power can be 2.2 to 4.5 times less expensive to develop than photovoltaic (PV) solar energy. The study, published in the journal *Nature* in April 2012, mentioned the cost gap between the two technologies was expected to continue until at least 2020. Considering that the government's additional adder for small wind farms of less than 50-MW installed capacity is 4.5 baht/kwh compared to 6 baht/kwh for solar farms, wind energy investment can be a more attractive option provided that suitable sites can be found.

The government needs to fund research and development and/or create incentives for the private sector to improve wind turbine technology, in order to achieve higher power output at a lower cost and at a lower wind power class. It is necessary to find sites suitable for mixed land use. For example, an onshore wind farm could be established in agricultural or animal husbandry areas, like those in the Welsh island of Anglesey or in Australia.

Despite the difficulties in developing reliable and cost-effective wind farms, advances in wind turbine technology along with development of an interconnected smart grid offer a promising future for wind power in some countries in ASEAN and Asia.

Hydroelectric Power: Strategic Location and Public Support
Hydroelectric power has been a staple source of energy for many countries in ASEAN and Asia for several decades. Thailand, as an example, has

extensive experience with hydroelectric dams. Dams owned and operated by the Electricity Generating Authority of Thailand (EGAT) accounted for almost 13.2 percent of the country's total electricity-generating capacity in 2007 as per EPPO (2012). In addition to power generation, hydroelectric dams have many other uses including irrigation and flood management, and as tourist attractions. The country's largest multipurpose hydroelectric dam, the Bhumibol Dam, is a very cost-effective generator, according to a 2011 EGAT study.

In most cases, to generate sufficient hydroelectric power, it is necessary to construct a dam with supporting infrastructures. This requires large areas of land upstream to the dam for creation of a reservoir. Many people, forests, and animals must be removed from those areas. As in many other countries, the key issue with developing hydroelectric power in Thailand is public opposition, especially from people living in or around the prospective sites. Thus, future development may be limited to small-scale projects that are the most economical and environmentally friendly. Government needs to raise public awareness of the benefits of hydroelectric dam projects and clearly explain their potential impacts. Also, it is important that local residents are compensated in a transparent and fair manner.

Another key problem with large hydroelectric power projects is that some rivers suitable for such projects in ASEAN flow through more than one country. A prime example is the Mekong River. Building a dam on this river upstream of other countries requires intricate cooperation and negotiation. There is a Mekong River Commission that groups representatives from Thailand, Vietnam, Laos, and Cambodia. The Xayaburi dam project in northwestern Laos has clearly shown the difficulty of developing a joint natural resource. While Laos' government supports the project because the electricity generated from the dam would provide a major source of income, the project has been put on hold since late 2011 because of concerns about potential harm to the environment and to the livelihoods of people living downstream to the dam.[15] Further discussions are required to convince Cambodia and Vietnam that their concerns will be addressed with minimum adverse impacts.

Despite many obstacles, hydropower offers many advantages over other renewable energy sources. Hydropower based on a large hydroelectric dam is more reliable than wind and solar power. Hydropower can serve as the baseload for electricity generating, while wind and solar cannot without major investments in electricity storage capacity and technology. Currently, micro hydropower dams built along small rivers provide significant benefits to local communities in water management and irrigation.

Nuclear Power: Technology, Security, and Waste Management
Electricity derived from nuclear power is almost CO_2-free. But when we consider its full life cycle, from construction of the plant to the disposal of the nuclear spent rods, a nuclear power plant can produce significant emissions (1 to 288 grams of CO_2 produced per kwh of energy). However, this is still significantly less than that of a natural gas power plant (1 to 443 grams of CO_2 per kwh) or a coal-fired plant (1 to 1050 gram of CO_2 per kwh) as per EPPO (2012).

ASEAN countries currently do not possess the technologies required to build key components and to operate a large-scale modern nuclear facility. They also lack the uranium ore/mine. Nuclear power development would therefore require significant technology and resource transfers from advanced countries. That raises concerns about nuclear proliferation. Several countries in Asia such as Japan, South Korea, India, and China, in comparison, possess technology sufficiently to build and operate large-scale modern nuclear power plants.

Security to prevent nuclear proliferation involves complex schemes to control nuclear technology, nuclear energy sources, and by-products from reprocessing of spent nuclear fuel (plutonium). One proposal calls for establishing an international authority under the control of developed nuclear nations. This authority would supply less-developed countries with safeguarded nuclear fuel for their reactors. The fuel would always remain under the control of the supplier. When the fuel is spent, it would be removed and replaced with more fuel controlled by the supplier. Most developing countries have rejected this option because it would put their domestic power programs under foreign control.

A nuclear power plant also requires strict adherence to operation and security procedures at the site. Human error in conjunction with failure of backup systems and/or impacts from natural disasters can have catastrophic consequences such as that at the Chernobyl plant in the former Soviet Union in 1986 and at the Fukushima-Daiichi plant in Japan in 2011.

Nuclear waste management is another key issue. To date, there has been no consensus as where to store spent fuels long term, which often means thousands of years. Because of fears of potential harm to local communities, strong opposition arises whenever suggestions are made for a storage site. In the United States, a plan to make the Yucca Mountain in Nevada a long-term repository was suspended after fierce opposition from residents and nongovernmental organizations (NGOs). Without a solution in sight, most spent fuel in the United States is now stored at each reactor location.

Another concern about waste management is the high-temperature water released from the plant. Most nuclear power plants require large quantities of water, mostly for cooling. The cooling water is not

Table 8.2   Fifteen-year Ethanol Production Plan (2008–2022) (Unit: Million liters/day)

	Short term				Middle term	Long term
	2008	2009	2010	2011	2012–2016	2017–2022
Target	3	3	3	3	6.2	9
Online plants' capacity	1.6	1.7	2.9	2.9	N/A	N/A
Actual production	0.92	1.1	1.16	1.42*	N/A	N/A

Notes: 1. Adapted from Preechajarn and Prasertsri (2011).

2. *Average capacity utilization during January–February 2011.

Source: Ministry of Energy. Copyright © Ministry of Energy.

radioactive, but it is returned to rivers at high temperature and can kill fish and create other problems.

Despite all this, nuclear power is still a key potential energy source because of its relatively low CO_2 emissions compared to fossil fuels and its ability to reliably supply energy at low cost. What we need is a careful examination of the real costs/risks and benefits of nuclear power plants.

Biofuels: Food vs. Energy Security

Biofuels are produced from renewable biological resources such as solid biomass, liquid fuels, and biogases. They are widely used in transportation and electricity generation.

Thailand, as many other countries in ASEAN and Asia, has long recognized the importance of biofuels to help reduce its reliance on oil imports. The government adopted a 15-year biodiesel and ethanol plan as a part of the Alternative Energy Plan 2008–2022. The plan set ambitious targets for ethanol production at 6.2 million liters/day for 2012–2016 (see Table 8.2), and for biodiesel production at 3.64 million liters/day in 2016.

Most ASEAN countries are well suited for large-scale development of biofuels because of their extensive agricultural bases. Thailand and Malaysia, for example, are leading producers of palm oil, a first-generation feedstock for biofuel. What is needed is advancement in the technology to convert second-generation feedstock into biofuel and to increase the yield and efficiency of agricultural practice.

Challenge for Renewable Energy Development

Land-Use Intensity and Scalability

At first glance, renewable energy may seem to offer unlimited energy supply. But in reality, with current technologies, many renewable energy projects are land-intensive and require sites with certain conditions, and thus are limited in potential. The estimates of land-use intensity for different types of renewable energy in terms of acres/ gigawatt hours (gwh)/ yr vary. These invite public debate on the suitability and limitation of renewable technology that clearly need public support for land acquisition and appropriation and tax incentive to siting energy facilities, including transmission lines.[16] Biomass is the most land-use-intensive energy source by far, about 550 acres/GWh/year (AGWY) or over 70 times of solar energy usage on average for the same electricity.[17] Wind (30 AGWY) and hydropower (180 AGWY) also require quite large areas.[18] Solar panel (7 AGWY) and solar thermal (4 AGWY) are medium land-use ones.[19] Comparatively, the most attractive sources in terms of land use are geothermal (2 AGWY) and nuclear power (1 AGWY), which actually require less land area than do natural gas (5 AGWY) and coal (2 AGWY).

The land-use requirement of some renewable energy sources can be reduced through distributed power generation technology and planning. For example, instead of building a large solar farm, we can use rooftop solar panels for small-scale, local power generation.

Land use also relates intrinsically with scalability of renewable energy. Because it is very land-intensive, biomass is not scalable to sufficiently support large-scale energy demands. To increase amounts of biomass supply, more areas to grow biomass are required and the risk of deforestation in plantation areas increases as the renewable energy demand/price increases. These limitations must be considered as part of a long-term green energy plan. Thus, for Asian nations, renewable energy policy is also implicitly interrelated to land reform and urban–rural income distribution policy.

Smart Grid

A smart grid provides significant increases in power usage efficiency. It is also suitable for energy trading in ASEAN and Asia countries, especially for countries with common land borders. Smart grid can be an essential part of energy security policy in countries such as Singapore that have limited land for new power plants. In 2012, Malaysia and Singapore discussed the possibility of a private-sector energy-trading project. The Malaysian sellers can build their power plants more efficiently knowing that they will have buyers not only domestically but also abroad. Such projects can reduce development costs via the economy of scale and help developers secure financial support.

If we can expand the smart grid in Southeast Asia, we can create an efficient power network that can route power load to where it is needed the most while promoting the economies of all the countries involved. However, careful consideration of proper trading procedures and openness of transactions without undue interference from governments are essential. (See next section on China and the third industrial revolution initiative with "energy internet" policy.)

Slowing the Growth of Energy Demand

In addition to the development of renewable energy paradigm, attention needs to be paid on how we can slow the growth of energy demand while continuing to promote economic activities. Reduced energy demand will help stabilizing level of CO_2 emissions and balance investments in new power plants. Reducing electricity usage is one of the most cost-effective and easiest approaches. Consumers need to be incentivized to change their behavior and reduce excessive energy usage. There are several simple means to reduce energy demand including the following.

Ban the Incandescent Bulb
We should replace all incandescent light bulbs with compact fluorescents (CFLs) or newer light-emitting diode (LED) technology bulbs, which can reduce electricity use by up to 7 percent. A CFL bulb costs up to twice as much as an incandescent, but it lasts 10 times as long. Replacing incandescent bulbs can be done relatively easily nationwide by creating incentives for people to switch. Many countries have set targets to eliminate incandescent bulbs and programs to promote the use of LEDs.

Promoting Energy-Efficient Appliances
Modern household appliances are much more energy efficient than older appliances, and consumers should be encouraged to upgrade when appropriate. Efficiency standards should be raised through various means such as lower tax rates for more efficient appliances and programs, promoting use of such appliances. This would make those appliances more attractive price-wise.

Energy-Promoting Efficient Buildings
Building construction is responsible for a large share of electricity consumption, raw materials usage, and waste generation. Green buildings not only have less impact on the environment but also have higher real estate values. They are attractive to buyers because they have lower operating costs and offer a more healthful environment. The Leadership in Energy and Environmental Design program in the United States certifies buildings that meet standards for environmental quality, materials use, energy efficiency, and water efficiency. There also is a program that

supports retrofitting older buildings to reduce energy use. The building industry can become a leader in energy saving and carbon reduction by establishing standards/codes encouraging or requiring designers and architects to fashion buildings with natural light, rooftop solar modules, reduced water usage, and efficient lighting. ASEAN and Asian countries, with the exception of Japan, Singapore, and South Korea, in general, lag behind the developed countries on efficiency standards for commercial and residential buildings.

Restructuring Transportation

The transportation sector uses a large share of energy, usually in the form of refined liquid fossil fuels and, to a lesser extent, compressed natural gas. A public mass transportation system is by far the most efficient means to transport large numbers of people. But while most countries recognize the importance of developing a mass transit system, their actual policies often run counter to this goal.

Many countries maintain very low gasoline taxes or even subsidize the cost of gasoline sold to consumers. The main reason that most governments rely on for continuing support of low gasoline tax or subsidy is to support growing industrial activities and to control inflation. The result is that people do not have an incentive to conserve energy or to use public transportation.

Restructuring the gasoline taxation system can help improving transport system efficiency. Tax revenues can be used to build or improve mass transit systems. These improvements will prompt more people to use the systems instead of their cars. This will mean more efficient energy usage and less traffic congestion, which in turn means less pollution and higher productivity. Another potential area that is worth considering is setting up congested zones and collecting fees from cars entering the zones. Congestion fees may be suitable for large metropolitan areas with severe congestion such as inner Bangkok metropolitan areas.

Green Energy Economy: In Summary

With reasonably well-developed industrial sectors, well-educated human capital, and available natural resources, ASEAN and Asian countries are well positioned to become leaders in developing green energy economy. There are several clear advantages including the following:

1. Long peak sun hours and plentiful suitable land make it much more suitable for solar energy development than many countries in other regions.

2. Large agricultural base favors biofuels development.
3. Wind power is very promising in some countries such as Vietnam, with advances in low wind speed technology and strong government support.
4. Extensive experience with hydroelectric power projects, several suitable areas, and technical know-how are advantageous.
5. Some countries such as Thailand have reasonably well-developed physical infrastructure. It has wide coverage of the national power grid along with respectable transportation and logistics networks.
6. Shale gas can play crucial role for future energy supply of the region in the form of importation via LNG carriers or domestic production in China.

There are many aspects that ASEAN and Asian countries can improve. Excluding a few countries in Asia (most notably Japan and South Korea), Asian countries are less well developed in technology and human capital relative to Western nations. This aspect illustrates one of the key areas that present some limitations to green energy economy and shale gas development. But it also presents a great opportunity for growth in high-tech industries supporting the development. Another key area of limitations of some Asian nations is lack of political stability and long-term supporting policy relative to the more developed nations such as the United States.

Most countries in ASEAN and Asia lag far behind the United States in energy efficiency standards, in terms of both consumer usage and government policy. For example, from the energy-saving plan from the Power Development Plan 2012, Thailand's target is to save 1,170 MW/year, or about 3 percent of the total energy consumption, by 2030. Data from the Northwest Power Conservation Council in the United States show that the United States has increased its energy savings every year from 1978 to 2007, resulting in more than 30,000 MW/yr saved—more than 25 times Thailand's target for 2030.

Reinforcing Positive Developments: Future of Sustainable Development in Asia

The world is changing, as it has always. But this time, we are moving toward a great major change in energy paradigm, sustainable development through green energy economy. This is an exciting moment in our history comparable to the first industrial revolution when steam power gave rise to the widespread industrial developments. Green energy economy offers a way to a brighter future by reducing our dependency on conventional fuels to energy sources that can be sustained over a longer term.

Japan: Renaissance of Renewable Energy, Side Effects from the Fukushima Incident

In the past decades, the Japanese government adopted nuclear power as a means to support the nation's economic growth. In a way, this paradigm was necessary and successful until the consequential cost of such plan became obvious from the tragedy at the Fukushima Nuclear power plant in 2011. Japan was forced to adapt. The future of nuclear power in Japan became uncertain with strong indicators of phasing out of nuclear power in 2030.

Although renewable energy has always been a subject of interest in Japan, since the event, the country has seen a significant rise of interest in this area. One of the most important initiatives the Japanese government undertook was an introduction of a feed-in tariff for renewable energy. The idea behind this program is to provide assurance that the government will purchase energy produced from renewable energy sources at a fixed price that would hopefully provide basis for industrial growth in this area.[20] The tariff covers various forms of renewable energy such as solar, wind, biomass, hydro power, and geothermal. This positive development paves the way for future growth and strengthens Japan as a world economic powerhouse.

China: From World Factory to Renewable Energy Industry Leader and Innovator

China, arguably the world factory, is aware of its need for renewable energy development early on in their quest for economic growth since China has long struggled to secure energy resources to keep up with the ever-growing demand at home. (See "China National Offshore Oil Corporation and Its Quest for China's Energy Resources" case study.) The country invested in a number of hydroelectric projects, which partly pushed the renewable energy share for electricity generation to approximately 17 percent in 2007. China became the world's largest manufacturer of solar panels by 2010. It is clear that China is growing its industrial bases into the renewable energy market in addition to its expansion into the shale gas development.

According to the government-backed Chinese Renewable Energy Industries Association, renewable energy industries in China help creating jobs rapidly totaling up to 1.12 million in 2008 and growing every year.[21] China combines its strength on industrial production at low competitive cost with domestic needs to expand electricity to support the needs of the people and industries. This results in a platform for growth with enormous advantage. Chinese manufacturers can enjoy significant efficiencies producing solar panels supporting both domestic and international market. This positive development can, in turn, lead to further development of human resources in terms of education and research and development in this area. The positive cycle, if continues, can strengthen China to be not only the world's leading manufacturer of solar power equipment but also the world's leading innovator.

It is important to note that the third industrial revolution is possible if there is a sufficient shift toward renewable energy like solar on building and household level; in the near future, these renewable are expected to be sufficient and able to connect to a smart intergrid similar to Internet communication technology rapid development in the last few decades.[22] These new smart grids with "hydrogen" and other storages would revolutionize the way we produce and consume electricity. As Internet transforms marketing and sales of goods and services efficiently at little or no cost, this inexpensive green electricity would laterally allow small and medium enterprises to prosper. Chinese Premier Li Keqiang, in December 2013, determined to lead the world in the third industrial revolution by initiating "energy internet" and "intercontinential backbone network" programs to combat its serious pollution issues and for sustainable economic development.[23] (See also "the Construction of Shenzhen Carbon Market" case study.) Indeed, it remains to be seen how this game-changing concept would evolve over the next decade.

India: Convergence of Factors Supporting Solar Power Development

In India, key factors (population, highly suitable environmental factor, and substantially reduction of the price of solar panels, lacks of widespread electricity grid) are coalescing forming a viable basis for significant growth in solar energy development. India is densely populated, being the world's second-most populated country, and has high solar insulation. The price of solar panels has been declining mainly driven by significant growth in the solar panel manufacturing industry in China. Combining these factors with the lack of widespread electricity grid introduces a very positive scenario. In recent years, India has seen significant growth in grid-connected solar power from just 10 MW as of December 2010 to 2,208.36 MW by January 2014. The growth rate is phenomenal but the total produced solar energy is still very small compared to the country's total energy demand.

The country is facing severe electricity deficit that often runs between 10 percent and 13 percent of daily need.[24] Part of this huge deficit comes from growth of the middle-class population in India. Demand for electricity increases substantially and in inverse relationship with the poverty rate. The government appears to realize that it is facing a serious problem and appears to commit to support renewable energy development as evidence from various government's policies and supports. However, land in India is a scarce resource. Therefore, large-scale solar power plants on dedicated land may not be suitable in many cases as a 20- to 50-MW solar power plant generally needs approximately 1 square kilometer of land.[25] A more suitable approach is distributed solar power generation such as rooftop solar panels connecting to a local grid. This approach is also viable for areas without connection to the national grid, which is numerous in India. Unlike China, India can embrace private lead initiative for "energy internet" programs for "distributed capitalism" as a game-changing transformation discussed earlier in chapter 6.

We are seeing the transformation of Asia from the old role of manufacturing bases for the world and nations that rely on importation of technology from the developed nations. With Japan's increasing focus on renewable energy and China's emergence as the titan in renewable equipment manufacturers, the future is bright and exciting. The key is to continuously reinforce these positive developments to create long-term positive cycle. Today, Asia is standing at a unique position.

Many factors that used to hinder development can actually be turned into fuels for future growth. The rise of a large segment of population from the poor and the growth of the middle class in many countries, particularly India and China, can serve as the basis for further investments in renewable energy and related manufacturing industries. This development drives government's policy to support greater growth in renewable energy because its need to achieve energy security as well as meet its population's demand. These factors are converging to produce a strong basis for an exciting future of renewable energy in Asia.

Case Study

The Construction of Shenzhen Carbon Market

Bin Ye

China is a developing country, enjoying rapid economic growth, with a large population. Its rapid industrialization and urbanization, shifting away from rural agrarian society, have increased energy consumption demands. This change has been highlighted by the "Transformation and Structural Adjustment" theme of economic development of the 18th National Congress of China. The Chinese government is actively promoting market-oriented reforms in the field of environmental protection having made great strides in reducing carbon emissions. The construction of environmental resources market is the latest initiative, designed to create a market means to resolve the allocation of environmental resources.

Carbon Emission Status of China
Over the past 30 years, China has witnessed rapid and sustained economic growth. However, this growth also leads to surging energy consumption and severe environmental pollution. China's carbon emission increased rapidly. In 2011, its carbon emission increased to 8715 Mt, accounting for 26.75 percent of global carbon emission, becoming the largest single emitter. The Chinese government has promised that carbon emissions per unit of GDP in 2020 will decrease by 40 to 45 percent compared with 2005. China has officially launched carbon emission trading pilots in its seven provinces and cities, actively trying to enhance energy saving and emission-reduction incentives through market mechanism.

Economy Development and Carbon Emission Status of Shenzhen City
Shenzhen is China's first special economic zone. The policy of reforming and opening up China, pursued by Deng Xiaoping, was first implemented in Shenzhen. Shenzhen has grown from a small fishing village to one of the largest and most prosperous cities in China over the past 30 years. Its population has grown from over 300,000 inhabitants to more than 13 million, roughly double the size of Hong Kong's population; and its GDP has increased from 40 million US dollars to over 200 billion US dollars, equal to approximately 80 percent of Hong Kong's. Shenzhen has considered energy saving and the reduction of emissions as an important means to promote economic development and transformation away from low-wage manufacturing and high-skill and technology industry.

Between 2008 and 2013, Shenzhen's energy consumption per unit of GDP declined by about 16.33 percent, meeting the initial energy-saving target in "The Eleventh Five-Year Plan" from the central government in Beijing. In 2012, Shenzhen's energy consumption per unit of GDP was 0.451 tons of standard coal per 10,000 yuan (price of 2010), lower than the average national and provincial levels.

As a rapidly industrializing and urbanizing emerging economy, Shenzhen has three emission features that can be summarized as: two highs, one fast, and one low. In other words, the proportion of carbon emissions from industries are high, within the industry the proportion of carbon emissions from manufacturing are also high, carbon emissions from transportation are increasing fast, and carbon emissions per capita are low. In the long run, Shenzhen will utilize increasing amounts of carbon emissions changing the emission structure: the total quantity of carbon emissions from manufacturing will continue to increase, but the development of high-end manufacturing will speed up the decrease of carbon intensity of manufacturing, and the growth rate of carbon emissions will slow. Conversely, urbanization will increase the proportion of carbon emissions from transportation, commerce, and residence. At present, the proportion of carbon emissions from Shenzhen's transportation is significantly lower than the level of developed countries, but the carbon emissions from transportation will be the major driving force of Shenzhen's carbon emission growth in future. It can be forecasted that, while the carbon intensity of manufacturing will decrease and eventually weaken, the growth of carbon emissions from transportation, commerce, and residence will continue to increase.

The Development of Shenzhen Carbon Market

Shenzhen is emerging as a new carbon market. China has actively been participating in fighting and preventing climate change. Shenzhen, as one of the 13 pilot cities to work with low carbon development, has made progress in tackling climate change by promoting low-carbon urban development and piloting the carbon emissions trade.

On June 18, 2013 the industrial sector of Shenzhen carbon trading market was launched. Through the end of October 2013, in Shenzhen's carbon market, the cumulative trading volume was exceeded 200,000 tons of CO_2 with a cumulative turnover of about 15 million yuan. The initial trade price was 28 yuan and a March 2014 price of 83 yuan.

From 2010 to 2015, the goal of Shenzhen is to reduce its carbon intensity (carbon emission amount per GDP) by 21 percent, with the target of the industrial sector being an even higher decline of 25 percent. Through the data reported by enterprises, the computer system will automatically generate allowance allocation results. For the 635 covered enterprises, the rate of descent of the average carbon intensity surpasses 30 percent. The range of emission reduction vastly exceeds Shenzhen's target of reducing carbon intensity by 21 percent, setting a good example for the whole municipality in energy saving and emission reduction, by having found a new method with the double binding of total allowance and carbon intensity, which connects allowance allocation with the quality of economic development.

China National Offshore Oil Corporation and Its Quest for China's
Energy Resources

Pongsak Hoontrakul

Founded in 1982, China National Offshore Oil Corporation (CNOOC) is one of China's three national oil companies. Its largest subsidiary, CNOOC Ltd, which has been publicly listed on the Hong Kong and New York exchanges since 2001, engages primarily in offshore operations and increasingly in overseas operations, including in Australia, North America, and Central Asia.

CNOOC Ltd was once the darling of investors because it pursued a pure upstream focus, acquiring many energy reserve assets overseas to serve China's fast economic growth. In June 2005, it made an $18.5 billion cash offer to take over the American oil firm Unocal Corp. but withdrew the bid after fierce lobbying from a group of US congressmen concerned about national security risks. CNOOC Ltd still has managed to acquire many overseas assets over the years. In 2012, CNOOC took over Canada's energy company, Nexen, for over USD 15 billion to gain new energy offshore exploration in western Africa, the North Sea, the Gulf of Mexico, and oil sands project in Alberta along with other reserves.[26] Still its total oil and gas production overseas in 2015 is projected to shrink to 819,000 barrels of oil equivalent, a −18 percent year-on-year growth compared to 2014.

CNOOC increased its capital expenditure from $6.4 billion in 2011 to an estimated $16 billion in 2014, a nearly 150 percent increase, although its oil and gas production has been lower than expected.[27] Four of the ten offshore oil and gas exploration projects were delayed. Two large gas field projects, Liwan 3–1 and Lufeng 7–2 in the South China Sea, could not commence production volume of up to 40,000 barrels per day in 2014 as planned.[28] CNOOC is also venturing the deepwater activities in China with limited success. Block 43/11 with 1,500–3,000 meter water depth (mwd) in the Pearl River Mouth Basin of South China Sea, block 29/06 with 500–1,500 mwd in Eastern South China Sea, and block 04/35 with 2,500 mwd in the East China Sea are among the fine examples of its deepwater activities.[29] With weak execution at home, CNOOC's overseas assets will deliver stronger revenue growth than its offshore operations. The company's US assets are still the main growth driver, especially the shale gas reserves from the Eagle Ford project in Texas and the Niobrara project in Wyoming.[30]

As of January 21, 2014, CNOOC Ltd had a market capitalization of $80 billion. CNOOC Ltd is projected to have total revenue and net profit for 2015 at 303 billion RMB ($48.87 billion) and 69.3 billion RMB ($11.18 billion), respectively, representing year-on-year growth of 4.5 percent and 9.6 percent, respectively.[31] After an oil-rig incident in the waters of the Paracel Islands, South China Sea, that sank one Vietnamese naval ship and killed 53 people in May 2014, the high political tension between China and Vietnam along with few selected ASEAN nations becomes more than a dispute over sovereignty, as well as how to handle international law over the sea.[32] It remains to be seen how CNOOC would manage to grow its business in these seemingly troubled areas.

Notes

1. S. Major, T. Commins, and A. Noppharatana, "Potential of Wind Power for Thailand: An Assessment," *Mj Inter Sci Tech J.*, 2008, 2:02, 255–266.
2. Ibid.
3. "Technically Recoverable Shale Oil and Shale Gas Resources: An Assessment of 137 Shale Formations in 41 Countries Outside the United States," *Independent Statistics & Analysis, US Energy Information Administration, US Department of Energy (EIA)*, June 2013 (http://www.eia.gov/ analysis/ studies/worldshalegas/pdf/overview.pdf).
4. Ibid.
5. Ibid.
6. See more discussion by Samantha Azzarello, "Energy Price Spread: Natural Gas vs Crude Oil in the US," February 11, 2014 (http://www.nasdaq.com/article/energy-price-spread-natural-gas-vs-crude-oil-in-the-us-cm325685) and Jason Channell, Timothy Lam, and Shahriar Pourreza, "Shale & Renewable: A Symbiotic Relationship," *Citi*, September 12, 2012: Fig. 19 on p. 11.
7. Channell et al., "Shale & Renewable: A Symbiotic Relationship," Fig. 19 on p. 11 and Fig. 17, p. 11. More discussion see David Hewitt and Horace Tse, "The Shale Revolution: Part 1," *Credit Suisse*, December 2012: 32–43.
8. Thai Research Foundation (TRF), Final Report. "Policy Research to Support the Development and Usage of Renewable Energy and to Increase Efficiency in Energy Usage of Thailand," 2007.
9. R.A. Alvarez, S.W. Pacala, J.J. Winebrake, W.L. Chameides, and S.P. Hamburg, "Greater Focus Needed on Methane Leakage from Natural Gas Infrastructure," *Proceedings of the National Academy of Sciences of the United States of America*, 2012, 109(17).
10. Suthep Chimklai, *ASEAN Interconnection, Briefing on ASEAN Power Grid*, Electricity Generating Authority of Thailand (EGAT), March 14, 2013, presentation, pp. 2–25 (http://portal.erc.or.th/aern/images/Panel%201–1%20 Briefing%20on%20ASEAN%20Power %20Grid.pdf).
11. C.S. Greacen and C. Greacen, "Proposed Power Development Plan (PDP) 2012 and a Framework for Improving Accountability and Performance of Power Sector Planning." Accessed June 2012 (http://www.palangthai.org/

PDP2012-Eng.pdf/). For more discussion see EPPO,"Assumptions and Summary of Draft PDP 2010," Accessed June 2012 (http://www.eppo.go.th/power/pdp/seminar-17feb2553/assumptions-PDP2010.pdf/).

12. Ibid. More discussion see J. Tollefson, "Air Sampling Reveals High Emissions from Gas Field," *Nature*, February 7, 2012 (http://www.nature.com/news/air-sampling-reveals-high-emissions-from-gas-field-1.9982/).

13. Thai Research Foundation, "Policy Research."

14. Channell et al., "Shale & Renewable," 1–88.

15. Harvey, Rachel, "Burma Dam: Why Myitsone Plan is Being Halted," *BBC*, September 30, 2011, Accessed February 2012 (http://www.bbc.co.uk/news/world-asia-pacific-15123833/); Raybould, Alan, ed., "Laos Defies Neighbors on Dam Project," *Reuters*, June 23, 2011, Accessed June 2012 (http://www.reuters.com/article/2011/06/23/laos-dam-idUSL3E7HN1L320110623/).

16. Martin LaMonica, "Figuring Land Use Into Renewable-Energy Equation," May 29, 2010 (http://www.cnet.com/news/figuring-land-use-into-renewable-energy-equation/).

17. P. Brown and G. Whitney, "U.S. Renewable Electricity Generation: Resources and Challenges," *Congressional Research Service*, August 2011 (http://archive.nationalaglawcenter.org/ assets/crs/R41954.pdf).

18. Ibid.

19. Ibid.

20. Wharton School, University of Pennsylvania, "Renewable Energy for Japan: A Post-Fukushima Quest," Accessed March 2014 (http://knowledge.wharton.upenn.edu/article /renewable-energy-japan-post-fukushima-quest/).

21. A. Jäger-Waldau, "PV Status Report 2013," Joint Research Center of the European Commission, European Commission, September 2013. More discussion see The New York Times, "China Leading Global Race to Make Clean Energy," Accessed March 2014 (http://www.nytimes.com/2010/01/31/business/energy- environment/31renew.html? pagewanted=1&_r=2).

22. Jeremy Rifkin, *The Third Industrial Revolution: How Lateral Power is Transforming Energy, the Economy, and the World* (New York: Palgrave Macmillan), 2011, 35–36, ISBN 978–0-230–11521-7. More discussion see Renewable Energy World, "Report Projects Massive Solar Growth in India," Accessed March 2014 (http://www.renewableenergyworld.com/rea/news/article/2011/12/report-projects-massive-solar-growth-in-india?cmpid=SolarNL-Tuesday-December13–2011).

23. Liu Zhenya, "Science Daily: Smart Grid and the third industrial revolution," *stdaily*, Retrieved December 5, 2013 (www.stdaily.com).

24. The New York Times, "China Leading Global Race to Make Clean Energy," Accessed March 2014 (http://www.nytimes.com/2010/01/31/business/energy-environment/31renew.html? pagewanted=1&_r=2).

25. Renewable Energy World, "Report Projects Massive Solar Growth in India," Accessed March 2014 (http://www.renewableenergyworld.com/rea/news/article/2011/12/report-projects-massive-solar-growth-in-india?cmpid=SolarNL-Tuesday-December13–2011).

26. Euan Rocha, "CNOOC Closes USD15.1 Billion Acquisition of Canada's Nexen," February 25, 2013 (http://www.reuters.com/article/2013/02/25/us-nexen-cnooc-idUSBRE91O1A420130225).

27. Thomas Wong, Horace Tse, and Kelly Chen, "CNOOC Ltd: Downgrade to NEUTRAL on Lower Production Growth," *Asia Pacific/China Equity Research Oil & Gas Exploration & Production*, Credit Suisse, January 21, 2014: 1 (https://doc.research-and-analytics.csfb.com/docView?language=ENG&source=ulg&format=PDF&document_id=1028171371&serialid=FuUWJDpO057VscG5QmvfEQ37rAil9rl7K4VyD6NmYE8%3D).

28. Ibid., pp. 13–16.

29. Ibid.

30. Ibid., pp. 7–8.

31. Ibid., p. 1.

32. Nguyen Thi Lan Anh, "The Paracels: Forty Year On," *RSIS Commentaries*, No. 109/2014, S. Rajaratham School of International Studies, Nanyan Technological University, Singapore, June 9, 2014.

9

Natural Disasters and Fragile Supply Chains: The Great East Japan Earthquake and the Thai Floods in 2011

Shigeyuki Abe and Pongsak Hoontrakul

Introduction: Disaster-Prone Asia

Contemporaneous with rising climate change, natural disasters have become increasingly frequent in the world over the years. The highest ever was in 2007, when there were more than 1,000 disasters.[1] Natural disasters can be classified into two main categories: (1) severe or extreme weather events, including meteorological events such as storms, hurricanes, and high winds, and hydrological events such as floods, drought, and bushfires; and (2) geophysical events such as earthquakes, tsunamis, and volcanic eruptions. It is particularly noteworthy that weather-related disasters in particular are increasingly frequent with steeper upward trend than geophysical events.[2]

From 1990 to 2011, Asia experienced nearly 40 percent of the world's natural disasters, and suffered almost 80 percent of the total death toll. Approximately 58 percent of Asia's natural disasters occurred in East Asia. In 1990–2011, countries prone to natural disasters were China (681 disasters), India (604), the Philippines (529), Indonesia (412), Bangladesh (312), Japan (291), Iran (193), Vietnam (177), Pakistan (166), Thailand (119), Hong Kong (103), and Sri Lanka (81).[3] The Asia-Pacific region is particularly prone to geophysical events, hydrological events, and meteorological events. Earthquakes and tsunami in Japan in March, floods in Pakistan in August–September and in Thailand in August–November, and tropical storms in Philippines in December are among the fine examples of the natural catastrophes in Asia in 2011 alone.[4] Urbanization has also amplified the scale of potential losses from such disasters.

Specifically in March 2011, an earthquake and tsunami killed more than 15,000 people in eastern Japan, whereas in the last quarter of that year, floods in Thailand's central provinces and parts of Bangkok killed more than 800 people. In both cases, natural disasters disrupted both domestic production and regional, even international, supply chains. The two cases show that natural disasters can affect not only a domestic economy but also economies in the rest of the world, given the extent of interconnected production networks in this globalized era. The costs need to be evaluated carefully so that we can be better prepared.

The Great East Japan Earthquake

On March 11, 2011, a 9.0-magnitude earthquake struck off the east coast of Tohoku, Japan. The devastation of the Great East Japan Earthquake was further amplified by two tsunamis. Three prefectures—Miyagi, Fukushima, and Iwate—were inundated. The Fukushima-Daiichi nuclear power plant meltdown followed (see Figure 9.1).

Considering the magnitude and severity of this triple disaster, disaster preparations proved on the whole to be effective. Many buildings in Sendai, the largest city in the earthquake-affected area, shook severely but suffered little major damage. This was evidence that Japan's building codes, revised following the Hanshin-Awaji earthquake of 1995, functioned very well in enforcing the adoption of quake-resistant building technology. In addition, regular tsunami evacuation drills had been practiced in the region, and tsunami warnings were issued within three minutes of the earthquake, enabling many people to safely evacuate.

What Japan did not learn from the Hanshin-Awaji earthquake was the need to protect the supply chain. The 1965 earthquake severed the trunk roads from western to eastern Japan, so most automobile manufacturers could not obtain necessary parts and could not quickly return to normal production. The 2011 earthquake likewise halted the delivery of intermediate products to the main factories. And because the supply chain has been extended Asia-wide in recent years, the earthquake affected not only Japan but also the world.

The Nikkei stock market index plunged about 16 percent during the week of the earthquake, severely affecting other stock markets around the globe. The Group of 7 (G7) convened a special meeting on March 17 for concerted actions to calm the markets.

For the first quarter of 2011, Japan—the third largest economy in the world—experienced a 3.7 percent contraction in real gross domestic

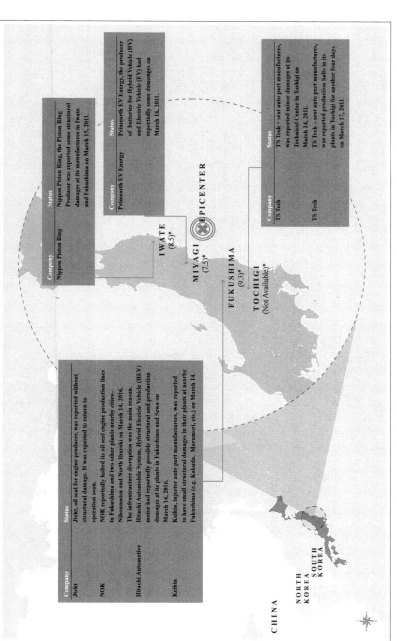

Figure 9.1 The 311 Earthquake Fukushima—Eastern Japan (on March 11, 2011)

Note: * The estimated maximum tsunami heights observed (in meter).

Source: 1. Wikimedia Commons, "Tsunami map Tohoku 2011" (http://commons.wikimedia.org/wiki/File:Tsunami_map_Tohoku2011.svg).
2. Takahashi, 2011, Fig. 12, p. 9. Copyright © 2014, Pongsak Hoontrakul.

product (GDP). The World Bank estimated the economic cost of the earthquake at US$235 billion. Insured losses were estimated at $34.6 billion. The cost from the supply chain disruption was immeasurable. It was considered the costliest natural disaster in human history.[5]

After the earthquake, a serious power shortage loomed in eastern Japan. Supply from the stricken nuclear power plants was shut off as the plants were closed. And demand was at its typical summer peak. Manufacturers dealt with the problem by rotating production times, shifting production to holidays, employing rolling blackouts, and coordinating production schedules to avoid peak-load periods.

Intermediate Goods Trade and Supply Chain Development in Asia

After years of trade frictions, Japan and the United States signed the Plaza Accord in 1985 to devalue the dollar. This led the yen–dollar exchange rate to soar from 240 to 120 yen/dollar almost within one year. Japanese manufacturers could not remain competitive in world markets. They moved plants en masse to Southeast Asia; this diversion toward production abroad eventually created the Asia-wide supply chain that we see now. Japan shifted production of low-value and intermediate-value goods to Southeast Asia, especially Thailand and Malaysia, and later to Indonesia and China. It kept high-value and high-tech production at home, or shifted them to other advanced countries like Taiwan and South Korea.

The extent of the Asia-wide supply chain can be seen in the structure of trade flows. Asia's newly industrialized countries and China have very high "vertical specialization."[6] Production was once highly "vertical integrated" into a handful of large manufacturers. With the modern supply chain, production was separated into small fragments/firms.[7] Each "vertical specializing" firm is an expert on particular tasks, work, or component production within the division of labor required to produce a finished product like an iPad or a car. Vertical specialization is measured by how much imported contents are embodied in a country's gross exports. In 2004, Japan's specialization index was 12.2. South Korea's was 33.9; Hong Kong's was 27.5; and Taiwan's was 41.1; for China, it was 35.7.[8] Thus, in order to export, Asia's newly industrializing countries and China must import intermediate goods (or components) worth 30 to 40 percent of the value of their exports.[9]

A typical example of this vertical specialization is the finished iPhone that China exports. China's value-added share of its iPhone exports is less than 5 percent. In other words, 95 percent of the value must be procured through the supply chain. When the Apple iPad 3 equipped with 32 gigabytes (GB) of NAND flash[10] memory and 4G long-term evolution (LTE)[11] wireless capacity was, for example, broken into teardown small components in 2012, the preliminary bill of materials (BoM) represents about half of the suggested retail price of about USD700.[12] The cost analysis of each component shows over 70 percent of the BoM derived from high-precision and semiconductor-related components like display and touch screen (USD127), wireless module (USD 41.5), NAND Flash (USD 33.6), dynamic random access memory (DRAM; USD 13.9), and electromechanical component (USD 50.50).[13]

The European Union (EU) and the United States are major destinations of Asia's exports, although exports to those areas have declined from about 33.8 percent of Asia's total exports in 1999 to 24.5 percent in 2010.[14]

Domestic demand and demand from other Asian countries have gradually increased. One thing we need to consider, however, is the components/finished products trade structure. Asia has developed an extensive production network by intense foreign direct investment and export promotion policies, helped by the development of free-trade agreements. Asia's supply chain is used mainly to export finished products to the United States, the EU, and Japan. When those markets are hit by a global economic crisis, the trade in components shrinks by multiple factors. As a result, Asian countries will be affected seriously and simultaneously. As the supply chain trade has expanded, the vulnerability of each Asian country has also increased.

At least 1,135 factories in Japan were affected by the earthquake, according to a survey by the newspaper Yomiuri Shimbun.[15] Key industrial sectors were severely impacted:

Automobile Industry

Each car consists of 20,000 to 30,000 parts; any missing part can cause a halt in production. The earthquake caused many bottlenecks in the supply of electronic components, plastic parts, and specialized materials. The fall in operating rates (supply disruption) was worse than the Lehman Brothers bankruptcy (sudden loss of demand) because of the breadth and depth of supply part inputs to automakers. Figure 9.1 shows selectively the auto parts companies' damage status and the state and speed of recovery among the companies that suffered damage. Some medium-value components like piston rings and disk brake pads could be temporarily outsourced elsewhere. But quite a few highly specialized components like batteries for hybrid vehicles and electric vehicles (HVs/EVs) are not readily available elsewhere. For example, most of the electrolytic fluids for lithium-ion batteries and chemicals for aluminum capacity were produced by the Okuma plant of Tomiyama Pure Chemical Industries. Thus, the Big Three—Toyota, Honda, and Nissan—were forced to lower their operating rates and halt their overseas operations. General Motors in the United States and Ford and Renault in Europe had great difficulties finding alternative part suppliers. All auto parts firms worldwide were materially impacted whether or not they suffered direct damage in the quake.

Specialty Chemical Sector

Specialty chemicals are used in a wide range of sectors from electronics to consumer durables, from autos to semiconductors. Specialty-derivative and fine-chemical supply is crucial to many key sectors like personal computers (PCs) and liquid-crystal displays (LCDs). Mitsubishi Chemical Holdings Co., for example, lost its plants in Kashima and Shirakawa to the quake. Production halts to quite a few materials like bismaleimide triazine (BT) resin, produced exclusively in Japan, halted the global supply line of semiconductors (see the Mitsubishi Gas Chemical case study).

Electronic Components and Consumer Electronics

Figure 9.1 also illustrates a selected list of major electronics and component plants. These include some of listed firms such as Alphs, Panasonic, Rohm, and Hitachi. Nearly all these firms reported no major damage directly from the quake. But they all suffered severely from the indirect impacts. Unstable power supplies disrupted plant operations, particularly in the high-tech and high-value plants with delicate production lines. With only one to two weeks in inventories, the decentralized production and supply chain was severely challenged. Flat-screen TV panel production, for example, required semiconductor input like image sensors, game console chips, and DRAM. But the plants for Toshiba lines in Iwate Prefecture and the Alps Electric and the Sony plants in Kyushu and Tagajo cities in Miyagi Prefecture were forced to suspend their semiconductor operations. They cut their output by up to 30 percent.

Online Games and Advertising

The losses extended to cyberspace and the service sectors. Entertainment industries like online games and amusement arcades suffered from restraint in leisure consumption and rising prices of basic goods. Since these services typically operate on a pay-as-you-go business model, they were severely impacted. In addition, manufacturers that were experiencing problems due to the earthquake spent less on advertising, particularly in online media.

The Great Thai Floods

The Thai floods in the last quarter of 2011 also severely disrupted the supply chain in Asia, particularly in automotive and high-tech component manufacturing. Even up to mid-2012, Thai manufacturers could not deliver enough hard disks and other products to meet world demand.

Past damage from flooding in the Chao Phraya River basin was largely confined to the agricultural sector. But not this time. The 2011 floods caused the most damage ever.[16] The floods displaced more than three million people.[17] They affected over 660,000 workers and more than 14,000 factories in 20 provinces,[18] and crippled at least six industrial estates,[19] as shown in Figure 9.2. About 180 square kilometers (112 square miles) of Bangkok and adjoining Samut Prakarn province were inundated in varying degrees.[20] The submerged electronics and automobile industries represented about 20 percent and 15 percent of Thailand's export, respectively.[21] Thailand's fourth quarter GDP fell 9 percent year on year and 10.7 percent quarter on quarter due to widespread supply stoppages and damaged logistics systems in the three months of floods.[22] This was worse than during the 1997 financial crisis. Naturally, global industrial production, especially in the automobile and technology sectors, was hit substantially[23] (see Figure 9.2).

Unlike in the case of the Japan earthquake, the Thai floods caused supply chain disruptions in low- to intermediate-value production. This was resolved effectively as the components were readily replaceable from other production bases. Thailand's National and Economic Development Board estimated the cost of the flood damages at 328 billion baht ($10.7 billion). That depressed Thailand's overall economic growth in 2011 to 0.1 percent, compared with the initial estimate of 3.8 percent.[24] In the fourth quarter of 2011, Thailand's overall industrial output fell 21.8 percent as capacity utilization fell to 46.4 percent. The recovery process was relatively fast after the water drained from the seven affected industrial estates in December 2011; by March 2012, production levels for most products resumed to the preflood level.

Thai manufacturing production index had plunged over 40 percent during the production disruption from the great flood.[25] The three most heavily impacted sectors were hard disk drives, integrated circuit and electronic components, and vehicles.[26] Exports fell drastically in November: an 84 percent fall for transportation equipment; 77.2 percent for office machines, mainly hard disk drives; 73 percent for information technology (IT) equipment; and 58.7 percent for electric and electronics products.[27] There was a complete shutdown for integrated circuit and semiconductor devices.

Here is a closer examination of the flood impact on selected products:

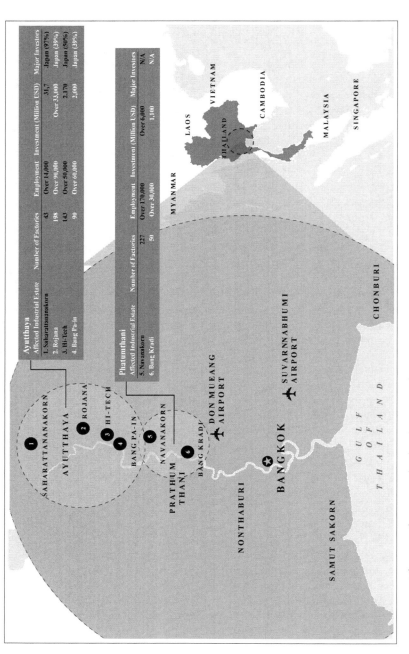

Figure 9.2 The 2011 Thai Great Flood and Impacts of Industrial Estates in Ayutthaya and Pathumthani

Note: Assuming 30 Thai Baht = 1 USD.
Source: Saicheua and Fongarunrung, 2011, slide p. 14. Copyright © 2014, Pongsak Hoontrakul.

Hard Disk Drives and PCs

Thailand is the second largest producer of hard disk drives in the world. It accounts for a quarter of global output. Thailand exported $12.42 billion in hard disk drives in 2010. Figures 9.3a and 9.3b show the impact of the floods on the hard disk drive supply chain. Exports were seriously impacted and bounced back strongly the following year.

China is the largest importer of Thailand's hard disk drives; it uses them to assemble PCs. As Figure 9.4 shows, China's PC exports fell after the Thai floods. In order to keep PC production going, China imported more disk drives from Malaysia to compensate. China exports PCs to the United States, Hong Kong, the Netherlands, and Japan. Despite the stoppage of hard disk drive imports from Thailand, China restarted its PC exports by early 2012, as illustrated in Figure 9.4.

Digital Cameras

A similar pattern can be seen in digital cameras and camera lens products from Figures 9.5 and 9.6. Lighter-weight interchangeable lens cameras are dominated by Japanese brands like Canon and Nikon. According to a Camera & Imaging Products Association report in November 2011, the Thai floods caused the interchangeable lens camera shipment volume to fall by half month on month, to 770,000 units, and compact digital cameras to fall by a third, to 7.42 million units. By December, the industry started to substitute production and parts procurement and normalized its line. Canon, for instance, relocated its printer plants to Vietnam and to Korat in northeast Thailand, away from its submerged Ayuthaya plants. JVC Kenwood shifted some Thai production back to its Yokosuka Plant in Japan.

Automobile Industry

Thailand's vehicle output fell to 1.4 million units in 2011, compared to 1.6 million units in the previous year. Half of the unit and components production is for export. Only two out of 13 auto plants in Thailand were directly impacted by the deluge. The large Honda plant was made inaccessible behind a 10-meter-high (11-yard-high) water dam in the Nikom Rojna industrial estate. Several small original equipment manufacturer (OEM) auto parts suppliers were badly hit.[28] The lack of parts

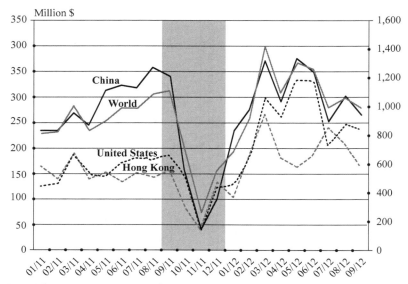

Source: Thai Customs Department and Author's calculation. Copyright © 2014, Shigeyuki Abe and Pongsak Hoontrakul.

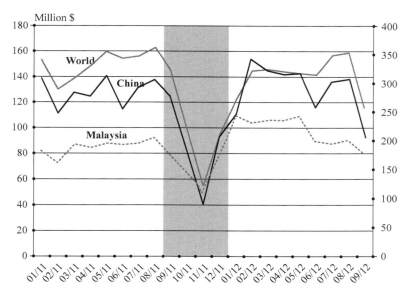

Figure 9.3 The Impact of the Floods on the Hard Disk Drive Supply Chain. (a) Exports to Thailand and (b) Exports to Japan.

Source: Japanese Customs & Author's Calculations. Copyright © 2014, Shigeyuki Abe & Pongsak Hoontrakul.

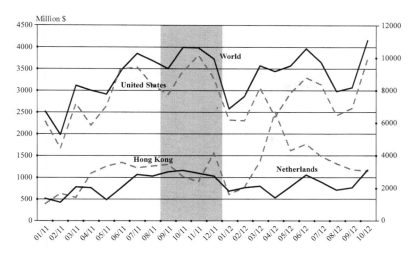

Figure 9.4   PC: Exports of China

Source: China Customs & Author's Calculations. Copyright © 2014, Shigeyuki Abe & Pongsak Hoontrakul.

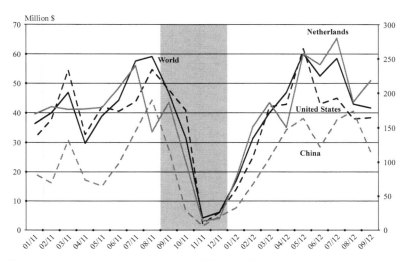

Figure 9.5   Digital Camera: Exports of Thailand

Source: Thai Customs Department and Author's Calculation. Copyright © 2014, Shigeyuki Abe & Pongsak Hoontrakul.

forced Honda to cut output at all six of its plants in the United States and Canada. The General Motors assembly lines in Rayong, 100 kilometers (62 miles) away from the submerged area, were severely impacted due to parts, goods, and services bottlenecks.[29]

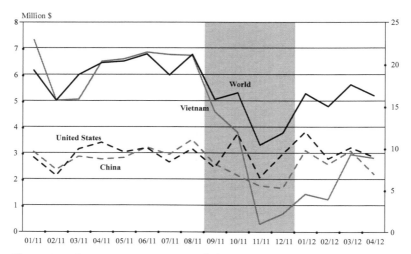

Figure 9.6   Camera Lenses: Imports of Thailand

Source: Thai Customs Department and Author's Calculation. Copyright © 2014, Shigeyuki Abe & Pongsak Hoontrakul.

The flood hurt Japan's export of engines, as shown in Figure 9.7. The largest drop was in December. It took four months for exports to the United States, China, the UK, and Brazil to recover to the preflood level. Because Thailand is a major parts and components supplier in the world market, the floods disrupted global automobile exports in general.

Comparing the Two Disasters

Crisis Management and Information Disclosure

Policymakers must address the dangers to citizens posed by natural disasters in a timely fashion. Japan's earthquake struck unexpectedly, followed by tsunamis and nuclear failure fallouts. These triple disasters caused widespread panic. Authorities could have alleviated this panic by making clear early on that Fukushima was not on the scale of the Chernobyl disaster in the former Soviet Union in 1986, instead of allowing worst-case speculation to spread in the mass media.

Unlike Japan's earthquake, the Thai floods took more than four months to unfold and could have been anticipated. The Thai government initially underestimated the gravity of the situation despite plenty of experts' warnings in the mass media. The monsoon brought major flooding and flash floods to northern and northeastern Thailand beginning in May. In late August, the heavy rains continued unabated. By

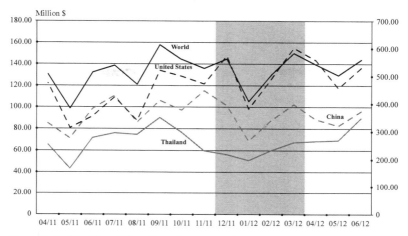

Figure 9.7   The Flood Hurt Japan's Export of Engines

Source: Japan Customs & Author's Calculations. Copyright © 2014, Shigeyuki Abe & Pongsak Hoontrakul.

then, the coordination failure in water management from upstream to downstream became obvious as nearly all of the dams were near breaking point.[30] Politically inexperienced leaders, blaming games among officials, and confusion from the Flood Relief Operation Centre were commonly cited reasons for the severity of the floods. The impact could have been mitigated if timely and accurate information had been provided.

In both Japan and Thailand, military personnel were used extensively during the crises. In Japan, the military was called in early, but in Thailand, it was a case of too little too late.

Low- vs. High-Value-Added Supply Chain

The big difference in the supply chain troubles of Japan and Thailand was the different level of value-added and the complexity of the components that the two countries produced. About 40 OEM-type auto parts manufacturers closed down because of the Thai floods. Shortly after, much of the lost production was replaced by supplies from other production bases like Indonesia and North America because OEM components can be readily produced anywhere, even if at higher cost. But it was impossible to replace Japanese-made high-tech and high-value-added products like BT resin and semiconductor components in a short period. Hence, the earthquake had huge consequences for industrial activity. Toyota and others encountered problems because of their system of sourcing components from the same geographical area.

Lessons for the Future

These two cases show that businesses need to rethink the very basics of their operations and the clustering concept for efficiency. Modern manufacturing is enabled by modern technology, low-cost transportation, and low tariffs. Module production makes it possible to situate in different locations the separate processes needed to make a product. Labor-intensive processes are located in countries that have abundant labor and low wages. The completed modules are brought together at a final assembly site. This supply chain production is very efficient and substantially lowers the prices of final products. However, we should realize that seeking too much efficiency often leads us to neglect security and reliability. In both Japan and Thailand, core parts production was concentrated in one area, and factories did not store sufficient surplus parts to use in case of disruptions to the supply chains. The result was that the natural disasters severely impacted manufacturing and supplies not only in the directly hit areas but also in unaffected areas of Japan and Thailand, and worldwide.

The solution to this problem extends from the old saying, "Don't put all your eggs in one basket." In fact, some Japanese multinational manufacturers have already shifted strategy and separated core suppliers into two or more locations, although this does mean having redundant suppliers. Alternatively, maintaining redundant inventory, although more costly, can help ensure that operations are not disrupted.

Case Study

Mitsubishi Gas Chemical and the BT Resin Global Scare in 2011

Pongsak Hoontrakul

The damage and disruption to factories from the March 2011 earthquake and tsunami in eastern Japan highlighted the country's importance to the global semiconductor process supply chain, particularly in supplying specialty chemicals.

BT resin is a special bonding chemical used in the third and fourth levels of semiconductor chip manufacture. Any prolonged halt in supplies would halt world production of many semiconductor process businesses, including integrated circuit chips, smartphones, and tablets. Mitsubishi Gas Chemical is the world's largest manufacturer of BT resin. In 2011, it accounted for half of the world output, while two other Japanese suppliers, Hitachi and Sumitomo, together accounted for 40 percent. In other words, 90 percent of the world's supply of a key material for modern information and communications technology (ICT) devices came from three Japanese firms. Fortunately, only

Mitsubishi Gas Chemical's plant was damaged.[31] But because different types of BT resins cannot be perfectly substituted, chip makers face high uncertainty when production at one manufacturer is halted. Apart from BT resin, there are at least four other specialty chemicals vital to the semiconductor process—E679, ACF, CMP slurry, and silicon wafer—that would be in short supply if their production in Japan was disrupted.[32]

On March 31, 2011, Mitsubishi Gas Chemical reported that its BT resin production line seemed to suffer minor damage, and a steady power supply was needed to restart it. Fortunately, the company was able to resume full pre-earthquake-level production from the beginning of May.

The disaster in Japan could cause huge impacts on Taiwan's high-tech sector. The stock prices of Siliconware Precision Industries Co. (SPI) and Advanced Semiconductor Engineering (ASE) could have plunged at least 25 percent if Mitsubishi Gas Chemical had not been able to resume BT resin production within a few months after the Taiwanese companies' 1 ½-month inventory was depleted.[33] The primary reasons were SPI and ASE could have lost their total sale 35–30 percent and 20–25 percent and dropped in earning per share as much as 30 percent and 25 percent, respectively, due to the BT shortage.[34]

Notes

1. Elain Prior, Nigel Pittaway, and Mark Tomlins, "Insurance and Extreme Events: Anomaly or Climate Change Trend?—Implications for Insurers," *Thematic Investing (Citi), Australia*, December 20, 2012: 1–38.
2. Ibid.; Shigeyuki Abe and S. Thangavelu, "Natural disasters and Asia: Introduction," *Asian Economic Journal*, 2012, 26(3): 181–187.
3. EM-DAT, The International Disaster Database (http://www.emdat.be/database).
4. Prior et al., "Insurance and Extreme Events."
5. "The World Bank Supports Thailand's Post-Floods Recovery Effort," *World Bank*, December 13, 2011 (http://www.worldbank.org/en/news/feature/2011/12/13/world-bank-supports-thailands-post-floods-recovery-effort), retrieved January 8, 2014. For more general discussion see T. Fomby, Y. Ikeda, and N. Loayza, "The Growth Aftermath of Natural Disasters," *World Bank Policy Research Working Paper No. 5002*, Washington, DC: World Bank, 2009.
6. R. Koopman et al., "Give Credit Where Credit is Due: Tracing Value Added in Global Production Chains," *NBER Working Paper No. 16426*, September 2010.
7. Ibid.
8. Ibid.
9. Ibid.
10. NAND flash is electronic data storage that requires no power to retain data by using floating-gate transistors. One of main drawbacks is that it has a finite

number of lifecycle or write-cycle, but it is a better choice for most of users. See more discussion by Jim Cooke, "Flash Memory 101: An Introduction to NAND Flash," eetimes.com and Micro Technology Inc, March 20, 2006 (http://www.eetimes.com/document.asp?doc_ id=1272118).

11. LTE stands for "long-term evolution" standard for wireless communication, typically known as 4G or fourth generation.

12. Andrew Rassweiler, "New iPad 32GB + 4G Carrier $364.35 Bill of Materials," *HIS*, March 16, 2012 (https://technology.ihs.com/389505/new-ipad-32gb-4g-carries-36435-bill-of-materials).

13. Ibid.

14. Authors' calculation based on UNComtrade bilateral trade data.

15. *Yomiuri Shimbun*, March 25, 2011.

16. Supavud Saicheua and Thanomsri Fongarunrung, "2012: The Good, the Bad and the Ugly," *Phatra Securities*, presentation on December 13, 2011, pp. 12–14.

17. Ibid.

18. "14,000 factories in 20 cities flooded", *Bangkokpost*, Oct 18, 2011 (http://www.bangkokpost.com/news/local/261960/over-14000-plants-in-20-cities-flooded).

19. Saicheua, "2012," 14.

20. Ibid., p. 18.

21. Anne Jirajariyavech et al., "Thailand 101: An Equity Investor's Guide to the Land of Smiles," *JP Morgan*, June 20, 2014: Fig. 18, p. 14.

22. Saicheua, "2012," pp. 14–20.

23. David Hensley and Joseph Lupton, "Global IP hit by Thai flood," *JP Morgan*, November 11, 2011: pp. 11–12.

24. Arkhom Termpittayapaisith, "Economic Policy and Conditions after Severe Flood in Thailand," August 3, 2012 (www.esri.go.jp/jp/workshop/120803/120803-03-1.pdf).

25. Saicheua, "2012."

26. Ibid. For more discussion see Kota Ezawa and Tsubasa Sasaki, "Eastern Japan Earthquake/Consumer Electronic/Electronic Components: Alert: Primary Damage from Quake Limited," *Citi*, March 14, 2011: 1–8.

27. Ibid.

28. OEM (original equipment manufacturer) components are purchased by another company and retailed under the purchasing company's brand name.

29. Steve Finlay, "Thailand Auto Industry Back on Track After Floods," *Wards Auto*, June 19, 2012 (http://wardsauto.com/asia-pacific/thailand-auto-industry-back-track-after-floods).

30. "Dams Near Breaking Point: More Flooding Likely as Excess Must be Released," *Bangkok Post*, October 1, 2011 (http://www.bangkokpost.com/news/local/259142/dams-near-breaking-point).

31. Kathrin Hille, "Smartphone Makers Face Chip Resin Shortage," *FT*, March 17, 2011 (http://www.ft.com/intl/cms/s/2/f02bb38c-4ff4-11e0-9ad1-00144-feab49a.html# axzz2wywYcZKn).

32. Rick Hsu et al.,"Semiconductor Contract Manufacture (SCM): Semis 101— How Crucial Japan is to the Food Chain," *J.P. Morgan*, March 22, 2011, 1–12.

33. Hsu et al., "Semiconductor Contract Manufacture."

34. Ibid.

References

Abe, Shigeyuki, "Impact of The Great Thai Floods on the International Supply Chain," *Malaysian Journal of Economic Studies*, 51 (Special Issue), 2014.

Abe, Shigeyuki and S. Thangavelu, "Natural disasters and Asia: Introduction," *Asian Economic Journal*, 2012, 26(3): 181–187.

Aghion, Philippe et al., "The Unequal Effects of Liberalization: Evidence from Dismantling the License Raj in India," *American Economic Review*, 2008, 98(4): 1397–1412 (http://www.aeaweb.org/articles.php?doi=10.1257/aer.98.4.1397; http://www.princeton.edu/~reddings/pubpapers/ABRZ_AER_Sept2008. pdf).

Akamatsu, Kaname, "A Historical Pattern of Economic Growth in Developing Countries," *Journal of Developing Economies*, March–August, 1962, 1(1): 3–25.

Alex Yao, "2014 China Internet Outlook: Investment Continues While Early Movers Approach Return Stage," *J.P. Morgan*, January 9, 2014: 1–88.

Alvarez, R. A, S. W. Pacala, J. J. Winebrake, W. L. Chameides, and S. P. Hamburg, "Greater Focus Needed on Methane Leakage from Natural Gas Infrastructure," Proceedings of the National Academy of Sciences of The United States of America, 2012.

Anand, R. and V. Tulin, "Disentangling India's Investment Slowdown," *IMF Working Paper 14/47*, March 24, 2014.

Anand, R. et al., "Potential Growth in Emerging Asia," *IMF Working Paper 14/2*, January 13, 2014.

Anh, Nguyen Thi Lan, "The Paracels: Forty Year on," *RSIS Commentaries*, No. 109/2014, S. Rajaratham School of International Studies, Nanyan Technological University, Singapore, June 9, 2014.

Arayasantiparb, Athaporn, "1H'14 Thai Strategy: The Magic of Abenomics," *UOBKayhian*, January 10, 2014 (http://research.uobkayhian.com/content_ download.jsp?id= 19512&h=7487db4b18866f75529483d51e31fd49).

Arayasantiparb, Athaporn, "Strategy—Thailand: The Japan Effect and More," *UOBKayHian*, 2014: 1–2 (http://research.uobkayhian.com/content_download.jsp?id=19512&h= 7487db4b18866f75529483d51e31fd49).

Ariff, M. and H. Hill, *Export-Oriented Industrialisation* (Hoboken: Taylor & Francis), 2012.

Aristotle (b. 384–d. 322 BC), "Politics," See more details discussion of "Aristotle's Political Theory," at http://plato.stanford.edu/ entries/aristotle-politics/.

Arman, Helmi, "ASEAN Economics Long View: Indonesia: En Route to a Top-10 World Economy by 2025," *Asia Pacific, Economics, Citi Research*, March 20, 2013: 1–35 (https://ir.citi.com/qkmmp1WC%2fe3%2bW5lRWDaqFNK7YrFG d1Psy403a%2fEmpAt2tmrIZinuaCx3Bj%2b7bbTV9k6HYSRMAmU%3d).

Arman, Helmi, "Indonesia Macro View—Prospects 2014: How Does Macro Stabilitization Mix with Elections?" *Citi*, December 9, 2013.

Arora, Tony, "Indian PM Visit Put India Back in Step with Reform Momentum," *Bangkok Post*, June 4, 2012 (http://www.bangkokpost.com/business/economics/296453/pm-visit-puts-india-back-in-step-with-reform-momentum).

ASEAN, *ASEAN Economic Community in Chartbook 2012* (Jakarta: ASEAN Secretariat), January 2013: 1–64 (http://www.miti.gov.my/cms/ document-storage/com.tms.cms.document.Document_a6d0d796-c0a81573–26b77801-cda8bcf8/AEC%20Chartbook%202012.pdf).

ASEAN, *Master Plan on ASEAN Connectivity* (Jakarta: The ASEAN Secretariat), reprint in January, 2011: 1–91 (http://www.asean.org/resources/publications/asean-publications/item/master-plan-on-asean-connectivity-2).

Asian Development Bank, *Overview of Greater Mekong Subregion: Economic Cooperation Program*, March 2012, p. 11 (http://www.gms-eoc.org/uploads/resources/61/attachment/GMS%20Economic%20Cooperation%20Program%20Overview.pdf).

Ashraf, Sajjad, "Rise of China and India: Global Game Changer?" *RSIS Commentaries no 024/2013*, the S. Rajaratnam School of International Study, Nanyan Technology University (NTU), Singapore, February 7, 2013.

Aziz, Mohshin and Jaroonpan Wattanawong, "ASEAN Open Skies: What Is It, What It Means to US?," *Maybank Kim Eng*, June 21, 2013.

Azzarello, Samantha, "Energy Price Spread: Natural Gas vs Crude Oil in the US," February 11, 2014 (http://www.nasdaq.com/article/energy-price-spread-natural-gas-vs-crude-oil-in-the-us-cm325685).

Balakrishnan, Ravi et al., "Surging Capital Flows to Emerging Asia: Facts, Impacts, and Responses," *IMF Working Paper 12/130*, May 1, 2012.

Bangkok Post, "Dams Near Breaking Point: More Flooding Likely as Excess Must be Released," October 1, 2011 (http://www.bangkokpost.com/ news/local/259142/dams-near-breaking-point).

Bangkok Post, "14,000 Factories in 20 Cities Flooded," October 18, 2011 (http://www.bangkokpost.com/news/local/261960/over-14000-plants-in-20-cities-flooded).

Bangkok Post, "Banking in CLMV: Things to know before making an investment," September 3, 2012 (http://m.bangkokpost.com/business/310561 and http://scbeic.com/THA/document/topic_bkkpost_banking_clmv/ref:topic_all).

Bangkok Post, "Singapore Coy on Asia Spying Claims," November 30, 2013: 5.

Barrows, Ross et al., "Cloud Computing Part 2: Market Sizing, Barriers, Value Network & Outlook," *Global Communications Equipment Equities, Citi Research*, December 5, 2012: 1–20 (https://ir.citi.com/P8MtBwhA6nIY2kp90iUuICj0HzOm1a1cZ7G   4B9KRgHbKw%2bEsHGf4 Qz4zfpf9C9yDWiQ0LPbMZaM%3d; simon.weeden@citi.com Tel +44–20-7986–4204).

BBC, "Australia 'Spied on Indonesia President Yudhoyono," November 18, 2013 (http://www.bbc.co.uk/news/world-asia-24952229).

Beer, Michael and Vivan Tao, "Southeast Asia Transportation," *Asia Airlines Equities, CitiResearch*, February 20, 2014: 1–280 (https://ir.citi.com/dWFei3mu-Nj3SKnxpzLMCWRlRLQTpW02SA0yKuF9EjVgckyXOKKLevolW16zvJSu/yq4ENdpIRU=).

Bernanke, Ben, "Monetary Policy Since the Onset of the Crisis," speech delivered at the Federal Reserve Bank of Kansas City Economic Symposium, Jackson Hole, Wyoming, August 31, 2012 (http://www.federalreserve.gov/newsevents/speech/ bernanke20120831a.htm).

Berrisford, Carl, "Asia Pacific Equities: Myanmar in Transition," *UBS*, 2012: 1–11.

Bitzinger, R. A., "China's ADIZ: South China Sea Next?" *RSIS Commentaries non 219/2013*, S. Rajaratnam School of International Studies, Nanyang Technological University, Singapore, December 2, 2013.

Boone, Laurence et al., "ECB: Almost Like QE, but Not There Yet," *Bank of America Merrill Lynch*, June 2013: 1–12.

Borah, Rupakiyoti, "Rise of China and India: Global Game Changer?" *RSIS Commentaries no 118/2013*, S. Rajaratnam School of International Study, Nanyan Technology University (NTU), Singapore, June 27, 2013.

Bradsher, Keith,"China Leading Global Race to Make Clean Energy," *New York Times*, January 30, 2010. Accessed March 2014 (http://www.nytimes.com/2010/01/31/business/energy-environment/31renew.html?pagewanted=1&_r=2).

Brown, P. and G. Whitney, "U.S. Renewable Electricity Generation: Resources and Challenges," *Congressional Research Service*, August 2011 (http://archive.nationalaglawcenter.org/ assets/crs/R41954.pdf).

Buiter, Willem and Ebrahim Rahbari, "Trade Transformed: The Emerging New Corridors of Trade Power," *Citi GPS: Global Perspectives & Solutions*, October 18, 2011: 1–80 (https://www.citivelocity.com/citigps/ReportSeries.action?recordId=1).

Buiter, William et al., "2014 Investment Themes: A World in Transition: Tapering, Restructuring and Reform," *Citi GPS: Global Perspectives & Solutions*, January 13, 2014: 24–25 (https://www.citivelocity.com/citigps/ReportSeries.action?recordId=23).

Camus, Miguel R., "Megawide-GMR May Bag P17.5bn PPP Deal," *Philippine Daily Inquirer*, December 13, 2013 (http://business.inquirer.net/156125/megawide-gmr-may-bag-p17–5b-ppp-deal).

Carrie Yu, "2013 Outlook for the Retail and Consumer Products Sector in Asia," *PWC*, 2013 (http://public.adequatesystems.com/pub/attachment/233954/035 2133891623116136497245262 5-fr.pwc.com/PwC%20-%20Etude%20Asia%20 outlook%20030413%20 basse%20def.pdf? id=882391).

Ceraso, Chris et al., "Yen and You: The Competitive Edge: Global Autos," *Credit Suisse*, July 01, 2013: 43–58.

Chakravarty, V. and C. S. Ghee, *Asian Mergers and Acquisitions: Riding the Wave* (Singapore: Wiley Publishers), 2012.

Chan, Vincent et al., "China Market Strategy: Urbanization and Its Limits," *Credit Suisse Equity Research*, March 13, 2013: 1–72.

Chan, Vincent, Victor Wang, Dick Wei, Evan Zhou, and Frances Feng, "Sino Hotspot Series: Internet Finance," *Credit Suisse*, January 2, 2014: 1–56 (https://doc.research-and-analytics.csfb.com/docView?language=ENG&source=ulg&format=PDF&document_id=1027329381&serialid=8eAbN9%2fPPyGY1T QzKiIyVlMXZT0RuanH0scnmqWnMMM%3d).

Chang, Bao, "China Playing a Rising Role in ASEAN Business," ChinaDailyAsia.com, October 11, 2013 (http://www.chinadailyasia.com/business/2013–10/11/content_15092349 .html).

Channell, J., H. R. Jansen, A. R. Syme, S. Savvantidour, E. L. Morsea, and A. Yuen, "Energy Darwinsim: The Evolution of the Energy Industry," *Citi GPS: Global Perspectives & Solutions*, October 2, 2013 (https://www.citivelocity.com/citigps/ReportSeries. action?recordId=21).

Channell, Jason, Timothy Lam, and Shahriar Pourreza, "Shale & Renewable: A Symbiotic Relationship,"*Citi Research*, September 12, 2012. Accessed April 2013 (http://www.4is-cnmi.com/knowledge-pge-research/Citigroup-Shale-renewables-symbiotic-r.pdf).

Chawla, Jatin and Akshay Sazena, "Tata Motors Ltd.: The Story Has More Legs Part 2," *Credit Suisse Equity Research*, January 9, 2014.

Chellaney, Brahma, "Coming Water Wars," *International Economic*, Fall 2009 (http://www.international-economy.com/TIE_F09_Chellaney.pdf).

Chik, Leon Andrew Hsu, and Ebru Sener Kurumlu, "Shenzhou International: Headwinds to Growth Dissipating," *J.P. Morgan*, September 23, 2013: 1–22.

Chimklai, Suthep, "ASEAN Interconnection, Briefing on ASEAN Power Grid," Electricity Generating Authority of Thailand (EGAT), March 14, 2013, presentation, pp. 2–25 (http://portal.erc.or.th/aern/images/Panel%201–1%20 Briefing%20on%20ASEAN%20 Power%20Grid.pdf). and Electricity Generating Authority of Thailand (EGAT), "ASEAN Power Grid," (http://www2.egat.co.th/apg/index.php?option=com_ content&view=article&id=69 &Itemid=466).

Chua, Hak Bin et al., "Asia Macro Weekly: India: Do Politics Matter for Economics?" *GEM Fixed Income Strategy & Economic for Asia, Bank of America Merrill Lynch*, May 16, 2013: 1–21.

Chua, Hak Bin et al., "Asia: Demographic Divide & Peaks," *GEM Economics— Asia, Bank of America Merril Lynch*, August 23, 2013: 1–20.

Chua, Johanna et al., "Asia Macro and Strategy Outlook: Is the Emerging Asia Growth Story Losing Its Luster?" *Citi*, October 25, 2013 (https://ir.citi.com/0IT%2b%2f%2b72H6Zh DTjLeX790kvKO49%2f3Ca5M6r3pS7cXlM2P w045N0%2fbpf5nkwRBLdJKrKUKv1dScY%3d).

Chua, Johanna et al., "Asia Macro Flash: Disruptive Techonology and Asia's Changing Export 'Beta'," *Citi*, November 18, 2013 (https://ir.citi.com/ QHN7s%2B5xiA76Rgw 8dBenZyfyGaVQq G8yu7AZS%2B4bFBxLgiq3FZj% 2FGVatOOCc2AAW).

Chui, Michael, James Manyika, Jacques Bughin, Richard Dobbs, Charles Roxburgh, Hugo Sarrazin, Geoffrey Sands, and Magdalena Westergren,

"The Social Economy: Unlocking Value and Productivity through Social Technologies," McKinsey Global Institute, July 2012: 1–184 (http://www.mckinsey.com/insights/high_tech_telecoms_ internet/the_social_economy).

CIA World Factbook (2011). *CitiGroup*, "Smartphones-The GEMs Telco Study for 2013," November 2012.

ComScore, "In India, 1 in 4 Online Minutes Are Spent on Social Networking Sites," August 19, 2012 (https://www.comscore.com/Insights/Press_Releases/2012/8/In_India_1 _in_4_Online_Minutes_are_Spent_on_Social_Networking_Sites.

ComScore, "2013 India Digital Future in Focus," press release, August 22, 2013 (https://www.comscore.com/Insights/Press_Releases/2013/8/comScore_ Releases_the_2013_India_Digital_Future_in_Focus_Report).

Cooke, Jim, "Flash Memory 101: An Introduction to NAND Flash," eetimes.com and Micro Technology Inc, March 20, 2006 (http://www.eetimes.com/document.asp?doc_ id=1272118).

Craig, R. S. et al., "Development of the Renminbi Market in Hong Kong SAR: Assessing Onshore–offshore Market Integration," *IMF Working Paper 13/268*, December 24, 2013.

Craig, Sean, Changchun Hua, Philip Ng and Raymond Yuen, "Development of the Renminbi Market in Hong Kong SAR: Assessing Onshore—Offshore Market Integration," *IMF Working Paper*, May 2013: 1–23.

Croissant, A. et al., *Democratization and Civilian Control in Asia* (Basingstoke: Palgrave Macmillan), 2013.

Daswani, Anil et al., "Global Gaming: Maximum Bullish in 2014: A Watershed Year for Macau and the US," *Citi Research Equities*, January 6, 2014: 1–236.

Davies, Paul J., "Asian Debt: Beware of Bubbles," *Financial Times*, May 22, 2013 (http://www.ft.com/intl/cms/s/0/acd43be0-bec9–11e2–87ff-00144feab7de.html# axzz2nY0pjd9z).

Devalier, Izumi and Rupali Sarkar, "A Pretty Big Deal: Everything You Need to Know About the Trans-Pacific Partnership," HSBC Global Research, December 18, 2013.

DinodiaCapital, "Social, Mobile, Analytics & Cloud: The Game Changers for the Indian IT Industry," June, 2013: 27 (http://www.saviance.com/whitepapers/SocialMobileAnalyticsCloud.pdf).

Dobbs, R., S. Lund, T. Koller, and A. Shwayder, "QE and Ultra-Low Interest Rates: Distributional Effects and Risks," McKinsey Global Institute, November 2013: 1–72.

Dobson, William, *The Dictator's Learning Curve: Inside the Global Battle for Democracy* (Doubleday) (New York: Anchor Book), 2012.

Dr. Reddy's, "Investor Presentation," February 2014 (http://www.drreddys.com/investors/pdf/drreddys-investor-presentation.pdf.

EGAT, "Corporate Social Responsibility Report 2011—Electricity Generating Authority of Thailand," 2011: 1–88 (http://www.egat.co.th/en/images/sustainable-dev/csr-report/EGAT-CSR-Annual-2011-en.pdf).

EPPO,"Assumptions and Summary of Draft PDP 2010." Accessed June 2012 (http://www.eppo.go.th/power/pdp/seminar-17feb2553/assumptions-PDP2010.pdf/).

Ezawa, Kota and Tsubasa Sasaki, "Eastern Japan Earthquake/Consumer Electronic/Electronic Components: Alert: Primary Damage from Quake Limited," *Citi*, March 14, 2011: 1–8.

Feenstra, R., "New Product Varieties and the Measurement of International Prices," *The American Economic Review*, 1994, 84(1): 157–177.

Felman, J. et al., "ASEAN5 Bond Market Development: Where Does It Stand? Where Is It Going?" *IMF Working Paper 11/137*, June 1, 2011.

Fernquest, Jon, "News Makes Up Larger Piece of Online Pie," Bangkok Post, November 26, 2013 (http://www.bangkokpost.com/learning/work/381793/what-new-in-business-news-november-26-2013).

Fineman, Dan and Siriporn Sothikul, "Thailand Market Strategy: Profiting from Early Elections," *Credit Suisse*, December 6, 2013.

Finlay, Steve, "Thailand Auto Industry Back on Track After Floods," *Wards Auto*, June 19, 2012 (http://wardsauto.com/asia-pacific/thailand-autoindustry-back-track-after-floods).

Fisher, Mas, "How China Stays Stable Despite 500 Protests Every Day," *The Atlantic*, January 5, 2012 (http://www.theatlantic.com/international/archive/2012/01/how-china-stays-stable-despite-500-protests-every-day/250940/).

Fomby, T., Y. Ikeda, and N. Loayza, "The Growth Aftermath of Natural Disasters," *World Bank Policy Research Working Paper No. 5002*, Washington, DC: World Bank, 2009.

Freedom House, "China's New Leadership Declares War on Social Media," September 23, 2013 (http://www.freedomhouse.org/blog/chinas-new-leadership-declares-war-social-media).

Friedman, George, "The Geopolitics of China: A Great Power Enclosed," *Stratfor*, June 15, 2008: 1–11.

Friedman, Norman, *The Fifty-Year War: Conflict and Strategy in the Cold War* (Annapolis: Naval Institute Press), 1999.

Friedman, Thomas L., "The Lesser-Known Arab Wakening," *Bangkok Post*, December 2, 2013.

Fukuyama, Francis, "The Middle-Class Revolution," *Wall Street Journal*, June 28, 2013 (http://online.wsj.com/news/articles/SB10001424127887323873904578571472700348086).

Garcha, Kulbinder, Randy Abrams, and Achal Sultania, "The Wireless View 2014: Smartphones—A Slowing Disruptive Force," *Credit Suisse*, January 6, 2014: 1–81 (https://doc.research-and-analytics.csfb.com/docView?language=ENG&source= emfromsendlink&format=PDF&document_id=805847640&extdocid=805847640_1_eng_pdf&serialid=VKIqPfyGKvPXILC6%2bF%2bpFCXU1PjBAqhenh6L1lN6AVE%3d).

Geiger, Thierry, "Charting ASEAN's Competitiveness Landscape," *World Economic Forum Blog*, June 6, 2013 (http://forumblog.org/2013/06/charting-aseans-competitiveness-landscape/).

Gelblum, Ehud et al., "Comm Equipment and Data Networking: Recasting Citi's Global Smartphone Model and 2014 Update," *Global Communications Equipment Equities, Citi Research*, March 10, 2014: 1–15 (https://ir.citi.com/Zpghh/MHa2M89we7g0Yle Gt2+If8m1Y96V8t5j973Mpx5qt9Zg2qpg==).

Ghosh, Anjan et al., "Indian Pharmaceutical Sector," *ICRA Rating Feature*, March 2012: 23–24 (http://icra.in/Files/ticker/Indian%20Pharmaceutical%20Sector.pdf).

Gill, Amar, Eric Fishwick, and Anna Tantuico, "Asia Graying: Investment Implications of Rapid Ageing," *CLSA*, December 2012.

Gisbourne, Ian, "Strategy—Thailand: New Frontiers CLMV," *Phatra Securities*, January 17, 2013: 1–83.

Goble, C. and L. H. Ong, "Social Unrest in China," *London: Europe China Research and Advice Network*, 2013 (http://www.euecran.eu/Long%20Papers/ECRAN%20Social% 20Unrest%20in%20China_%20Christian%20Gobel%20and%20Lynette%20H.%20Ong.pdf).

Gollin, D., "Getting Income Shares Right," *Journal of Political Economy*, 2002, 110: 458–475.

Gong, Sophie, "Myanmar Awards 20 Offshore Oil and Gas Exploration Tenders," *ibtimes*, March 26, 2014 (http://www.ibtimes.com/myanmar-awards-20-offshore-oil-gas-exploration-tenders-1563719).

Gonsalves, J. B., "An Assessment of the Biofuels Industry in Thailand," *A Review for United Nations Conference on Trade and Development*, September 19, 2006.

Gore, A., *Our Choice: A Plan to Solve the Climate Crisis* (Emmaus, PA: Rodale Books), 2009.

Gray, S. et al., "Developing ASEAN5 Bond Markets: What Still Needs to Be Done?" *IMF Working Paper 11/135*, June 1, 2011.

Greacen, C. S. and C. Greacen, "Proposed Power Development Plan (PDP) 2012 and a Framework for Improving Accountability and Performance of Power Sector Planning." Accessed June 2012 (http://www.palangthai.org/PDP2012-Eng.pdf/).

Greenwald, Glenn, Ewen MacAskill, and Laura Potras, "Edward Snowden: The Whistleblower Behind the NSA Surveillance Revelations," *Gaurdian*, June 10, 2013 (http://www. theguardian.com/world/2013/jun/09/edward-snowden-nsa-whistleblower-surveillance).

Gupta, Surajeet Das, "The Jaguar–Land Rover Turnaround," *Business Standard*, February 12, 2014 (http://www.business-standard.com/article/beyond-business/the-jaguar-land-rover-turnaround-113082001080_1.html).

Hackett J., ed., *The Military Balance* (The International Institute for Strategic Studies, Oxfordshire: Routledge Journals), 2010.

Hale, Jeremy, Maya Bhandari, and Maximilian Moldachi, "Foreign Exchange Forecasts: November 2013," *Citi Research*, November 21, 2013: 1–31.

Han, Becky, "Shenzhou International Group Holdings: Solid 2013 Results: Vietnam Expansion on Track," *Standard Chartered*, March 25, 2014.

Hargreaves, Rupert, "Why Does Tata Motors Look Significantly Undervalued?" *The Motley Fool*, January 16, 2014.

Harvey, Rachel, "Burma Dam: Why Myitsone Plan is Being Halted," *BBC*, September 30, 2011. Accessed February 2012 (http://www.bbc.co.uk/news/world-asia-pacific-15123833/).

Hayutin, Adele, "Population Age Shifts Will Reshape Global Work Force," Standford Center of Longevity, April, 2010 (http://longevity3.stanford.edu/wp-content/uploads/2012/10/Pop-Age-Shifts_Work-Force_April-2010_v2_FINALWEB_0.pdf).

He, Laura, "Facebook: Mobile Growth Take Off in Emerging Markets," *Forbes*, October 21, 2012 (http://www.forbes.com/sites/laurahe/2012/10/21/facebook-mobile-growth-takes-off-in-emerging-markets/).

Hensley, David and Joseph Lupton, "Global IP Hit by Thai Flood," *J.P. Morgan*, November 11, 2011: 11–12.

Hewitt, David and Horace Tse, "The Shale Revolution: Part 1," *Credit Suisse*, December 2012: 32–43.

Hille, Kathrin, "Smartphone Makers Face Chip Resin Shortage," *FT*, March 17, 2011 (http://www.ft.com/intl/cms/s/2/f02bb38c-4ff4–11e0–9ad1–00144-feab49a.html #axzz2wyw YcZKn).

Ho, Simon, Muzhi Li, and Paddy Ran, "Chinese Banks: Digital Stormtroopers at the Gate," *Global Communications Equipment Equities, Citi Research*, March 11, 2014: 1–52 (https://ir.citi.com/qFC87i81AZ3VMaJ7HQwZ8QA/tbL7tagU0 2S6EzBf+o3P6cjVx7HRMQ==).

Hongzhou, Zhang, "China is Marching West for Food," *RSIS Commentaries No.023/2014*, S. Rajaratnam School of International Studies, Nanyang Technological University, Singapore, February 4, 2014.

Hoontrakul, Pongsak, "Globalization and Trilemma," *Journal of Review of Pacific Basin Financial Markets and Policies*. World Scientific, Singapore, December, 1999.

Hoontrakul, Pongsak, "Lessons from Wikileaks: Is This the World Turning Point?" *Matichon Daily Newspaper*, January 25, 2011 [Thai].

Hoontrakul, Pongsak, "Thailand's 1997 Banking Crisis: Recoveries from Assets of Troubled Banks," discussion paper, International Association of Deposit Insurers (IADI), BIS, Basel, September 8, 2013.

Hoontrakul, Pongsak, David Walker, and Julapa Jagtiani,"The Global Financial Crisis and Implications for Thailand," discussion paper, International Association of Deposit Insurers (IADI), Bank of International Settlements (BIS), Basel, June 20, 2012.

Hooper, P., M. Spencer, M. Wall, and G. Moec, "World Outlook: A Leap Back to Trend Growth," *Deutsche Bank Research*, December 11, 2013: 1–71.

Hsieh, Pasha L., "The Roadmap for a Prospective US-ASEAN FTA: Legal and Geopolitical Considerations,"Journal of World Trade,January,2012:1–35(http://works.bepress.com/cgi/viewcontent.cgi?article=1013&context=pasha_hsieh).

Hsu, Rick et al.,"Semiconductor Contract Manufacture (SCM): Semis 101—How Crucial Japan is to the Food Chain," *J.P. Morgan*, March 22, 2011: 1–12.

IFC, "Indonesia's Infrastructure Investments: Finally Taking Off." Accessed January 2014 (http://www.ifc.org/wps/wcm/connect/region__ext_content/

regions/east+asia+and+the+pacific/news/indonesia+infrastructure+investm ents).

Iley, Richard et al., "Asia Ex-Japan: Key Macro Themes For 2014," *BNP Paribas*, January 2014.

IMF, "Global Financial Stability Report (GFSR): Responding to the Financial Crisis and Measuring Systemic Risk," April 2009 (http://www.imf.org/ External/Pubs/FT/GFSR/ 2009/01/ and http://www.imf.org/external/pubs/ft/ gfsr/2009/01/pdf/summary.pdf).

Infosys, "Impact of SMAC on Enterprise Software Applications." Accessed April 8, 2014 (http://www.infosysblogs.com/supply-chain/2014/04/impact_of_ smac_on_enterprise_s.html).

Inquirer,"Ayala to Venture into 'Green' Hydropower Projects with Sta. Clara." Accessed August 2011 (http://www.business.inquirer.net/money/breaking-news/view/20110420–332221/Ayala-to-venture-into-green-hydro-power-projects-with-Sta-Clara/).

IMF, "Global Financial Stability Report (GFSR): Responding to the Financial Crisis and Measuring Systemic Risk," April 2009 (http://www.imf.org/ External/Pubs/FT/GFSR/ 2009/01/ and http://www.imf.org/external/pubs/ft/ gfsr/2009/01/pdf/summary.pdf).

IMF, *World Economic Outlook: Slowing Growth, Rising Risk* (Washington, DC: Imfbookstore), 2011 (http://www.imf.org/external/pubs/ft/weo/2011/02/pdf/ text.pdf and also available at http://en.wikipedia.org/wiki/List_of_countries _by_future_GDP_(PPP)_ estimates).

Isnawangshi, A., V. Klyuev, and L. Zhang, "The Big Split: Why Did Output Trajectories in the ASEAN-4 Diverge After the Global Financial Crisis?" *IMF Working Paper 13/222*, October 30, 2013.

Jager-Waldau, A., "PV Status Report 2013," Joint Research Center of the European Commission, European Commission, September 2013.

Jensen, Robert, "The Digital Provide: Information (Technology), Market Performance and Welfare in the South India Fisheries Sector," *Quarterly Journal of Economics*, August 2007 (https://www.chinadialogue.net/article/ show/single/en/6753-Why-India-and-China-should-leave-the-Yarlung-Tsangpo-alone).

Jha, Prem Shankar, "Why India and China Should Leave the Yarlung Tsangpo Alone," *Chinadialogue*, March 5, 2014 (https://www.chinadialogue.net/arti-cle/show/single/en/6753-Why-India-and-China-should-leave-the-Yarlung-Tsangpo-alone).

Jin, Zhongxia, "The Use of RMB in International Transactions: Background, Development and Prospect," *Peoples Bank of China*, 2011 (http://china.ucsd. edu/_files/renminbi/ pdf-rmb-JinZhongxia.pdf).

Jirajariyavech, Anne et al., "Thailand 101: An Equity Investor's Guide to the Land of Smiles," *J.P. Morgan*, June 20, 2014: 1–49.

Jittapong, Khettiya and Viparat Jantraprap, "NCPO Delays 4G Auction by a Year," *The Bangkokpost and Reuters*, July 18, 2014 (http://www.bangkokpost. com/business/telecom/421221/ncpo-delays-4g-auction-by-a-year).

Joyce, Tom, Javier Guzman, and Jeff Ryan, "The Great Unwind: The Implications of Bernanke Taper Delay," Presentation in Bangkok, *Deutsche Bank Research*, September, 2013.

Kalra, A. and D. Lalmalsawma, "Social Media Not a Game Changer in 2013 Election," *Reuters*, September 25, 2013 (http://blogs.reuters.com/india/2013/09/25/social-media-not-a-game-changer-in-2014-elections/).

Kalra, Sanjay, "ASEAN: A Chronicle of Shifting Trade Exposure and Regional Integration," *IMF Working Paper 10/119*, May 1, 2010.

Kanno, Masaaki and Masamichi Adachi, "Macroeconomic Impacts of Japan/China dispute," *J.P. Morgan*, October 6, 2012: 1–5.

Kaplan, Robert D., "The Geopolitics of Shale," *Stratfor*, December 19, 2012 (http://www. stratfor.com/ weekly/geopolitics-shale?utm_source=freelist-f&utm_medium= email&utm_campaign=20121219&utm_term=kaplan&utm_content=readmore&elq=d6c1712f55064d7aabde82c8b958d525).

Kaplan, Robert D., "The India–China Rivalry," *Stratfor*, August 25, 2012 (http://www.stratfor.com/weekly/india-china-rivalry#axzz3CLaXw7lr).

Kaplan, Robert D., "Elections Don't Matter, Institutions Do," *Stratfor*, January 15, 2014 (http://www. stratfor.com/weekly/elections-dont-matter-institutions-do).

Kasahara, S., "The Flying Geese Paradigm: A Critical Study of Its Application to East Asian Regional Development," *United Nations Conference on Trade and Development, Discussion Paper #169*, April 2004.

Kasman, Bruce, David Hensley, and Joseph Lupton, "Global Data Watch: The Global Consumer is Lifting," *J.P. Morgan*, December 20, 2013: 1–4.

Kasman, Bruce, David Hensley, and Joseph Lupton, "Global Data Watch: The Supply Slide," *J.P. Morgan*, December 13, 2013: 1–4.

Kehoe, Timothy J. and Kim J. Ruhl, "Why Have Economic Reforms in Mexico Not Generated Growth?" *Journal of Economic Literature, American Economic Association*, December 2010, 48(4): 1005–1027.

Kemp, Simon, "Social, Digital & Mobile in APAC in 2014," *We Are Social*, January 23, 2014 (http://wearesocial.net/blog/2014/01/social-digital-mobile-apac-2014/).

Kersley, Richard et al., "Yen and You: The Competitive Edge," *Credit Suisse*, July 01, 2013: 1–121.

Kersley, Richard, Ed Westlake, and David Hewitt, "The Shale Revolution II," *Credit Suisse*, October 1, 2013.

Kewaleewongsatorn, Saengwit, "Ratings Boom for Political TV," *Bangkok Post*, November 14, 2013 (http://www.bangkokpost.com/news/politics/379713/ratings-boom-for-political-tv).

Kichikawa, Masayuki et al., "BOJ: Optimistic but Dovish," *Bank of America Merrill Lynch*, May 21, 2014: 1–7.

King, Stephen, "Reversal of Fortune: From Excess Liquidity to Financial Drought in the Emerging World," *HSBC Global Research*, September 4, 2013: 1–12 (http://www.scribd. com/doc/169344291/HSBC-Global-Research-Reversal-of-Fortune).

King, Stephen, Karen Ward, and James Pomeroy, "Global Economics—Deflation: The Hidden Threat," *HSBC Global Research, Macro Global Economics Q1 2014*, January, 2014: 1–94 (https://www.research.hsbc.com/midas/Res/RDV?p=pdf&key=gtkNdeNyMS&n= 398767.PDF).

Klaczek, Josh, "An Inflection Point on Leverage and Growth," *J.P. Morgan*, June 10, 2013: 11.

Klaczek, Josh, and Joy Wu, "Asia Banks & Corporate Credit: Cycles of Foreign Bank Lending: Pre-97 vs Pre-2013," *J.P. Morgan*, September 10, 2013: 1–10.

Klaczek, Josh, and Joy Wu, "Asia Banks & Corporate Credit: Looking for a Shift in the Capex Cycle," *J.P. Morgan*, September 29, 2013: 1–10.

Klaczek, Josh and Joy Wu, "Asia Banks: Looking Beyond 2q: Growth Correction vs Credit Crisis," *J.P. Morgan*, August 25, 2013: 1–52.

Koh, Jimmy et al., "Global Macro Outlook 2H2013: US QE Tapering dynamic & China Interbank Cash Crunch," *UOB Banking Group*, July 10, 2013.

Koopman, R. et al., "Give Credit Where Credit Is Due: Tracing Value Added in Global Production Chains," *NBER Working Paper No. 16426*, September 2010.

Korea, G. I., "Are Political Dynasties an Asian Things?" January 9, 2013 (http://rokdrop.com/2013/01/09/are-political-dynasties-an-asian-thing/#sthash.VBBxLh28.dpuf).

Kotoky, Anurag and A. Ananthalakshmi, "India 'Concerned' by China's Role in Port," *Reuters*, reprinted by *Bangkok Post*, February 8, 2013.

Krishnan, Ananth, "India's Trade Deficit with China Nears Record USD30bn," The Hindu, December 14, 2013.

Kuang, Melissa et al.,"Thailand: Banks: Correction Overdone, Valuation Attractive," *Goldman Sachs*, January 16, 2014: 1–39.

Kuroda, Haruhiko, "Quantitative and Qualitative Monetary Easing," Remarks at the International Council Meeting of the Brentton Woods Committee, Washington DC, October 10, 2013 (http://www.bis.org/review/r131016d.pdf?frames=0).

Kurumlu, Ebru Sener et al., "Asia Consumer 2014 Outlook and Strategy," *J.P. Morgan*, January 22, 2014.

Kurumlu, Ebru Sener, Shen Li, and Henry Tan,"Prada S.P.A," *J.P. Morgan*, April 3, 2014: 1–21.

Kurumlu, Ebru Sener, Shen Li, Henry Tan, and Celine Pannuti, "Baby Boosts and Consumption," Asia Pacific Equity Research, *J.P. Morgan*, 2013, 1(17): 1–18.

Kwock, Alvin et al., "China Technology EDGE: Five Landscape-Changing Policies to Watch," *J.P. Morgan*, March 18, 2014: 1–20.

Kwock, Alvin, Gokul Hariharn, William Chen, and Masashi Itaya, "Asian Technology: E-commerce Hardware Winner & China Technology Landscape Changing Policies," *J.P. Morgan*, March, 2014: 1–32 (https://markets.jpmorgan.com/research/ArticleServlet?   doc=GPS-1347867–0&referrerPortlet=EQCASHASIA_accordion).

Kwock, Alvin, J. J. Park, Gokul Hariharn, and Chi-Chu Tschang, "EM Mobile Data Tipping Point: Brands, Whitebox, Carriers—Same Trend, Varying Fate," *J.P. Morgan*, March 12, 2013: 1–32.

Kwong, Lucia and Ryan Li, "Asia Real Estate Handbook," Part 1, *J.P. Morgan*, June 12, 2012 (https://markets.jpmorgan.com/#research.article_page&action=open&doc= GPS-872705–0).

LaMonica, Martin, "Figuring Land Use Into Renewable-Energy Equation," May 29, 2010 (http://www.cnet.com/news/figuring-land-use-into-renewableenergy-equation/).

Lake, Fiona et al., "Not Your Older Brother's Asia Financial Crisis," *Goldman Sachs, Portfolio Strategy Research*, 2013: 18–19.

Leone, Steve (Assoc. Ed.), "Report Projects Massive Solar Growth in India," *Renewable Energy World*, December 9, 2011. Accessed March 2014 (http://www.renewableenergyworld.com/rea/news/article/2011/12/report-projects-massive-solar-growth-in-india).

Levin, Doron, "The Real Winner in the China–Japan Row," *CNN*, November 1, 2012 (http://features.blogs.fortune.cnn.com/2012/11/01/the-real-winner-in-the-china-japan-row/?iid=HP_LN).

Leviter, L, *The ASEAN Charter: ASEAN Failure or Member Failure?* 2010 [e-book]. Accessed April 1, 2014 (http://nyujilp.com/wp-content/uploads/2013/02/43.1-Leviter.pdf).

Li, Muzhi, Ravi Sarathy, and Gregory Zhao, "China Education Service: Class Apart," *Citi Research*, February 7, 2014.

Lim, Benajamin Kang, "China Princeling Emerges from Defection Scandal," *Reuters*, June 19, 2007 (http://www.reuters.com/article/2007/06/19/us-china-party-yu-idUSPEK15174020070619).

Lim, Soo Chong et al., "China Property Sector: A Credit Primer," *J.P. Morgan*, May 9, 2013 (https://markets.jpmorgan.com/research/EmailPubServlet?action=open&hashcode=g1ucdn71&doc=GPS-1122980–0.pdf).

Limsamarnphun, Nophahun, "India Funds Three-Nation Road," *The Nation Daily Newspaper*, August 12, 2012.

Lipinsky, F. and L. Ong, "Asia's Stock Markets: Are There Crouching Tigers and Hidden Dragons?" *IMF Working Paper 14/37*, February 26, 2014.

Liptak, Kevin, "5 Takeaways from Obama's Trip to Asia," *CNN*, April 29, 2014 (http://edition.cnn.com/2014/04/29/politics/obama-asia-trip/).

Liu, Beck, "Offshore Renminbi Bonds—Outlook for 2014," *Global Research*, Standard Chartered Bank, February 5, 2014: 4 (https://research.standard-chartered.com/ configuration/ROW%20Documents/Offshore_Renminbi_bonds_%E2%80%93_Outlook_for_2014__05_02_14_02_42.pdf).

Long, Tina et al., "Global Beneficiaries if China Retires Its One-Child Policy," *Consumer Product—Hong Kong/China Equity Research, Bank of America Merrill Lynch*, May 22, 2013: 1–44.

Lorenzen, Hans, "Too Much Money, Not Enough Assets to Buy: Inside the Global Supply–Demand Imbalance," *Citi Research*, April 25, 2013: 1–15.

Lubin, David et al., "China & Emerging Markets: China Is About to Rebalance. How Will EM Be Affected?" *Citi GPS: Global Perspectives & Solutions*, July 16, 2012: 1–56 (https://www.citivelocity.com/citigps/ReportSeries.action?recordId=7).

Lund, Susan, James et al., "Game Changers: Five Opportunities for US Growth and Renewal," *McKinsey Global Institute*, July 2013: 1–18.

Lupton, Joseph and David Hensley, "Global FX Reserves Near $12 Trillion in 2013," *J.P. Morgan*, February 28, 2014: 1–5.

Mackintosh, Jampes, "Currency war," *Financial Times*, September 28, 2010.

Maddison, Angus, "Statistics on World Population, GDP and per Capita GDP, 1–2008 AD," University of Groningen, Appendix B, Table B-20, 1995: 1–35 (http://www.ggdc.net/maddison/other_books/appendix_B.pdf). And discussed by Derek Thompson, "The Economic History of the Last 2,000 Years in 1 Little Graph," June 19, 2012 (http://www.theatlantic.com/business/archive/2012/06/the-economic-history-of-the-last-2-000-years-in-1-little-graph/258676/).

Maguire, Raymond, "Thai Equity Strategy: Will Foreign Manufacturing Shift from Thailand," *Global Research UBS*, March 19, 2014: 1–11.

Mahbubani, Kishore,"Dynastic Asia," *Project Syndicate*, January 3, 2013 (http://www.project – syndicate.org/commentary/asia-s-children-of-the-powerful-come-to-power-by-kishore-mahbubani#BTWStvpQm4T7P7qb.99).

Mahindra, Anand, "Toward a Uniquely Indian Growth Model," *McKinsey & Company*, November, 2013 (http://www.mckinsey.com/insights/asia-pacific/toward_a_uniquely_indian_growth_model).

Major, S., T. Commins, and A. Noppharatana, "Potential of Wind Power for Thailand: An Assessment," *Maejo International Journal of Science and Technology*, 2008, 2(2): 255–266.

Malkani, Rohini and Anurag Jha, "India Macroscope: Looking Beyond Elections," *Citi*, March 7, 2014: 1–28.

Malkani, Rohini and Anrag Jha, "India Macroscope: Modiscope: Mandate, Mantra and More," *Citi*, June 6, 2014: 1–28 (https://ir.citi.com/2X%2BAZ%2BPU98EyYiBZ tSHQF3MogfwwxqprPr0%2B6aI0mazC%2FR9O6IAqwg%3D%3D).

Manpuria, Neha, Pinakin Parekh and Sean Wu, "Dr. Reddy's Laboratories Limited," *Asia Pacific Equity Research. J.P. Morgan*, March 6, 2014: 1–11 (https://markets.jpmorgan.com/research/email/rfpjhbri/GPS-1339563–0).

Manyika, James et al., "Disruptive Technologies: Advances That Will Transform Life, Business and the Global Economy," *McKinsey Global Institute*, May 2013: 1–176 (http://www.mckinsey.com/insights/business_technology/disruptive_technologies).

Manyin, M. E. et al., "Pivot to the Pacific? The Obama Administration's 'Rebalancing' Toward Asia," *CRS*, March 28, 2012 (http://www.fas.org/sgp/crs/natsec/R42448.pdf).

Maziad, S. and J. S. Kang, "RMB Internationalization: Onshore/Offshore Links," *IMF Working Paper 12/133*, May 1, 2012.

McCallum, Colin and Jennifer Gao, "Asia Telecoms Sector: Killer App: OTT Voice," *Credit Suisse*, March 13, 2014: 1–45 (https://doc.research-and-analytics.csfb.com/doc ViewPlanguage=ENG&source=ulg&format=PDF&document_id=806056360&serialid=EYyrVAffwugU8gnE%2fn92ozsCAqUDqmjSiok QjxtUoPM%3d).

Mercereau, B., *FDI Flows to Asia* (Washington, DC: International Monetary Fund, Asia Pacific Dept), 2005.

Middleton, Carl, "Thailand's Commercial Banks' Role in Financing Dams in Laos and the Case of Sustainable Banking," *International Rivers*, 2009: 1–39 (http://www.banktrack.org/manage/ems_files/download/thailand_s_commercial_banks_role_in_financing_dams_in_laos_and_the_case_for_sustainable_banking/110707_sustainablethaibanks_ir_dec09.pdf).

Millward Brown, *BrandZ Top 50: Most Valuable Chinese Brands 2013*, 2013.

Ministry of Energy, "Energy statistics of Thailand 2011." Accessed June 2012 (http://www.eppo.go.th/info/cd-2011/index.html).

Ministry of Energy, "Summary of Thailand Power Development Plan 2012–2030 (PDP2010: Revision 3)." Accessed June 2012 (http://www.eppo.go.th/power/PDP2010-r3/PDP2010-Rev3-Cab19Jun2012-E.pdf/).

Mishra, Neelkanth and Ravi Shankar, "India Market Strategy: Reforms: The Past and the Future," *Asia Pacific/India Equity Research, Credit Suisse*, November 8, 2012: 1–28.

Mishra, Neelkanth and Ravi Shankar, "India Market Strategy: India's Better Half: The Informal Economy," *Asia Pacific/India Equity Research, Credit Suisse*, July 9, 2013: 1–44.

Mishra, Neelkanth and Ravi Shankar, "India Market Strategy: India 2014 Outlook," *Asia Pacific/India Equity Research, Credit Suisse*, December 2, 2013: 1–21 (https://doc.research-and-analytics.csfb.com/docView?sourceid=em&document_id=x542738&serialid=oWQ%2FK9tP277%2FnsElvyt5TpcqhK9ligzL7emTfuWTSFA%3D).

Mishra, Neelkanth, Ravi Shangkar et al., "India Market Strategy: India: The Silent Transformation," *Asia Pacific/ India Equity Research, Credit Suisse*, March 13, 2013: 1–44 (https://doc.research-and-analytics.csfb.com/docView?sourceid=em&document_id=x501785&serialid=NsYgMCZ0S2w1efwkTBs%2fDZEkKVpQnxhT0f7uMVA%2bIyE%3d).

Mitra, Arnab and Akshay Saxena, "India Consumer Survey 2014: Rural Continues to Be the Bright Spot," *Credit Suisse*, 2014: 1–37.

Moe, T. et al., "Asia Pacific 2014 Outlook: Back on Track," *Goldman Sachs, Economics Research*, November 21, 2013.

Mohr, Alexander, "A Boost for Thai–EU Relations," *Nation Daily Newspaper*, February 28, 2013 (http://www.nationmultimedia.com/opinion/A-boost-for-Thai-EU-relations-30200854.html).

Morgan Stanley, *The China Files: Chinese Economy through 2020*, 2010 [image online]. Accessed April 1, 2014 (http://www.morganstanley.com/views/perspectives/ China_Economy_2020.pdf).

Mowat, Andrian et al., "China 2020: 130 Million Swing: How Demographics Change the Economy," *Emerging Market Equity Research, J.P. Morgan*, May 31, 2011: 1–31.

Mowat, Andrian et al., "Battered by Bonds: Perspectives and Portfolios-Lite," *J.P. Morgan*, June 10, 2013: 1–48.

Mukherjee, Krittivas, "India's Worldfloat a Challenger to Facebook," *The Strait Times Newspaper*, May 10, 2013.

Naraya, Anantha and Sagar Rastogl, "India IT Service Sector: The SMAC Pack," *Credit Suisse*, July 10, 2013 (https://doc.research-and-analytics.csfb.com/docView? language=ENG&source=ulg&format=PDF&document_id=101981 3371&serialid=KDTcan6WWDtwPyROhjt1Ubh5pCqDjCoE198IXqKWkEc %3d).

National Broadcasting and Telecommunications Commission (NBTC), "Thailand's 3G Auction Episode," June 16, 2013 (http://www.nbtc.go.th/wps/portal/NTC/!ut/p/c4/04_SB8K8xLLM9MSSzPy8xBz9CP0os3gTf3MX0wB3U08n8zAjA88 wCzNXM   09PA1MzE_2CbEdFALxking!/?WCM_GLOBAL_CONTEXT=/wps/wcm/connect/library+ntc/internetsite/eng/en_interesting_articles/en_interesting_articles_detail/ae185900400633288ac5ceabcb3fbcab).

National Intelligence Council (NIC), "Global Trends 2030: Alternative Worlds," USA, ISBN 978-1-929667-21-5, December 2012 (http://www.dni. gov/index.php/about/organization/global-trends-2030).

Naylor, Andrew, "China's Leadership Change 2012," *Cicero-group*, November 15, 2012: 1–10.

Ng, Eileen, "Malaysia Auto Sale to Slow after New High in 2013," *AP*, January 22, 2014 (http://bigstory.ap.org/article/malaysia-auto-sales-slow-after-new-high-2013).

Noi, Coh Sui, "Princelings Still Rule Despite Bo's Ouster," April 22, 2012 (http://guanyu9. blogspot. com/2012/04/princelings-still-rule-despite-bos.html).

Normand, John, "JP Morgan Currency Timelines: From the Brentton Woods breakup to the EMU Crisis," *J.P. Morgan*, August 14, 2013.

Nusantoro, Ella, Priscilla Tjitra, and Jahanzeb Naseer, "Indonesia Consumer Survey 2014: Small Tickets to a Better Future," *Credit Suisse*, 2014: 1–125 (https://doc.research-and-analytics.csfb.com/docView?language=ENG&source=ulg&format=PDF&document_id=1029607411&serialid=96t%2fiJvRXsfm %2baxcYSaB2Z0BlMWKJSUB%2fDzaQgoWCvE%3d).

O'Rourke, Ronal, "China Naval Modernization: Implications for US Navy Capacities—Background and Issues for Congress," *CRS*, September 5, 2013 (http://www.fas.org/ sgp/crs/row/ RL33153.pdf).

Organisation for Economic Co-operation and Development, "Programme for International Student Assessment," 2009 (http://www.oecd.org/pisa/).

Osius, Ted et al., "Enhancing India–ASEAN Connectivity," a report of the (Center for Strategic & International Studies) CSIS Sumitro Chair for SE Asia Studies and the Wadhwani Chair for US-India Policy Studies, NY: Rowman & Littlefield, June 2013: 1–104 (http://csis.org/files/publication/130621_Osius_EnhancingIndia ASEAN_WEB.pdf).

Panigirtzoglou, N., M. Lehmann, and J. Vakharia, "Flow & Liquidity: Severe Balance Sheet Shrinkage," *J.P. Morgan*, November 22, 2013: 1–18.

Parente, Stephen L. and Edward C. Prescott, "A Unified Theory of the Evolution of International Income Levels," *Research Department Staff Report 333*, *Federal Reserve Bank of Minneapolis*, March, 2004 (http://apps.eui.eu/Personal/rma-rimon/ courses/parenteprescott333.pdf).

Park, J. J., Jay Kwong, and Jesper J. Koll, "Sony: Still a Long Way to the End of Tunnel," *J.P. Morgan*, February 7, 2014: 1–20.

Patnaik, I., A. Shah, and N. Singh, "Foreign Investors under Stress: Evidence from India," *IMF Working Paper 13/122*, May 22, 2013.

Pehrson, Chirstopher J., "String of Pearls: Meeting the Challenges of China's Rising Power Across the Asian Littoral" (www.StrategicStudiesInstitute.army.mil), the US Government, July 2006: 6–8 (http://www.strategicstudiesinstitute.army.mil/pdffiles/ pub721.pdf).

Pesek, Willia, "China's Xi Jingping Pumped Up on Political Testosterone," *Bangkok Post*, November 30, 2013.

Petri, Peter A., Michael G. Plummer, and Fan Zai, "The Trans-Pacific Partnership and Asia-Pacific Integration: A Quantitative Assessment," East–West Center Working Papers, *Economics Series 119*. October 24, 2011 (http://www.usitc.gov/research_and_ analysis/documents/petri-plummer-zhai%20EWC%20 TPP%20WP%20oct11.pdf).

Pieterse, J. Nederveen, "Dynamics of Twenty-First Century Globalization: New Trends in Global Political Economy," *Prace Instytutu Profilaktyki Spo\lecznej i Resocjalizacji*, 2011, 17: 107–132.

Pineda, Arthur et al., "Pan-Asian Telecoms: Affordable Smartphones and the Impact on Emerging Asia Telcos," *Citi Research*, January 5, 2013: 1–48.

Platzer, Michaela D., "US Textile Manufacturing and the Trans-Pacific Partnership Negotiations," *Congressional Research Services*, November 20, 2013: 1–26 (https://www.fas.org/sgp/crs/row/R42772.pdf).

Pornwasin, Asina, "Many Facebook Users Protest Against Amnesty Bill," *The Nation*, November 4, 2013 (http://www.nationmultimedia.com/politics/ Many-Facebook-users-protest-against-amnesty-bill-30218651.html).

Prasad, Subramania M. K., "Are You Riding the Digital Wave with an Assurance Surfboard You Can Rely On?" Tata Consultancy Services (TCS). Accessed January 2014 (http://www.tcs.com/resources/white_papers/Pages/Digital-Wave-Assurance.aspx).

Pratruangkrai, Petchanet, "Yuan to Become Major Currency in World Trade: HSBC," *The Nation*, April 25, 2014 (http://www.nationmultimedia.com/ business/ Yuan-to-become-major-currency-in-world-tradeHSBC-30232162.html).

Preechajarn, S. and P. Prasertsri, "Thailand Biofuels Annual 2011," *USDA Foreign Agricultural Service, Gain Report 2011*, July 7, 2011.

Prescott, Edward C., "Overcoming Barriers to Riches," Presentation at the seminar organized by Sasin of Chulalongkorn University, Bangkok, Thailand, 2005.

Prince, Bob and Amit Srivastava, "Bridgewater Daily Observations," Bridgewater Associates LP (www.bwater.com) May 20, 2009: 1–7.

Prior, Elain, Nigel Pittaway, and Mark Tomlins, "Insurance and Extreme Events: Anomaly or Climate Change Trend? – Implications for Insurers," *Thematic Investing (Citi), Australia*, December 20, 2012: 1–38.

Rahbari, E. and D. Kupciuniene, "Global Economic View: Slow Trade, Fast Trade Transformation," *Citi GPS: Global Perspectives & Solutions*, March 11, 2013.

Rahbari, Ebrahim and Deimante Kupciuniene, "Global Economic View: Slow Trade, Fast Trade Transformation," *Citi Research*, March 11, 2013: 1–20.

Ramanreet, S., "Social, Mobile, Analytics & Cloud: The Game Changers for the Indian IT Industry," Dinodia Capital Advisors, June Private Ltd, 2013: 1–50 (http://www.saviance.com/whitepapers/SocialMobileAnalyticsCloud.pdf).

Rassweiler, Andrew, "New iPad 32GB + 4G Carrier $364.35 Bill of Materials," *HIS*, March 16, 2012 (https://technology.ihs.com/389505/new-ipad-32gb-4g-carries-36435-bill-of-materials).

Raybould, Alan, ed., "Laos Defies Neighbors on Dam Project," *Reuters*, June 23, 2011. Accessed June 2012 (http://www.reuters.com/article/2011/06/23/laos-dam-idUSL3E7HN1L320110623/).

Razavi, Shamin and Bintang Hidayanto, "Power Projects in Indonesia You Should Know," *Asian-Power*, October 21, 2013 (http://asian-power.com/project/commentary/power-projects-in-indonesia-you-should-know-about).

Redman, Alexander and Fan Cheuk Wan, "Opportunities in an Urbanizing World," *Emerging Market Research Institute, Credit Suisse*, 2012: 1–52 (https://publica-tions.credit-suisse.com/tasks/render/file/index.cfm?fileid=88E9D3D8–83E8-EB92–9D5DAF8ECA39029A).

Renewable Energy World, "Report Projects Massive Solar Growth in India." Accessed March 2014 (http://www.renewableenergyworld.com/rea/news/article/2011/12/report-projects-massive-solar-growth-in-india?cmpid=SolarNL-Tuesday-December13–2011).

Rick, Hsu et al., "Semiconductor Contract Manufacture (SCM): Semis 101—How Crucial Japan Is to the Food Chain," *J.P. Morgan*, March 22, 2011: 1–12.

Rifkin, Jeremy, *The Third Industrial Revolution: How Lateral Power is Transforming Energy, the Economy, and the World* (New York: Palgrave Macmillan), 2011: 1–304.

Ristimaki, Sasu-Petri, Glen Campbell, and Sean Johnstone, "Telecoms and Social Media—a Communications Value Transfer," *Global Telecom, Bank of American Merrill Lynch*, 2013: 1–24.

Rocha, Euan, "CNOOC Closes USD15.1 Billion Acquisition of Canada's Nexen," *Reuters*, February 25, 2013 (http://www.reuters.com/article/2013/02/25/us-nexen-cnooc-idUSBRE91O1A420130225).

Rodriguez, V. and A. Soeparwata, "ASEAN Benchmarking In Terms of Science, Technology, and Innovation from 1999 to 2009," *Scientometrics*, 2012, 92(3): 549–573.

Rosgen, Markus and Yue Hin Pong, "M&A: Asia Buys Commodities, Foreigners Buy Financial and Consumer," *Citi Research*, November 12, 2012: 1–14.

Saicheua, Supavud and Thanomsri Fongarunrung, "2012: The Good, the Bad and the Ugly," Phatra Securities Pcl, presentation on December 13, 2011.

Sakawee, Saiyai, "Thailand Grew by 33% in 3 Months to 24 Million Users," *Techinasia*, September 6, 2013 (http://www.techinasia.com/facebook-thailand-grows-to-24-million-users-infographic/).

Salamatian, Karim P., "Consume 2013 Outlook: Momentum Change," *Credit Suisse*, January 2, 2013: 1–5 (https://doc.research-and-analytics.csfb.com/docView?language=ENG&format=PDF&source_id=em&document_id=100633 1291&serialid=dWVfQ%2Bkg3%2FPz8qOLa5j%2FsRZ8VCTSs8l%2B8qC%2 Bc56YnVI%3D).

Salidjanova, Nargiza and Iacob Koch-Weser, "Third Plenum Economic Reform Proposal: A Scorecard," *U.S.–China Economic and Security Review Commission, U.S. government*, November 19, 2013. Accessed May 8, 2013 (http://origin.www. uscc. gov/sites/default/files/Research/Backgrounder_Third%20Plenum%20 Economic%20Reform%20Proposals--A%20Scorecard%20(2).pdf).

Schumpeter, Joseph A., *Capitalism, Socialism and Democracy* (New York: Harper), 1975 [orig. pub. 1942].

Schwab, Klaus, "2014 Will Make or Break the Economy," *Bangkok Post*, January 13, 2014 (http://www.bangkokpost.com/opinion/opinion/389247/2014-will-make-or-break-the-economy).

Scrutton, Alistair, "Indian PM Warns of Rising China," *REUTERS*, reprinted by *Bangkok Post*, September 8, 2010.

Sethi, I., L. Kong, M. C. Koh, "ASEAN: Transportation & Airports," Goldman Sachs, December 9, 2013.

Shanagher, Tim and Daisuke Takato, "Japan Outlook 2014: The Year to Deliver on Expectations," *Credit Suisse*, December 16, 2013: 1–30.

Shankland, Stephen, "IBM Sells its x86 Server Business to Lenovo for USD2.3 Billion," *News.CNET.com*, Jan 23, 2014 (http://news.cnet.com/8301–1001 _3–57617651–92/ibm-sells-its-x86-server-business-to-lenovo-for-$2.3-billion/).

Sheets, Nathan and Robert A. Scokin, "Perspectives: Our Global Top 10—A Tour of the Post-Crisis World Economy in 10 Easy Charts," *Citi Research*, July 5, 2013: 1–20.

Shen, Minggao et al., "China & India Equity Strategy: Two Plays, One Portfolio," *Citi Research*, October 8, 2010: 1–60.

Shen, Minggao, Shuang Ding, and Enjiang Cheng, "China Macro View: SFTZ: Testing the Waters of Reform," *Citi Research*, August 27, 2013: 1–15.

Shirvaikar, Ashwin, Philip Stiller, Tomasz Smilowicz, Robert Schlaff, and Donal Fandetti, "UPWARDLY MOBILE II: A Long and Winding Road for Mobile Payments—Eight Crucial Questions, Answered," *Citi GPS*, November, 2012: 1–60 (https://ir.citi.com/ %2fOx67RG%2b6opqS844%2bjuDL13WNBhvedM sna%2b7HXAEvK7UCB4n9nSlgQ%3d%3d0).

Shu, Chang, Dong He, and Xiaoqiang Cheng, "One Currency, Two Markets: The Renminbi's Growing Influence in Asia-Pacific," *BIS Working Paper Number 446*, Monetary and Economic Department, Bank for International Settlements, Basel, Switzerland, April 2014: 5 (http://www.bis.org/publ/work446.pdf).

Shvets, Viktor and Chetan Seth, "APAC—Competitive Edge: Separating Winners from Losers," *Macquarie*, March 21, 2013: 1–63.

Shvets, Viktor and Chetan Seth, "ASEAN 4—Risks & Returns," *Macquarie*, August 16, 2013: 1–63 (https://www.macquarieresearch.com/rp/d/r/pub-lication.do?f=E&pub _id=7210925&file_name=ASEAN4_160813e157384. pdf&uid=NzQ2MjQ4).

Shvets, Viktor and Karim P. Salamatian, "APAC: Consumption S Curve: Winners & Losers as Asian Consumer Evolve," *Credit Suisse*, August 6, 2012: 1–70 (https://doc.research-andanalytics.csfb.com/docView?language=ENG&sour

ce=ulg&format=PDF&document_id=992377261&serialid=SRAMg9dFM3xI E%2fv%2bbxaFowhh3ka8j0uG%2fgO1v%2b5ro%2bU%3d).

Song, Sophie, "Six Dramatic Reforms from China's Third Plenum," *International Business Times*, November 15, 2013. Accessed May 8, 2013 (http://www. ibtimes.com/six-dramatic-reforms-chinas-third-plenum-1472754).

Srinivasan, T. N., "China and India: Growth and Poverty, 1980–2000," discussion paper, Standford Center for International Development, September 2003: Table 3: p. 14 (http://web.stanford.edu/group/siepr/cgi-bin/siepr/?q=system/ files/shared/pubs/ papers/pdf/credpr182.pdf).

Srinivasan, T. N., "The Shift in the Balance of Power," Standard Chartered Research, January 2011.

Stratfor, "China Next Generation of Leaders, Looking to 2012," September 17, 2012 (http://www.marketoracle.co.uk/Article22759.html).

Sukkumnoed, D., *Better Power for Health: Healthy Public Policy and Sustainable Energy in the Thai Power Sector* (Department of Development and Planning, Aalborg University), 2007.

Sullivan, James R., "JPM Telcos: Travel with Sully: In-Depth on VoLTE with SingTel," *J.P. Morgan*, March 17, 2014.

Sullivan, James R. et al., "The Economics of Wireless Data—Part One: The Importance of Population Density and Spectrum," *J.P. Morgan*, May 4, 2011.

Sullivan, James R. et al., "The Economics of Wireless Data—Part Two: Valuing Air," *J.P. Morgan*, December 11, 2011: 1–51.

Sullivan, James R. et al., "The Economics of Wireless Data—Part 3: What LTE Means for Asia," *J.P. Morgan*, March 26, 2012: 1–108.

Takahashi, Kohei, "Autos and Auto Parts: Earthquake Update," *J.P. Morgan*, March 22, 2011: 1–13.

Tan, Alan Khee-Jin, "Toward a Single Aviation Market in ASEAN: Regulatory Reform and Industry Challenges," *ERIA Discussion Paper Series*, October 2013: 1–42 (http://www.eria.org/ERIA-DP-2013–22.pdf).

Tansubhapol, Thanida, "Beijing Eyes Train Deal: Premier Wen Calls for Fair, Open Competition," *Bangkok Post*, 2012 (http://www.bangkokpost.com/ news/ local/322448/beijing-eyes-train-deal).

Teather, Edward, "ASEAN Linkages and Why They Matter," *UBS Investment Research*, June 24, 2011: 1–24.

Termpittayapaisith, Arkhom, "Economic Policy and Conditions after Severe Flood in Thailand," August 3, 2012 (www.esri.go.jp/jp/workshop/120803/120803–03–1.pdf).

Thai Research Foundation (TRF),"Final Report. Policy Research to Support the Development and Usage of Renewable Energy and to Increase Efficiency in Energy Usage of Thailand," 2007.

The Economist, "Democracy Index 2012: Democracy Is at a Standstill," The Economist's Intelligence Unit, January 2013 (https://www.eiu.com/public/ topical_report.aspx? campaignid=DemocracyIndex12).

The Economist, "India as a Great Power: Know Your Own Strength," March 30, 2013   (http://www.economist.com/news/briefing/21574458-india-poised-become-one-four-largest-military-powers-world-end).

The Economist, "Politics in Malaysia: Bumi, Not Booming," September 28, 2013 (http://www.economist.com/news/asia/21586864-ruling-party-returns-its-old-habits-race-based-handouts-bumi-not-booming).

The Economist, "Water in China: Desperate Measures," October 12, 2013 (http://www.economist.com/news/leaders/21587789-desperate-measures).

The Economist, "Getting the Messages," February 22, 2014 (http://www.economist.com/ news/ business/21596966-why-mark-zuckerbergs-social-network-paying-such-whopping-sum-messaging).

The Nation, "Thailand Close to Achieve 3mn Auto Production Milestone," April 2, 2014 (http://www.nationmultimedia.com/business/Thailand-close-to-achieve-3mn-auto-production-mile-30230641.html).

The New York Times, "China Leading Global Race to Make Clean Energy." Accessed March 2014 (http://www.nytimes.com/2010/01/31/business/energy-environment/31renew.html? pagewanted=1&_r=2).

Tilton, Andrew et al., "Asia Economics Analyst: ASEAN's Half a Trillion Dollar Infrastructure Opportunity," *Goldman Sachs, Economics Research*, May 30, 2013 (13/18): 1–18 (http://www.btinvest.com.sg/system/assets/14801/ ASEAN%20infras %20opportunity.pdf.

Tilton, Andrew et al., "Asia Economics Analyst: A Deep Dive into Regional Financial Flows: Possible Impact of US Fed Tapering," *Goldman Sachs, Economics Research*, September 6, 2013 (13/32): 1–25.

Tilton, Andrew et al., "Asia Economics Analyst: Diverging Fortunes—the Emerging Asia Outlook for 2014," *Goldman Sachs, Economics Research*, November 21, 2013 (13/43): 1–12.

Tollefson, J. "Air Sampling Reveals High Emissions from Gas Field," *Nature*, February 7, 2012 (http://www.nature.com/news/air-sampling-reveals-high-emissions-from-gas-field-1.9982/).

U.S. Department of Energy, "Wind Energy Resource Potential," Energy Efficiency and Renewable Energy Wind and Hydro Power Technologies Program, 2006 (http://www.eere.energy.gov/windandhydro/).

U.S. Department of Energy (EIA), "Technically Recoverable Shale Oil and Shale Gas Resources: An Assessment of 137 Shale Formations in 41 Countries Outside the United states," *Independent Statistics & Analysis, US energy Information Administration, US Department of Energy (EIA)*, June 2013 (http://www.eia.gov/ analysis/studies/worldshalegas/pdf/overview.pdf).

Ved, Mahendra, "Political Dynasties Face a Tough Time across Asia," March 30, 2013 (http://www.eastasiaforum.org/2013/03/30/political-dynasties-face-a-tough-timeacross-asia/).

Vermeulen, F. and H. Barkema, "Learning through Acquisitions," *Academy of Management Journal*, 2001, 44(3): 457–476.

Viboonchart, Nalin and Jen Rita, "Malaysia's Eco-Car Ambitions: New National Automotive Policy Envisions the Country as an Energy-Effi cient Vehicle Hub, but Even Generous Incentives Might Not Be Enough to Woo Big Players to a Small Market," *Bangkok Post*, February 3, 2014 (http://www.bangkokpost.com/business/marketing/392981/ malaysia-s-eco-car-ambitions).

Viet Nam News and AsiaNewsNet, "Vietnam's Textile Exports Set for Strong Growth in 2014," January 7, 2014 (http://asianewsnet.net/Vietnams-textileexports-set-for-strong-growth-in – 55833.html).

Wang, Eva and Kenny Lau, "Pacific Textile Group," *Credit Suisse*, November 25, 2013.

Wang, Joy, Simone Yeoh, Sumedh Samant, and Hoy Kit Mak, "ASEAN Property: Crouching Lion, Hidden Dragon," *J.P. Morgan*, April 28, 2013: 1–220.

Weeden, Simon et al, "Cloud Computing: Every Silver Lining Has a Cloud," *Citi Research*, September 5, 2012: 1–116 (https://ir.citi.com/d0BRCdnv8T9NuI3-OY5SF68IpYth HBgeUdTYu3LS7x7bb%2fKiXnTaWsIaSrzyQOX91P152yj0D E%2f0%3d).

Wei, Dick and Evan Zhou, "China Internet Sector—Part One, The New Thumb Economy," *Credit Suisse*, May 26, 2013.

Wei, Zheng Kit and Brian Tan, "ASEAN Economic Long View: Singapore Swing-Refocusing on ASEAN Regionalization," *Asia Pacific, Economics, Citi Research*, December 4, 2012: 1–45 (https://ir.citi.com/Zm%2ffnwe7sD0v9l1rVsxjf00tcm EH6OVlPyAzX9tPdLJ4PVq1eGpHWD%2bxleGmla0xY1FdHpNbZ4A%3d).

Wei, Zheng Kit, Helmi Arman, and Jun Trinidad, "ASEAN Macro Flash: ASEAN-Bound FDI Continued to Catch Up with China in 2012," *Citi Research*, June 28, 2013: 1–7 (https://ir.citi.com/xmORZempYjFDQL0DcYHpylJj8CT5y-QgOh24Eg7QTOm XUNRr5UAWKfQ%3D%).

Wei, Zheng Kit, Helmi Arman, and Jun Trinidad, "ASEAN Macro View: Chartbook: Current Accounts—A Saving–Investment Perspective," *Citi Research*, August 27, 2013: 1–12.

Wei, Zheng Kit, Jun Trinidad, Helmi Arman and Brian Tan, "ASEAN Macro Flash: Should We Worry About Wage Inflation in ASEAN?" *Citi Research*, December 3, 2012: 1–17.

Wharton School, University of Pennsylvania, "Renewable Energy for Japan: A Post-Fukushima Quest," October 3, 2013. Accessed March 2014 (http://knowledge.wharton.upenn.edu/ article /renewable-energy-japan-post-fukushima-quest/).

Wharton School, University of Pennsylvania, "Road to the Chinese Dream? Xi Jinping's Third Plenum Reform Plan," December 10, 2013. Accessed May 8, 2013 (https://knowledge.wharton.upenn.edu/article/road-chinese-dream-xi-jinpings-third-plenum-reform-plan/).

Wheeler, D. et al., "Does the World Need Securitization?" *Citi Research*, December 12, 2008: 549–573 (http://www.americansecuritization.com/uploadedFiles/Citi121208_ restart_ securitization.pdf).

Wikipedia, "Princelings." Accessed March 2014 (http://en.wikipedia.org/wiki/Princelings).

Winkels, Mitchel et al., "The Global Social Network Landscape: A Country-By-Country Guide to Social Network Usage," *eMarketer*, July 2013: 1–40 (http://www.optimediaintelligence.es/noticias_archivos/719_20130715123913.pdf).

Wipro, "In Conversation with Bill Fearnley, Jr." Accessed January 2014 (http://www.wipro.com/ Documents/resource-center/in-conversation-with-Bill-Fearnley.pdf).

Wong, Thomas, Horace Tse, and Kelly Chen, "CNOOC Ltd: Downgrade to NEUTRAL on Lower Production Growth," *Credit Suisse*, Asia Pacific/China Equity Research Oil & Gas Exploration & Production, January 21, 2014: 1 (https://doc.research-and-analytics.csfb.com/docView?language=ENG&source=ulg&format=PDF&document_id=1028171371&serialid=FuUWJDpO057VscG5QmvfEQ37rAil9rl7K4VyD6NmYE8%3D).

Wongruang, Piyaporn, "545,00 Sign Web Petition to Stop Bill," *Bangkok Post*, November 6, 2013 (http://www.bangkokpost.com/breakingnews/378353/545000-sign-web-petition-to-stop-bill).

Woodford, Michael, "Methods of Policy Accommodation at the Interest-Rate Lower Bound," *Working Paper*, Columbia University, September 16, 2012: 1–99.

World Bank, "The World Bank Supports Thailand's Post-Floods Recovery Effort," December 13, 2011 (http://www.worldbank.org/en/news/feature/2011/12/13/world-bank-supports-thailands-post-floods-recoveryeffort), retrieved January 8, 2014.

World Economic Forum (WEF), "Global Risk Report 2012," Seventh Edition, *The Risk Response Network*, Geneva, March 2012 (http://www3.weforum.org/docs/WEF_GlobalRisks_Report_2012.pdf).

World Economic Forum (WEF), "The Vulnerability of Elites: Geopolitical Risk in 2013," The Global Agenda Council on Geopolitical Risk, World Economic Forum in Dubai, November 2012 (http://www.weforum.org/docs/WEF_GAC_GeopoliticalRisk_2013.pdf).

World Economic Forum (WEF), "Global Risk Report 2014," Ninth Edition, *The Risk Response Network*, Geneva, February 2014 (http://www3.weforum.org/docs/ WEF_GlobalRisks_Report_2014.pdf).

Wu, Thompson, "Lenovo Group Ltd—FY3Q14 Preview: Raising FY 14/15EEPS Alongside Global Smartphone Increase," *Credit Suisse*, Asia Pacific/Hong Kong Equity Research, IT Hardware, January 8, 2014.

Xi, Jinping, "The China Dream, The People's Dream," the inauguration speech at the National People's Congress on March 17, 2013 (http://cpc.people.com.cn/n/2013/ 0318/c64387-20819181.html) (in Chinese).

Yamanaka, T. and R. Muranaka, "Japanese Major Banks: In Initial Phase of Medium-Term Rally," *Credit Suisse*, September 9, 2013: 1–35.

Yang, Stanley and Sally Yoo, "Korea Internet: Focus on Overseas Business Momentum," *J.P. Morgan*, February 24, 2014: 1–27.

Yao, Alex and Yong Wang, "Those Disrupted by Mobile Internet: Taxi-Hailing," *J.P. Morgan*, March 3, 2014: 1–7.

Yao, Alex and Yong Wang, "A Deepening and Broadening Consumer Relationship with Mobile," *J.P. Morgan*, March 17, 2014: 1–8.

Yao, Alex and Yong Wang, "Baidu.com: Reverse Engineer 2014 Margin Guidance: What Assumptions Are Implied?" *J.P. Morgan*, March 18, 2014: 1–12.

Yao, Alex, "Youku Tudou Inc.: Increasing Uncertainties in Growth Outlook," *J.P. Morgan*, August 30, 2013: 1–13.

Yin, Kevin and Vivian Zhao, "China Consumer Survey 2014: Unlock the Power of 'Shopaholic'," *Credit Suisse*, February 14, 2014: 1–25.

Yu, Carrie, "2013 Outlook for the Retail and Consumer Products Sector in Asia," *PwC*, 2013 (http://public.adequatesystems.com/pub/attachment/233954/035 21338916231161364   972452625-fr.pwc.com/PwC%20%20Etude%20Asia%20 outlook%20030413%20basse%20 def.pdf?id=882391).

Yu, Michael, Joanne Cheung, and Adrian Mowat, "The 'Decision'—The Details: More on China's Reforms," *Asia Pacific Equity Research, J.P. Morgan*, November 17, 2013: 1–14.

Yuen Anthony et al., "The New American (Gas) Century: Transforming Sectors, Redefining the Global Natural Gas Order and Setting New Long Term Prices," *Citi Research*, January 30, 2014: 1–47 (https://ir.citi.com/DjqgfVP5dmDX9CG1la9WkD0Ah0U0G2Vc2 yj3H2ws4uWu3j4NxXTTIQ%3d%3d).

Zakaria, Fareed, "The Rediscovery of India," *McKinsey & Company*, November 2013.

Zhenya, Liu, "Science Daily: Smart Grid and the Third Industrial Revolution," *Std,* retrieved December 5, 2013 (www.stdaily.com).

Zhou, Y. S., "Explaining ASEAN-3's Investment Puzzle: A Tale of Two Sectors," *IMF Working Paper 13/13*, January 14, 2013.

Zhu, Helen et al., "Third Plenary: Ambitious Blueprint to Boost Sentiment," *Goldman Sachs*, November 18, 2013: 1–13.

Index

NOTE: Page references in *italics* refer to figures and illustrations.

U.S. Federal Reserve Bank (the Fed),
QE by, 3, 51, 53, 61
see also quantitative easing (QE)

Vallabhbhai, Sardar, 136
value transfer, social media economy
and, 113–15
value-added supply chains, low- *vs.*
high-, 229–30
vertical specialization, 12, 220
Vietnam
ASEAN and regional connectivity,
171–2
ASEAN textile tax incentives and,
179
energy and, 201, 207
income level of, 163, *165*
land connectivity of, *18, 173*
SMAC, human capital, and middle-
income trap, *121,* 121–2
see also Association of Southeast
Asian Nations (ASEAN)
VoLTE (Voice over long-term
evolution), 116

Wang Gongquan, 41
Wang Qishan, 45
wars, 7, 25–8, 35–6, *37,* 87, 134, 138,
151
waste management, nuclear, 202–3
water stress issues, 36, 151, 172
Web 2.0, social media economy and,
116
WeChat, 115, 117, 119
Weibo, 40, 115
Wen Jiabao, 36, 172
Western countries, rise and decline
of, 2–3
see also United States

WhatsApp, 108, 115
"white box" handsets, 110
wind energy, 197, 199–200, *200*
Wipro (case study), 122–4, *123*
wireless data
economic rise of India and, 147–8
economics of, 108–13, *109 (see
also* SMAC (social, mobility,
analytics, and cloud))
supply chains of, 220–1
workforce. *See* human capital
"work-outs," 54
World Bank, 137, 220
World Economic Forum, 20, 40, 167
WorldFloat.com, 10
World Trade Organization (WTO),
39, 44, 135, 143–4

Xi Jinping, 5, 30, 36, *38,* 40–1, 45,
135–6, 144
Xi Zhongxun, 36, *38,* 45

Yao Yilin, 45
Yellen, Janet, 3
yen
ASEAN and, 170
devaluation (case study), 74–6
yen-dollar exchange rate, 54, 58,
62–3, 220
yield curve, 66
Yoma Strategic Holding Ltd., 172
Yomiuri Shimbun (Japan), 221
Yuanqing, Yang, 103
Yudhoyono, Susilo Bambang, 43
Yulong, 110

Zardari, Bilawal Bhutto, *38*
zero interest rate policy, 3, 8, 17, 52–4
Zhou Enlai, 135

Printed in the United States of America